Space, Structure and Form

Interweaving Art, Math & Nature in Three-Dimensions

Space, Structure and Form

Rochelle Newman & Donna M. Fowler

Mathematics Consultant
Judith F. Moran, Ph.D

Photographer
Richard C. Newman

Illustrator, Drawings
Susan Libby

pythagorean
press

P.O. Box 5162
Bradford, MA
01835-0162

Brown & Benchmark
PUBLISHERS

Madison, WI Dubuque Guilford, CT Chicago Toronto London
Mexico City Caracas Buenos Aires Madrid Bogotá Sydney

About the collaborators:
Rochelle Newman is an artist and Professor Emeritus.
She has taught at Northern Essex Community College
and Bradford College, Haverhill, Massachusetts. She
has given workshops and lectures on the interdisciplinary
connections of art, math, & nature.

Donna M. Fowler is an artist and graduate, Magna Cum
Laude, of Bradford College. She resides in Bradford,
Massachusetts.

About the contributors:
Richard C. Newman is an artist and Chair of the Creative
Arts Division at Bradford College, Bradford, MA. He
was always there to capture the ever elusive image on
film.
Cover photo: Monument Valley, Arizona

Susan Libby is a graphic artist and illustrator who took
the concepts and translated them into beautiful images.

Judith F. Moran, Ph.D. is a faculty member at Trinity
College, Hartford, Conn. She has always been a strong
supporter of the connections between art and math.
It was, in fact, her discussions with Rochelle Newman
that began the journey that resulted in the
books published by Pythagorean Press.
The sole responsibility for this book, however, lies
with Pythagorean Press. Our mathematics consultant,
Dr. Judith Moran, was with us to correct our
errors and make suggestions for the improvement of
the mathematical content. But it was the Press that
ultimately made the choices. Suggestions and comments
from the readers are welcome.

ISBN 0-697-33058-3

Printed in the United States of America by Times Mirror
Higher Education Group, Inc. 2460 Kerper Bouldevard,
Dubuque, IA 52001

10 9 8 7 6 5 4 3 2 1

This book is dedicated to all things — great and small: galaxies to quarks; kittens to conundrums; sand grains to silver mountains, and to everything in between.

1% of sales is donated by Pythagorean Press to its Nurture Nature Fund for the support of environmental protection projects.

Acknowledgements

We wish to acknowledge, and affirm, the work of some of the organizations that toil to preserve a biocentric view of this earth. We link with these to forge a chain of responsibility that will encircle this planet.

The Audubon Society, The Body Shop, Ben and Jerry's Ice Cream, The Cousteau Society, Earthwatch, The Gorilla Foundation, Greenpeace, The Nature Conservancy, The National Arbor Day Foundation, Seventh Generation, The Rainforest Foundation, The Sierra Club, The World Wildlife Foundation.

In addition, we are grateful to:

Mary Calnan, Computer Illustration and Production Assistant
James F. Mahoney, Jr., Assistant to Donna Fowler

Science advisors:
Dr. Robert B. Cody, Jr. Ph.D.
Kenneth Holden
John F. Osborne Ph.D.

Professional artists:
Charles DiCostanzo
Arthur Silverman
Leslie Thompson
Wendy Waxman
Gilah Yelin Hirsch

Student artists:
Bradford College, Bradford, Mass.
Northern Essex Community College, Haverhill, Mass.

Contents

Preface

Life on Earth is an intricate network of mutually interdependent organisms held in a state of dynamic balance. The concept of life is fully meaningful only in the context of the entire biosphere.

Paul Davies
The Cosmic Blueprint

The structure of the Universe is of one piece; yet it masks itself in diversity and deceives us with its complexity. Science and Art both attempt to explore this structure in order to understand, and then make use of it. We ask questions, establish hypotheses, find some answers, and yet, the Universe is awesome. The more we learn, the greater the sense of mystery. The facts only serve to document the wonder. Our sensing of the cosmic order only deepens our admiration for all of creation — our aesthetic awareness of relationships which we call Beauty. We know only some of the " how" and the "what", but the essential questions of "who?" and "why?" remain.

We, citizens of this Earth, inhabit a minor planet rotating around a rather ordinary star only a million miles in diameter. We are located in the outer arm, three fifths of the way out from the center, of a spiral galaxy called the Milky Way, which is one hundred thousand light years from edge to edge and contains some 200 billion stars. It is one of a cluster of nineteen such galaxies spread throughout a region which would take three million lightyears to cross. Yet, it is only one of countless galaxies in the Universe.

But here we are! And conditions on this planet are unique. Life is what it is because of the special properties of this place and its perfect location, ninety-three million miles from the Sun. It has just the right size and mass to hold air and water, the essential plasma of life, to its surface. This planet has just enough spin, approximately one thousand miles per hour, to create a balanced cyle which allows for the Sun's heat to be absorbed by day and to be radiated out at night. There is just the right temperature range for life to survive. In addition, the earth is protected by a band of ozone which shields its inhabitants from the short-wave region of ultraviolet light, the most dangerous part of the Sun's radiation.

The Earth, our three dimensional biosphere, known to some as Gaia, is not a gentle place. Even though its diameter is almost 8,000 miles, we live essentially on the crust, a thin, solid surface layer resting on a core of radioactive metal. This layer is constantly shifting and realigning itself in response to internal stresses. The continents drift, pull apart, collide. Mountain ranges rise and fall. Earthquakes open and close the ground. Volcanoes attest to hot spots in the core of the earth. Yet, on this surface is found the entire spectrum of exquisite life as we know it, and life continues to beget life.

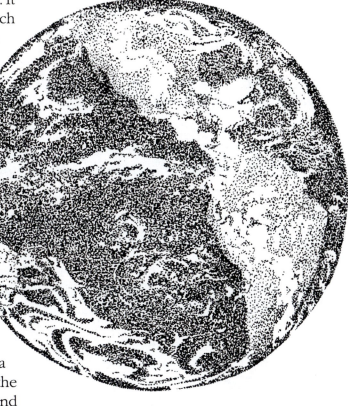

Conditions suitable for life have existed for some 4.6 billion years. However, humankind only appeared on this place about five million years ago, a mere tick on the vastness of the cosmic clock. Civilization itself is only several thousand years old — not much time to have learned how to behave as good citizens.

Our star will continue to give off heat and light for another five billion years. But will we humans with carelessness, greed and lack of foresight have destroyed our planet long before that time? Our world is defined by its limits. Our future depends upon accepting constraints and working within them. There is a point of balance and we must protect that: we who are the custodians of Gaia.

> *A future in which man replaces all other living things is no future at all.*
>
> *Carl Swanson*
> *Biologist*

Introduction

The space odyssey spirals us outward to the edges of the known. The boundaries shimmer and dissolve with our search. While inside the core, is the heart of things which knits what matters together.

As we shape our spaces, so our spaces shape us.

Winston Churchilll
20th Century statesman

The tapestry of three-dimensional space is woven of the strands of length, width and depth. Add movement through space and you gain the element of time, a fourth dimension. Once the astronauts stepped out of a shuttlecraft and onto the moon, the sense of our three-dimensional environs became much clearer to us than when we walked only on the relatively flat surface of the earth. Viewed from off that surface, the actual curvature of our planet is apparent, so is the compelling beauty of Earth, so is our place in the solar system, and so is our connection to this galaxy.

Even though, mathematically, space is an undefined term, within our solar neighborhood it has particular prop-

erties. The reality of matter is really space — more space than matter, more nothing than something, more movement than rest, more uncertainty than constancy. Constraints of gravity, mass, weight and materials, tightly define the freedom of structure.

The artist is extremely aware of the limits of space. Felt as a physical presence with physical properties, it is through this medium that all of the arts are expressed. Dance, music, theater, architecture, and sculpture, all manipulate the space/time experience.

Sculpture and architecture are the visual arts of three-dimensional space. Both architecture and sculpture require the experience and memory of movement, sight and touch. They make space intelligible by defining mass and boundary. The void of space is shaped into something tangible. Sculpture is active volume while architecture is active container. Both require structure that is manifested through forms. But, not just any object is elevated to the stature of sculpture nor is just any building considered architecture. More than mere presence is required to accomplish both of these arts. There needs to be an underlying clarifying concept and a strongly felt emotion which is articulated through the sensitive use of materials in organization.

In the past, these artforms were tied to the sacredness of Earth because the Earth was believed to have an energy and a spirit that flowed throughout the planet. The spirit was that of the female generative principle, both fruitful and fearsome simultaneously. Because of this, once upon a time, Gaia was treated as a living entity made fertile by a powerful sun. She was considered precious and she whispered words of wisdom and love through every rock, stream, and hill. Once she was tended, cared for, and given reverence for her bounties. Now she is mutilated, raped, and left to die. And we profane her at our peril.

Architecture and sculpture were joined to sacred spaces: special energy sites that held deep meaning for the peoples who knew those places. These two artforms were connected to these particular places and they, in turn, made the places holy. Every sacred place has its own topographic qualities: the shape of the land, the prevailing winds, the rock formations, the water bodies that flow through, the vegetal and animal life that exist there. In the design of a sculpture or an architectural structure, the polar alternatives ranged between echoing the form of the landscape or sharply contrasting it. In architecture, either choice acted as a mediating device between earthbound humans and the celestial sky. Impartial, but acknowledged, Nature was shaped in order to define the human place within it. Chaos was brought into order through form.

Many buildings that have earned the status of architecture related to mountains and the clefts between them. Some provided open areas that gave visual access to the grandeur of the mountain, while others deliberately, however stylized, mimicked the form. Cultures as diverse as the Mexican Aztec, the Ancient Egyptian, and the Mesopotamian utilized the pyramid. The mountain forms varied with subtleties that differentiated the underlying beliefs of individual cultures. Sculpture became the handmaiden to the architecture.

In the Twentieth Century, where have all the sacred sites gone? Have they been obliterated by shopping malls and parking lots? Have the avenues of the ancient pilgrims become four-lane highways rushing to nowhere in particular? When the shards of our civilization come to light ages hence, how will archaeologists interpret our culture? Will we be defined only by our material needs — by our fascination with gadgets of newness — by our desires for immediate gratification? Where will they find our spiritual center — in the basement of a quick sale, discount department store?

Only when we establish networks of interconnectedness can we truly call ourselves human in the best description. Only when our reach exceeds our grasp do we partake of the Cosmos.

1 Planar Pushups

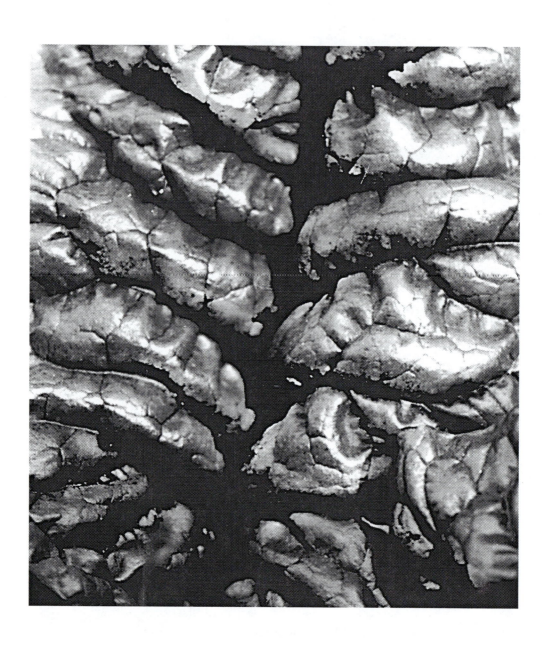

> Nothing exists except atoms and empty spaces ; everything else is opinion.
>
> Democritus
> Greek Philosopher 400 B.C.

Everything in our natural world exists in one of three states: solid, liquid or gas. Materials change from one state to another depending upon their inherent characteristics and the particular environmental conditions at a given time. Two main factors that influence change are pressure and temperature. Think of water, ice, and steam — three different states of the same substance. The study of materials and their properties falls within the realm of the natural sciences.

When studying the history of the life of our planet through its rocks, the science of geology can be likened to a diamond. From this stone the facets of other sciences, which deal with the specific aspects of the same diamond, can be cleaved. Petrology becomes the face on which the formation, alteration, and decay of rock is mirrored. Petrography is the face that describes, and then places, these solids into systematic classifications.

On the other hand, mineralogy can be likened to the facet that is the mirror of the soul of the diamond. It is the science that delves into the internal mystery of the gem's many substructures, as opposed to focusing on the diamond as a whole. This division lays down the foundation for the study of the inherent characteristics of rocks through their elements and compounds; the smallest units of matter from which they are composed. After this fragmentation has occurred, it is the science of crystallography, a subfacet of mineralogy, that seeks to explain the reconstruction of these elements into the orderliness underlying the beauty and symmetry of crystals.

Mineralogy is a science that requires the study and use of physics, chemistry, and mathematics. The use of mathematics, geometry in particular, lends the means by which artists can provide visual explanation to subjects, such as chemistry, which is the science of the realm of chemical elements. It is the quest of the physicist, however, to find that elemental unit that cannot be cleaved apart.

In this volume we will be concerned with solids, and as such, we may be likened to many of the scientists that work in those facets of the fields that we have just discussed. Our primary thrust will be to explore aspects of three-dimensional geometry. Mathematically, we are speaking of pure abstraction out of the arena of the natural and the physical. However, through art, ideas can be made concrete. Forms are created that become models for both naturally occurring phenomena and geometric ideas.

Mathematical Notation

Symbol	Example	Description of Terms

Lines

$\overleftrightarrow{AB}$

Line ($\overleftrightarrow{AB}$)
The tracing or connecting of points in space. A line has infinite length; however, it has no other dimensions. It can be named by any two of its points.

$\overrightarrow{AB}$

Ray ($\overrightarrow{AB}$)
A line that is bounded by an endpoint at one end, and extends infinitely in the other direction. It is named by its endpoint and any other point on its length.

$\overline{AB}$

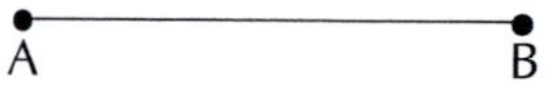

Line segment ($\overline{AB}$)
That portion of a line which is bounded by an endpoint at both ends. It is named by its endpoints.

$\overleftrightarrow{AB} \perp \overleftrightarrow{CD}$

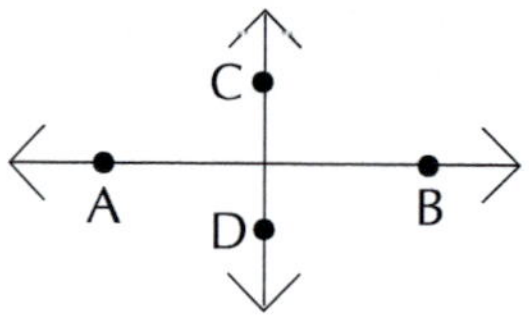

Is perpendicular to ($\perp$)
Two lines are perpendicular if they intersect at an angle of 90°.

Angles

$\angle ABC$

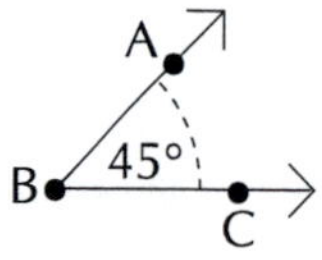

Angle ($\angle$)
Two rays sharing a common endpoint form an angle at the common ends.

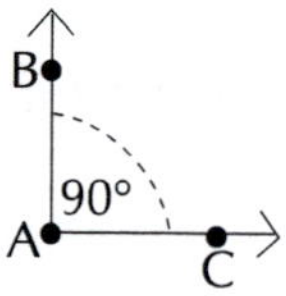

Right angle ($\square$)
An angle that has 90° between rays.

$\triangle ABC$

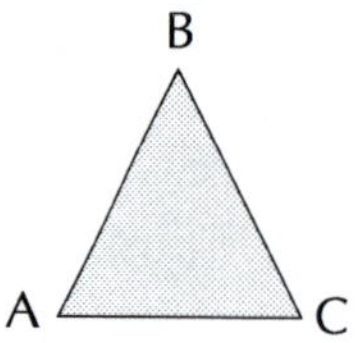

Triangle ($\triangle$)
A three sided polygon, or bounded planar surface.

Often symbols are used as a shorthand to replace the lengthy use of words. If the significance of these characters is not previously known, it is difficult to comprehend what is being communicated. It is for this reason that we include the chart on pages 2, 3, and 4, in which we

Description of Terms	Example	Symbol

Ratios

Ratio (: or /)
The mathematical comparison of numbers to each other. Sometimes these numbers are represented by letters.

16 to 10
or
A to B

16:10 or 16/10
or   or
A:B   A/B

Pi (π)
The ratio, or comparison, of the circumference of a circle to its diameter. It is approximately equal to 3.14.

Circumference
Diameter

π

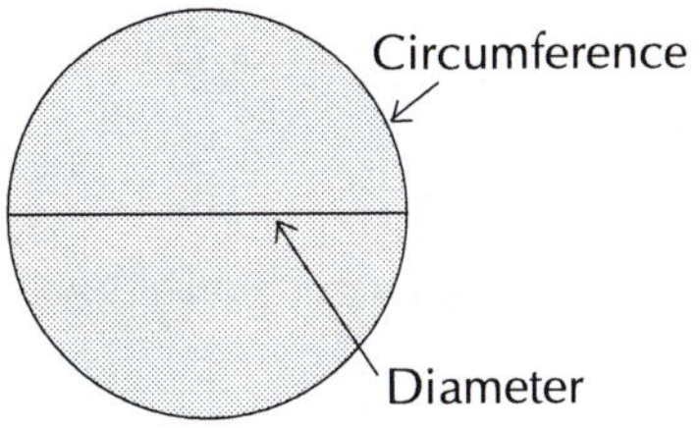

Relationships

Is equal to (=)

1+2 is equal to 2+1

1+2=2+1

Is approximately equal to (≈)

Pi is approximately equal to 3.14

π≈3.14

Is congruent to (≅)
Both geometric objects have the same size and shape.

Triangle ABC is congruent to triangle DEF

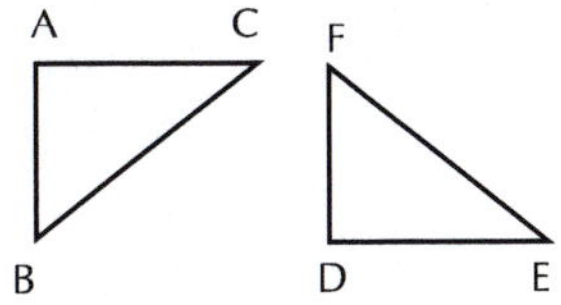

Is proportional, or similar to (~)
Both terms have the same shape, but are of different sizes.

Rectangle ABCD is similar to rectangle EFGH

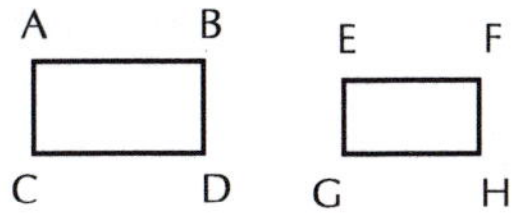

Is not equal to (≠)
Both terms are not equal.

64x2 is not equal to 2+1

64x2≠2+1

Is greater than (>)
The first term is larger than the second term. Notice the direction of the arrow: the narrower entity is next to the smaller end of the inequality symbol.

63 is greater than 21

63>21

translate some of the symbols used in this book. We begin with the longhand description of terms followed by the appropriate symbol. The chart on page 9 illustrates how many of these symbols can be put to practical use in the characteristic description of a simple rectangular sheet of paper.

Symbol	Example	Description of Terms
$A(B+C) \geq D(B+C)$	$A(B+C)$ is greater than or equal to $D(B+C)$	Is greater than or equal to $(\geq)$ The first term is larger than, or equal to, the second term.
$10 < 17$	10 is less than 17	Is less than $(<)$ The first term is smaller than the second term. Once again, notice the direction of the arrow.
$A+B \leq C+D$	$A+B$ is less than or equal to $C+D$	Is less than or equal to $(\leq)$ The first term is smaller than, or equal to, the second term.
$1+2=3 \therefore 3=2+1$	$1+2=3$ therefore $3=2+1$	Therefore $(\therefore)$ The second condition follows from the first as a conclusion.

Measurement

Linear

Symbol	Example	Description of Terms
$10''$	10 inches	Inches $('')$ A particular number of inches.
$2'$	2 feet	Feet $(')$ A particular number of feet.

Angular

Symbol	Example	Description of Terms
$45°$	45 degrees	Degrees $(°)$ A particular number of degrees in an angle.
$45°7'$	45 degrees 7 minutes	Minutes $(')$ A subdivision of a degree. There are 60 minutes in a degree.
$45°7'16''$	45 degrees 7 minutes and 16 seconds	Seconds $('')$ A subdivision of a minute. There are 60 seconds in a minute.

Subscripts and Superscripts

Symbol	Example	Description of Terms
x_4	denotes the fourth term in the sequence of $x_1, x_2, x_3, x_4, x_5, ...$	x sub n x_n) This marks the position of a particular term in a sequence.
10^3	10 times 10 times 10	X to the nth power (X^n) A particular number is multiplied by itself n number of times.

Above:
Gaia at work.

Gaia, often referred to as Mother Earth, or The Great Mother, is considered to be the eternal generative principal of our universe. She is supposedly charged with the soul responsibility of weaving The Great Tapestry of Life into an integrated and harmonious work of art. The yarns that she uses to do so come from the tangled skeins of Chaos.

The entire fabric becomes stronger than the individual strands when the delicate horizontal elements of the weft are intricately interlaced with the stronger vertical ones of the warp. The result is a completed piece that can withstand the stress of everyday wear and tear. Every strand is equally important in the design of the mantle that is meant to cover and protect all of her precious children.

Symmetry is the warp that forms the working structure of the piece, while elements, such as the Golden Ratio, are the weft threads that weave in and out of the warp. Depending on the perceived pattern, the symmetry may be hidden within the layers, leaving us to believe that there is only asymmetry, or the lack of order, present, when in truth, they both coexist. In this book, we consider the warp threads of symmetry in great detail, while the threads of such ideas as the Golden Ratio weave in and out.

> *Nature uses only the longest threads to weave her pattern, so each small piece of the fabric reveals the organization of the entire tapestry.*
>
> Richard Feynman
> 20th Century Theoretical Physicist

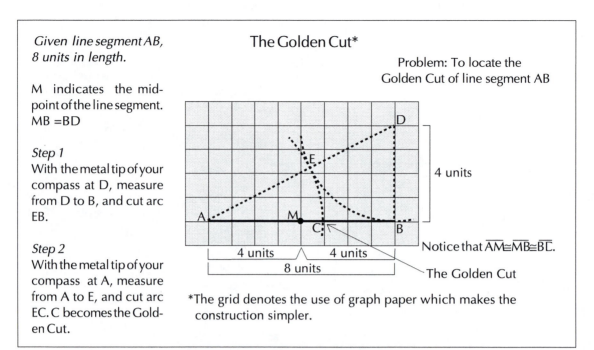

Given line segment AB, 8 units in length.

M indicates the mid-point of the line segment. MB =BD

Step 1
With the metal tip of your compass at D, measure from D to B, and cut arc EB.

Step 2
With the metal tip of your compass at A, measure from A to E, and cut arc EC. C becomes the Golden Cut.

The Golden Cut*

Problem: To locate the Golden Cut of line segment AB

4 units

4 units   4 units

8 units

Notice that $\overline{AM} \cong \overline{MB} \cong \overline{BC}$.

The Golden Cut

*The grid denotes the use of graph paper which makes the construction simpler.

In order to be able to understand the concept of the Golden Ratio, we must first come to terms with the idea of any ratio. A ratio is a comparison between things, and to be mathematically precise, it is a comparison of numbers only. As such, the kinds of things being compared do not come into account. For instance, we can compare 5 men to 3 women without resorting to gender by comparing only the number 5 to the number 3. Sometimes this is expressed as 5:3 or 5/3. The ratio 5/3 is an indicated division. When we actually carry out the operation:

$$\begin{array}{r} 1.666... \\ 3\overline{)5.000} \\ \underline{3} \\ 20 \\ \underline{18} \\ 20 \\ \underline{18} \\ 20 \\ \underline{18} \\ 2... \end{array}$$

We see that the ratio 5/3 can also be written as an infinite repeating decimal, 1.66666..... This particular ratio comes close to the numerical value of the Golden Ratio, which is sometimes referred to as Phi, or Ø, and is approximately equal to 1:1.618.

The Golden Ratio appears in very many places from relationships in nature to human constructs, such as the composition of paintings; to the ground plans in architecture; and to the layout of gardens. The Golden Ratio, however, unlike the ratio 5/3 is not obtained as a ratio of two integers, or positive whole numbers. Instead, it is a ratio of the lengths of two line segments. When this ratio appears, it tells us that if a line is divided at a particular point, which we shall call the Golden Cut, the smaller line segment is in relation to the larger segment as the larger segment is in relation to the whole line. This relationship can be expressed geometrically, as seen in the chart at the top of this page, as well as numerically. We have chosen to give some information about both ways of looking at this concept. The opposite page gives the proof of how a physical line segment can be given a numerical value. Thus, you can see a connection between space and number.

Golden Ratio Connections

Geometric Representation

On any line segment,   A ——————————————— B

there is a Golden Cut, labelled C,   A —————————— C ———— B
The Golden Cut

which can be calculated from either end.   A ———— C —————————— B
The Golden Cut

The Golden Cut separates $\overline{AB}$ into the Golden Ratio: $\overline{AC} = 1 : \overline{CB} = 1.618$.

A ———— 1 ———— C C ————— 1.618 ————— B

> Only when the line is divided precisely at this location does the unique relationship occur in which:
> $$\overline{AC} \sim \overline{CB}$$
> as
> $$\overline{CB} \sim \overline{AB}$$
> It is this fact that makes the Golden Ratio so significant.

Mathematical Proof of the Golden Ratio
(Requires the use of the Divine Proportion, the quadratic equation, and the quadratic formula.)

Let AC=x and CB=1.

A ———— x ———— • ———— 1 ———— B
                  C

We will now solve for x using the Divine Proportion, an equation that sets two ratios equal to each other.

$$\frac{AC}{CB} = \frac{CB}{AB}$$ = AB is to AC as AC is to CB =
$$\downarrow \quad \downarrow \quad \downarrow \quad \downarrow$$
$$x+1 \quad x \quad x \quad 1$$

$$\frac{x+1}{x} = \frac{x}{1}$$

> Divine Proportion
> $$\frac{AC}{CB} = \frac{CB}{AB}$$

We now cross multiply.

$$\frac{x+1}{x} = \frac{x}{1} = x+1 \cdot 1 = x \cdot x = x+1 = x^2$$

We now clear the equation with the use of the quadratic equation.

$$x+1 = x^2 = 0 = x^2 - x - 1$$

We now use the quadratic formula to solve for x. Notice that we substitute our numbers and then clear the fraction.

$$x = \frac{-b \pm \sqrt{b^2 - 4ac}}{2a} = x = \frac{1 \pm \sqrt{(-1)^2 - 4(1)(-1)}}{2(1)} =$$

> Quadratic Formula
> $$x = \frac{-b \pm \sqrt{b^2 - 4ac}}{2a}$$

$$\frac{1 \pm \sqrt{1+4}}{2} = \frac{1 \pm \sqrt{5}}{2} = \frac{1 \pm \sqrt{2.236}}{2} =$$

$$\frac{1 \pm \sqrt{2.236}}{2} = \frac{3.236}{2} = 1.618 = \varnothing = \text{The Golden Ratio}$$

Above:
Not only can paper be manu-
factured from trees, but the
bark of the tree suggests a
piece of paper.

The Euclidean plane is an abstraction used to examine geometric relationships in two dimensions. In Nature, a perfectly flat, rigid plane with no thickness does not exist. Rather, surfaces are twisted, convoluted, rough and irregular. In short, they are fractal.

A piece of paper lies somewhere between the perfection of mathematical abstraction and materials that occur naturally in our world. Even though it is constructed from natural resources, it does not exist without human intervention. It is a flimsy solid, unable to stand by itself or support anything else. Unlike living things, it has no bracing skeletal structure to give it stability until one starts to manipulate it.

Like the Euclidean plane, a piece of paper is an artifice. It represents a bounded portion of a plane purged of any irregularities. However, it is a useful fiction. It can function as a transition between the exploration of relationships in two and three dimensions. In this chapter we will examine ways to manipulate the plane to give it strength, stability and three-dimensionality. The humble sheet of paper is a powerful medium for exploring ideas that could be realized in more expensive and technically demanding materials. The chart on page 9 aids us in looking at the characteristics of a commonly used sheet of 8.5"x11" paper.

> *Except for the most primitive forms of life, all living things have a bracing "skeleton" — internal or external — which gives them stability and form.*
>
> Andreas Feininger
> The Anatomy of Nature

Characteristics of A Sheet of Paper

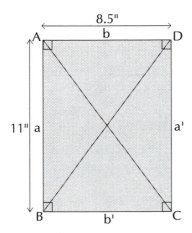

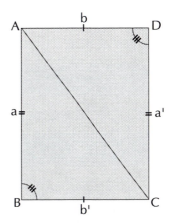

It is 8.5"x11".

It is called a rectangle. In this case rectangle ABCD.

It has length and width, and these can be named a and b.

It has opposite pairs of parallel congruent line segments which can be designated as a and a', and, b and b'.

It has four right angles which can be marked by a small square in each corner.

It has two diagonals, $\overline{AC}$ and $\overline{BD}$.

If one diagonal is used, the rectangle is divided into two congruent triangles: $\triangle ABC \cong \triangle ADC$.

Notice that because these triangles are congruent $\angle B \cong \angle D$, $\overline{AD} \cong \overline{BC}$ and $\overline{AB} \cong \overline{DC}$.

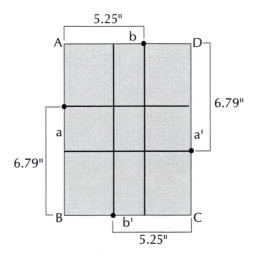

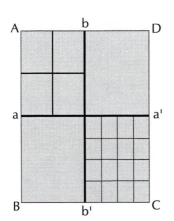

There are several ways in which this rectangle can be subdivided.

One of the simplest is to repeatedly divide the sides in half.

The ratio of the length of the rectangle to its width is a:b.

In real numbers it is 11:8.5, or 11/8.5, which reduces to 1:1.29.

To divide side b into two segments in the Golden Ratio, divide its length 8.5 by 1.618 which equals 5.25. We call the division point the Golden Cut. The same would hold true for the other side. Notice that these given unequal divisions.

The Pleated Plane

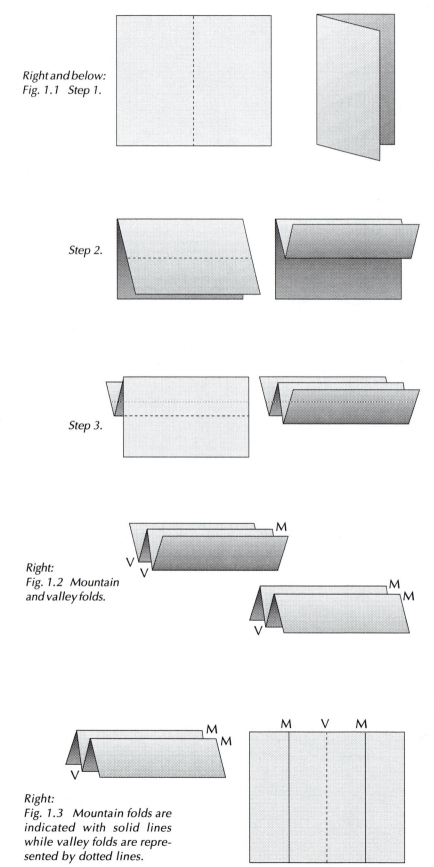

Right and below:
Fig. 1.1   Step 1.

Step 2.

Step 3.

Right:
Fig. 1.2   Mountain and valley folds.

Right:
Fig. 1.3   Mountain folds are indicated with solid lines while valley folds are represented by dotted lines.

The minute one puts a single fold into a piece of paper, its character changes. Try the following with an 8.5" x 11" piece of paper.

1. Fold the paper in half and crease between thumb and forefinger (Fig. 1.1). Notice there is a stability that did not exist before. It can now support its weight on edge, but it is not tremendously stable.

2. Lay the folded piece of paper flat with the centerfold at the top and fold one bottom edge up to it.

3. Turn the paper over and fold the other bottom edge the same way. With these two folds the paper has gained even more stability.

From this simple procedure, we now have the basis for the technique for examing the pleated plane and the vocabulary to describe it. If you lay the paper on two of its folds (Fig. 1.2) you will notice that the center fold rises. It is called a mountain fold (M). The two folds that the paper is resting on are called valley folds (V). If you turn the paper over, you will see two mountain folds and one valley fold. Diagrammatically, the folds in a piece of paper will be represented by using a solid line for a mountain fold and a dotted line for a valley fold (Fig. 1.3)

Paper folding can replace compass and straightedge in many geometric constructions. The fold functions as a line when the paper is opened. Increments between folds become units for measure.

There are several good books on

the subject of folded geometric constructions (see Further Reading). It is not our intent to duplicate those, but rather to use a combination of compass, straightedge, and folds, in order to explore three-dimensional ideas with some degree of accuracy.

We shall present paper folding constructions in the same format as the compass and straightedge ones. Instead of a compass icon, you will see a symbol of a piece of paper. This will be used to indicate that folding is an element of the construction.

Above:
Natural forms which suggest a pleated plane: the underside of a mushroom, the surface of a leaf, and elephant hide.

The following is one way to pleat the plane. Here we are not using the word plane in the true mathematical sense, but instead, are referring to a model in the form of a sheet of paper. Unless otherwise indicated, this will be the case from here on.

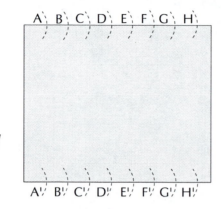

Fan Fold a Pleated Plane

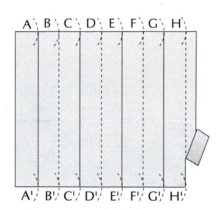

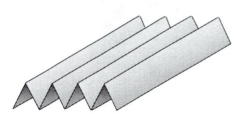

Given a sheet of lightweight paper*

1. Set your compass to whatever unit length you wish to use. Mark off consecutive units along a pair of parallel sides of the paper. Label points of intersection along one side A, B, C, ... and along the other A', B', C', ... as shown.

2. Lightly draw in segments AA', BB', CC', ...** . If the last strip is not congruent to the others, remove it. (This is easier than predetermining the number of congruent segments that will fit along the side of the paper.)

3. Fold AA' (M), BB' (V), CC' (M), DD' (V), and continue this way until all segments are folded.

Now the plane is fan folded.***

*If heavier weight paper is used, it may be necessary to **score** as well as fold.
**If you are very careful, you can fan fold without drawing guide lines first. Be sure to keep all pleats the same size.
***For a quick fold for studies, fold the paper in half, fold in half again, and fold in half once more. Open and recrease into alternating mountain and valley folds. Some accuracy will be sacrificed for speed.

Steps 1 and 2 in Construction 1 provide a foundation for many constructions. For example, try an M, M, V, V, ... sequence (Fig. 1.4), or an M, V, V, M, V, V, ... sequence (Fig. 1.5). See what kind of surface appears if you use a random folding sequence.

Skipping fold lines will result in further variations. Try V, M, V, skip, V, M, V, skip, V, ... (Fig. 1.6), or try counting off Fibonacci numbers before folding.

Unless you are prepared to be meticulous in your craftsmanship for the constructions in this text, you might as well go out and play baseball, or go fishing. You'll have more fun and will be considerably less frustrated.

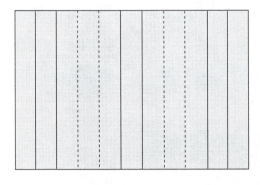
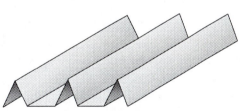

Left:
Fig. 1.4   M, M, V, V, ... sequence of folds.

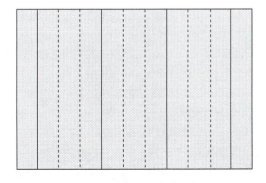
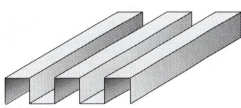

Left:
Fig. 1.5 M, V, V, M, V, V, ... sequence of folds.

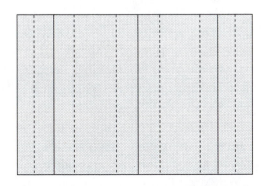
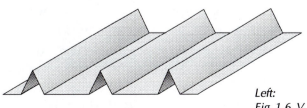

Left:
Fig. 1.6 V, M, V, skip, V, M, V, skip, ... sequence of folds.

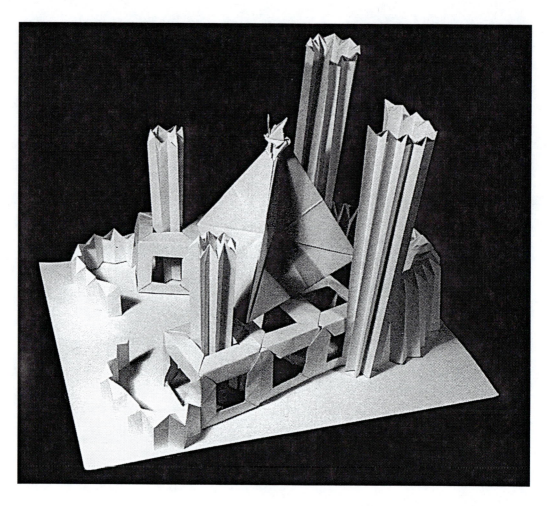

Above:
Ann MacLean. Folded fantasy dwelling. Modular structure of paper using different folding techniques.

The fan fold can be manipulated in other simple ways to create surface patterns, which, in turn, strengthen the paper. The original fan fold will be transformed by adding folds and turning some of the mountains into valleys and vice versa. Lightweight papers, such as typing bond, notebook paper, or tracing paper, are inexpensive and work relatively well for practicing the concepts. However, the folds soon lose their crispness.

Once the concept is mastered, a different paper may be desirable for creating artworks. Laser printer paper, lightweight, but somewhat more expensive, has a hard finish that is perfect for folding, and creases retain their hard edges. Where weight is not a factor in a finished artwork, this paper would be a good one to use. For a heavier project, Bristol works well if you first score fold lines with a pointed tool (an empty ball point pen is ideal). If even heavier materials are used, you may need to score fold lines with a mat or utility knife. This is extremely tricky and requires practice and patience. You may find that you must predetermine where all the mountain and valley folds will be on the finished piece, lightly pencil them in, and score on the mountain side of any fold. Some heavier materials (illustration board, plastics, sheet metal, wood, etc.) are not flexible enough to fold and reshape. They would need to be cut apart and reassembled. However, the paper model is valuable for investigating variations in forms, and so becomes a prototype.

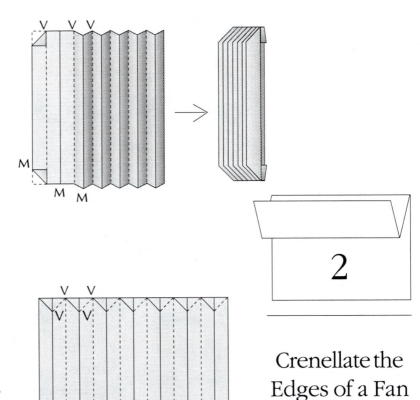

Given a closed, fanfolded piece of paper

1. Working along one edge of the paper, separate the pleats one at a time, each time folding the endpoint of the mountain fold over so that it rests on a valley fold. Bend the 45° fold in both directions so that it will be easier to manipulate. Fold the opposite edge in the same way.

2. Open and flatten the paper. You will notice a series of isosceles right triangles along the two edges. Each of these triangles is divided in half by one of the mountain folds of the original fan fold. One leg will be a mountain fold, the other a valley fold.

3. Crease each side of the isosceles right triangles into mountain folds and the center lines, or altitudes, into valley folds. You can do this by holding each pleat by the mountain fold and carefully pushing the triangle away from you.

4. Continue until all pleats are folded this way.

Now the fan fold is crenellated along the edges.

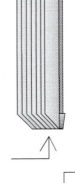

2

Crenellate the Edges of a Fan Fold

There are many interesting variations that you might try. One of them is skipping some mountain folds and crenellating others.

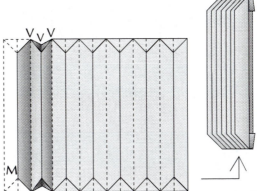

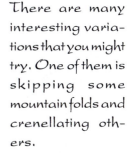

Step 1

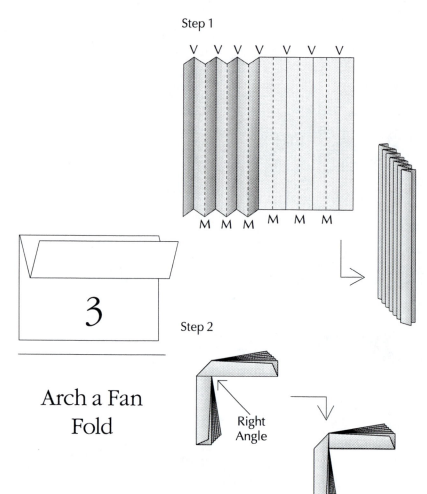

V V V V V V V

M M M M M M

3

Arch a Fan
Fold

Step 2

Right
Angle

Given a fan folded piece of paper

Initial Preparation
1. Refold the fan changing each mountain to a valley and vice versa, firmly creasing each pleat between your forefinger and thumbnail as you do so. This will make the piece more flexible and help you accomplish subsequent steps.

2. Crease the fan fold anywhere along its length so that it appears to form a right angle. The location and angle of this fold are actually arbitrary choices. The diagrams illustrate a 90° center fold. Open and fold in the opposite direction along the same crease, pinching firmly.

3. Open and flatten the piece of paper. You will see a series of trapezoids (such as ABCD) in which the nonparallel sides lie either on the edge of the paper or at 45° angles to the mountain and valley folds of the fan.

4. Turn all 45° creases into mountain folds beginning with EF. This is easiest to accomplish by pushing the fold up from the underside of the paper with one hand while pinching it into a mountain fold with the other.

Step 3

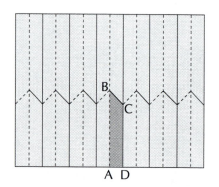

B
C
A D

Step 4

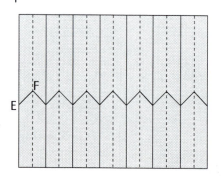

F
E

Step 5

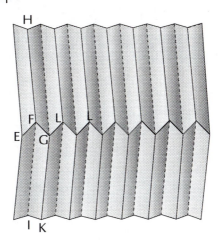

5. Adjust the fan folded pleats into the necessary mountain or valley folds. Begin by reinforcing mountain creases EF and FG. This time, however, rather than pinching the folds, crease them between your forefinger and thumbnail. This will naturally force FH into a mountain fold while FI will remain a valley fold. Crease as far up on each of these folds as possible, using your forefinger and thumbnail. Continue in this manner until all of the fan folded pleats have been firmly creased. After completing this step you will notice a slight arch in your paper.

Final Folding

1. With your left hand adjust pleat FH into a mountain fold and hold it. With your right hand adjust pleat FI into a valley fold. Pinch folds EF and FG together and hold them.

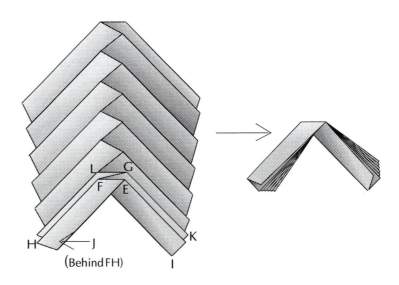

2. With your left hand adjust pleat GJ into a valley fold and hold it. With your right hand adjust pleat GK into a mountain fold. Pinch folds EF, FG, and GL together and hold them.

3. Continue in the same manner as in Steps 1 and 2. Alternate between left and right hands and mountain and valley folded pleats before pinching the 45° folds together.

Now when you open and stretch your paper, the fan is arched and can stand by itself.

A fan fold can be arched at any position along its length, and the angle of the fold can be any size desired. If either the position of the fold, or the angle of the fold, or a combination of both are changed, the resulting arches will look very different. Changing the angle of the first fold will alter the steepness of the arch. If the fan appears to be folded into an obtuse angle, the arch will be shallower (Fig. 1.7 A). An acute angle will give added steepness (Fig. 1.7 B).

You may want to experiment by creasing arches at more than one location on a single fan folded piece of paper. These creases should join at their endpoints along the edge of the folded fan (Fig. 1.7 C and D). When opened and flattened a diamond grid will appear. Diagonal lines will all become mountains, and the lines of the fan fold will all become valleys.

Work pleat by pleat and compress the pleats as you go.

Do multiple arches increase or decrease the manageability of the paper? What happens if the angles of these multiple folds have different sizes? What variations in form can you create? What happens if the paper has a drawing or design on it before you begin?

Sometimes it is easier to build large forms from either multiples of the same type of fold (modular building), or from groups of different types of folds. Using the same kind of paper will help you achieve unity. Experiment with different paper types and different joining techniques. The water in a water based adhesive might cause the paper to wrinkle. Therefore, if you wish to use an adhesive, make sure that you use one that is quick drying and not water based. Model cement is a good one to try. Use any adhesive sparingly.

Below:
Fig. 1.7 Folding patterns for different kinds of arches.

A. The angle of the arch will be obtuse.

B. The angle of the arch will be acute.

C and D. Creasing patterns for multiple arches.

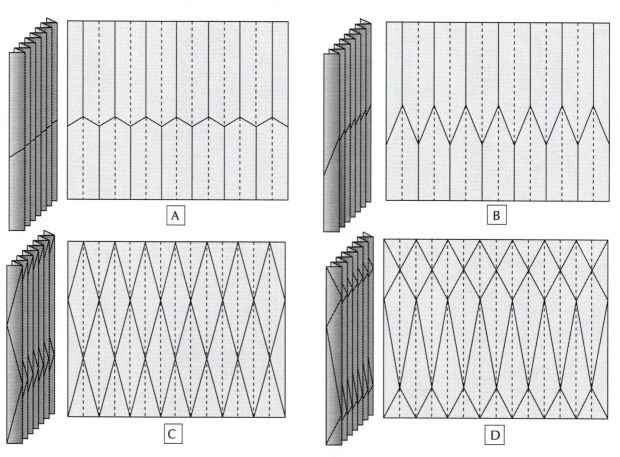

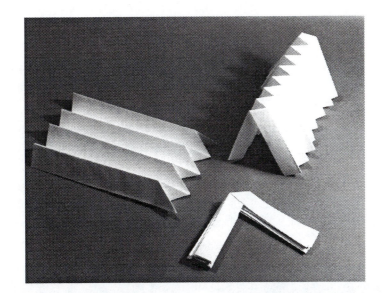

This page:
Folded units that can be used in multiples for building larger projects. These are fanfolds arched in different ways, and some are arched at more than one place.

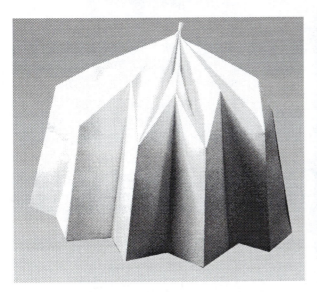

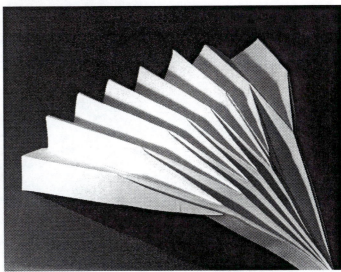

Step 1

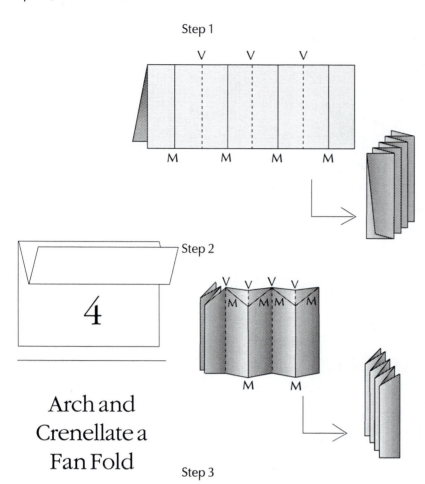

Step 2

4

Arch and Crenellate a Fan Fold

Step 3

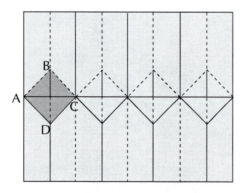

Step 4

Given a sheet of lightweight paper

Initial Preparation

1. Fold the paper in half lengthwise and then fanfold it.

2. Crenellate along the folded edge, remembering to crease all folds in both directions for ease of handling.

3. Open and flatten the paper. You will notice a series of squares (such as ABCD) joining one vertex to another along the original fold that halved the paper lengthwise. You will also notice that the mountain and valley folds in one half of the paper are opposite in orientation to those in the other half.

4. Reverse the direction of all folds in one half of the paper so that they match those in the other half. Although this can be accomplished in a variety of ways, the following technique works well.

   a. Begin by changing valley fold AB into a mountain fold. Push *up* on the valley fold from *underneath* the paper with one hand, and pinch it into a mountain fold from the *top* with the other.

   b. Change mountain fold BE into a valley fold. Push *down* on the mountain fold from the *top* of the paper with one hand, and pinch it into a valley fold from *underneath* with the other one.

   c. Reverse valley folds BF and BC into mountain folds. Push up from underneath and pinch from the top.

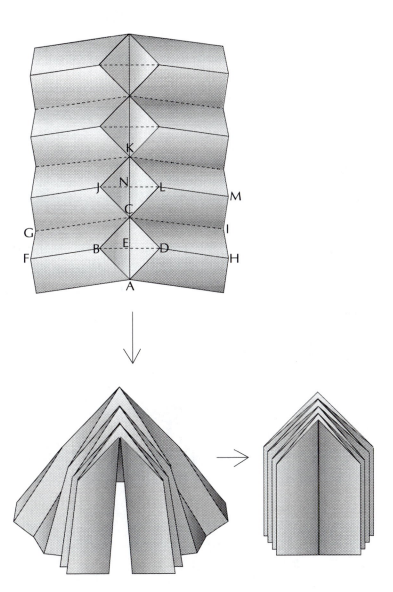

d. Turn CG into a valley fold. Push down from the top and pinch from underneath.

e. Continue in this manner, until all appropriate folds have been reversed. Now you will notice that your paper has begun to arch.

Final Folding

1. Using your right hand, gently pinch mountain fold DH as close as possible to D and hold it. Using your left hand, place your middle finger behind mountain fold BC and your thumb on the edge of the paper at A. Now, with your forefinger, gently push down on valley fold BD at E. Mountain folds DH and BF will pivot if you are not pinching too tightly at D. Finally, with your thumb, push A into C.

2. Readjust valley folds CG and CI if necessary. Using your right hand, gently pinch mountain fold LM as close as possible to L. Using your left hand, place your middle finger behind mountain fold JK, and with your forefinger, gently push down on valley fold JL at N. Finally, with your thumb, push A and C into K.

3. Fold the rest of the common vertices of the squares into the first group of three in the same manner as in Steps 1 and 2.

Now, when you open and gently stretch your paper, you have an arched fan fold creating a tunnel-like structure with a crenellated roof.

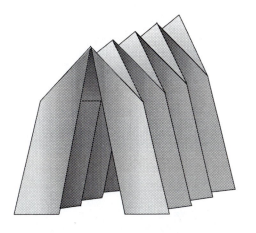

The Slit Plane

Folding the plane is an example of a single operation used to alter its form. Of course, complexity can result from multiple folds and surface embellishment. In this section, we will look at another way to manipulate the plane using a combination of operations.

Suppose you were given a sheet of paper and asked to stretch it in such a way as to lengthen it without adding or taking pieces away. The only way this can be accomplished is by cutting into the paper so that everything remains connected and no pieces are removed. We shall call this operation slitting.

There are several ways to slit the plane. The one shown in Fig. 1.08 would actually allow an 8.5" x 11" sheet of paper to form a closed path that a person could easily step through. Our interest, however, is in those slits that transform the plane in an aesthetic sense; those that produce surface patterns when light plays across the form or color is added.

On the opposite page, Figs. 1.09, 1.10 and 1.11 illustrate other patterns of slitting. In each, the structure of the piece is achieved by cutting on the dotted lines. The solid lines in Figs. 1.10 and 1.11 indicate where creasing is necessary.

Using scissors, an inexpensive and readily available paper, such as copier bond or notebook paper, will allow you to explore a technique quickly to see if it is appealing and worth investigating. To create an artwork you will probably want to use a heavier weight paper such as bristol. Using a mat or utility knife, instead of scissors, will help you get cleaner cuts and eliminate unwanted fold lines. Also, there is a variety of self-healing mats currently on the market which come in many different sizes. They provide a surface which makes cutting with a mat or utility knife much easier. Some are printed with grid lines which will enable you to keep your slits parallel, without having to first mark the slit lines with a pencil. As always, we encourage you to take these ideas further. You should never run out of rainy day activities.

Below:
Fig. 1.08 A slitting pattern that would transform the paper in such a way that a person could easily step through it. To create this pattern, first make the center slit where it is indicated by the dashed line. Then fold the paper in half along this slit and cut the plane along the remaining dashed lines. The closer together the slits, the larger the opening will be.

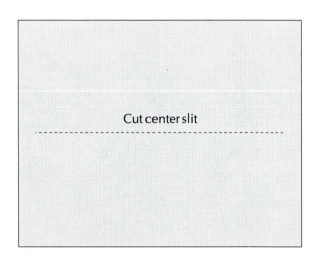

Cut center slit

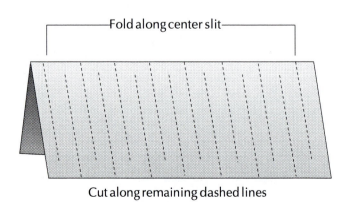

Fold along center slit

Cut along remaining dashed lines

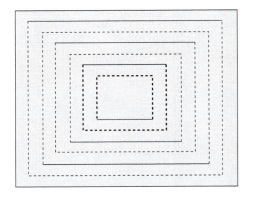

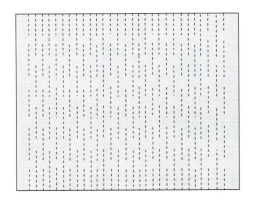

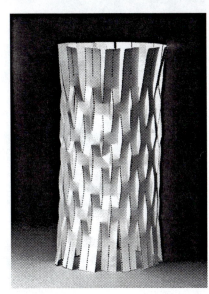

This page:
Slitting techniques. You can vary each of these patterns by using different spacing between slits. Use your imagination and have fun!

From top to bottom:
Fig. 1.09 Slitting a polygonal frame to form a series of similar polygons. Try this with several different shapes or try leaving the attachment on different sides.

Fig. 1.10 Slitting a net. This pattern becomes more interesting as the paper is stretched or folded.

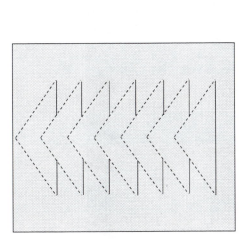

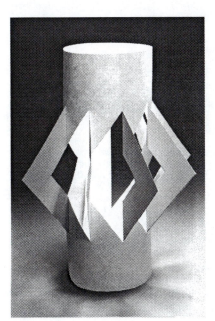

Fig. 1.11   Angular slits and parallel creases create a chevron fold. Although the diagram illustrates the use of an 8.5" x 11" sheet of paper slit at a specific angle, you are not restricted to using a rectangular piece of paper nor is the cut limited to this angle. Experiment for variations in form.

23

These facing pages:
Student works. Slit and folded
paper sculptures.

This page top and bottom:
Roseanne Porcelli

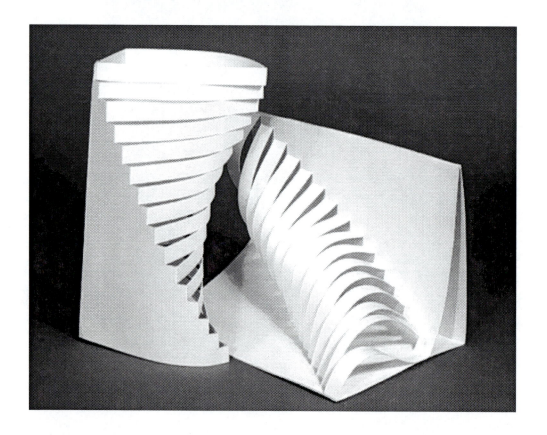

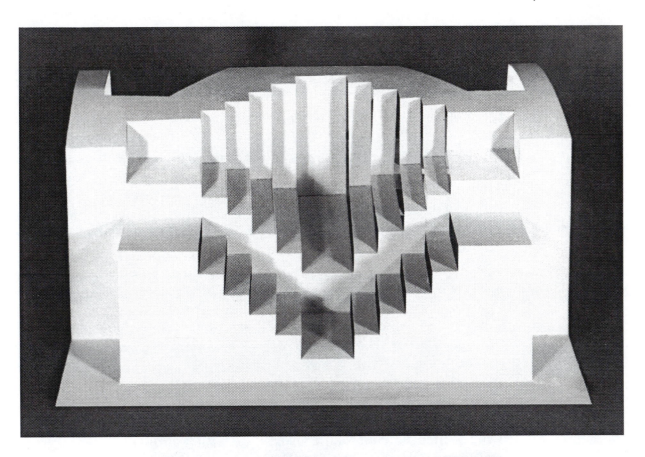

This page:
Two different views of the same work. Joseph Hastings.

The assignment limited the slits to one direction only with the use of mountain and valley folds. The paper had to be stiff enough to allow the work to stand by itself.

Inherent Symmetry

Opposite page:
The three art images derived from the natural world exhibit:
A. rotational symmetry
the fish have 3-turn symmetry but possess no reflection

B. reflectional symmetry
the relief sculpture of the green man exhibits reflectional symmetry through the vertical axis of the face.

C. a combination of both
the frogs have reflectional symmetry within the body. The frog is rotated three times within the hexagonal framework.
The flowers also possess reflectional symmetry. The single flower is rotated three times within the hexagon.

"The symmetry group of a periodic design is the collection of all isometries* which leave the design invariant; that is, they superimpose the design on itself so that it appears unchanged.

Doris Schattschneider
Mathematician

*translations, rotations, reflections, glide reflections

Space is the surround of us all. It is the invisible cloak that dictates our every turn. Everywhere it is the same. And everywhere, it forces our movements. We on this planet know only the spatial directions of length, width and breadth. We have always lived in space, but we have not always known that space is an actuality. Just as a fish lives in water, but is not conscious this medium directs its movement, so we exist in space but are not conscious of it. It is only when we bound it on the plane or place objects within it, do we sense its presence.

Practically, it exists as an undefined entity. It cannot be seen; it cannot be felt. Mathematically, space is an undefined term but for the visual artist space is the medium of expression. The visual artist explores its limits, gives it an aesthetic presence, and allows us to experience its power and beauty.

Symmetry is the all embracing concept that describes relationships in space. It describes the inherent relationship of parts to the whole within a single form. It also describes relationships in space of form to form. Everything found within our universe can be considered to be symmetrical or asymmetrical. Symmetry is directly related to repetition of arrangement, and we shall say than an object is inherently symmetrical if it possesses this quality. Conversely, we shall say that an object is inherently asymmetrical if it lacks such characteristics. We use the word inherent to differentiate between those symmetries than an object may have in-and-of itself, and the rigid body symmetrical movements that can be applied to an object.

To determine whether an object has rotational symmetry, turn the object to see if it can be superimposed on itself within the 360° of a circle. Because we can usually physically turn an object, we say that this operation of rotation is a performable one. The chart on page 32 shows the operation of rotation.

To determine whether an object has reflectional symmetry, imagine slicing the object in half and then placing a mirror along the cut edge. If the half-object and its reflection together, create an image of the original, we say that the original has reflectional symmetry. Because we cannot usually physically slice an object in half, but instead imagine the operation, we say that this operation is nonperformable. An artist, however, could construct a half-image and then reflect it to obtain a full one. The chart on page 33 illustrates the operation of reflection.

As examples, we have chosen to use the geometrical objects of a square, in two dimensions, and a cube, in three dimensions, since both of these are familiar to a great many people. In addition, these two objects possess both kinds of symmetry inherent within them. Mathematical language uses the word "fold" for describing a rotation. Since in this text we have used the word fold in a very different way, we choose to use the word "turn" which shall be consistent throughout this book.

In the plane, a geometrical object is referred to as a motif. This may begin as either an asymmetric or symmetric figure. In either case, it can be manipulated in three major ways. The motif can rotate about a point (called Point Groups); it can move along a line in very particular ways (called the Seven Line Groups);

or it can cover the surface plane in very defined ways (called the Seventeen Plane Groups.) But its degree of freedom of movement is constrained by the fact that it lies in the plane.

A motif can become an object when it moves into the third dimension. With the added dimension, the degree of freedom of movement increases. The object, whether asymmetric or symmetric, can also rotate about a point; it can move along a row; or it can slide through space.

For the artist, despite what appear to be very tight restrictions, the ways in which a motif or object can be altered is seemingly endless. The proportions and shape of it can vary while the symmetry moves stay the same. The intervals of space between motifs can stay constant or vary. The motifs can even overlap while keeping the symmetry moves the same. The motifs and objects can be colored in an arbitrary or symmetric manner and still the symmetry moves stay the same. Understanding what the moves are increases the artist's control over what he or she is doing. Artistic freedom grows out of comprehending limits.

On the following two pages, we offer a visual summary of the point, line, and plane groups in two dimensions. A simple asymmetric motif composed of two joined line segments is used throughout. The two segments of the figure are in the ratio of 1 to 1.618 with an angle between them of 45°. The motif can become a unit after performing a reflection or rotation operation on it. In order to have a reflection, it is necessary to take the motif up off the plane into the third dimension and back down onto the plane. Therefore, in some ways you need the third dimension in order to perform operations in the second.

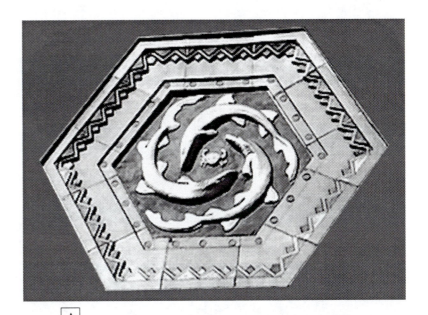

A

B

C

Symmetry Groups in Two Dimensions

The Point Groups

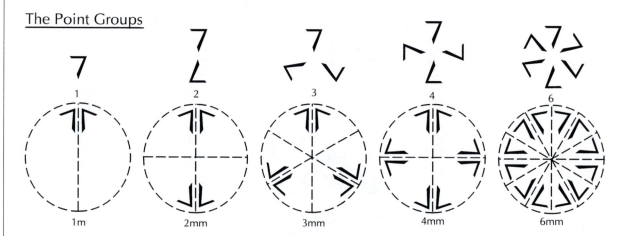

Notice both rotation and reflection about a rotation center

The Seven Line Groups

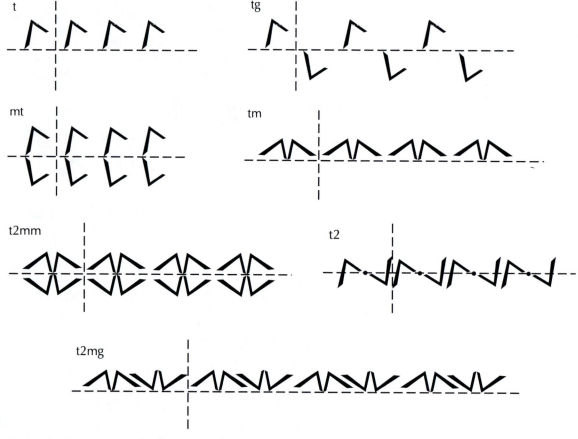

Notice both rotation and reflection. When a motif is first reflected, then slid, it is called a glide reflection.

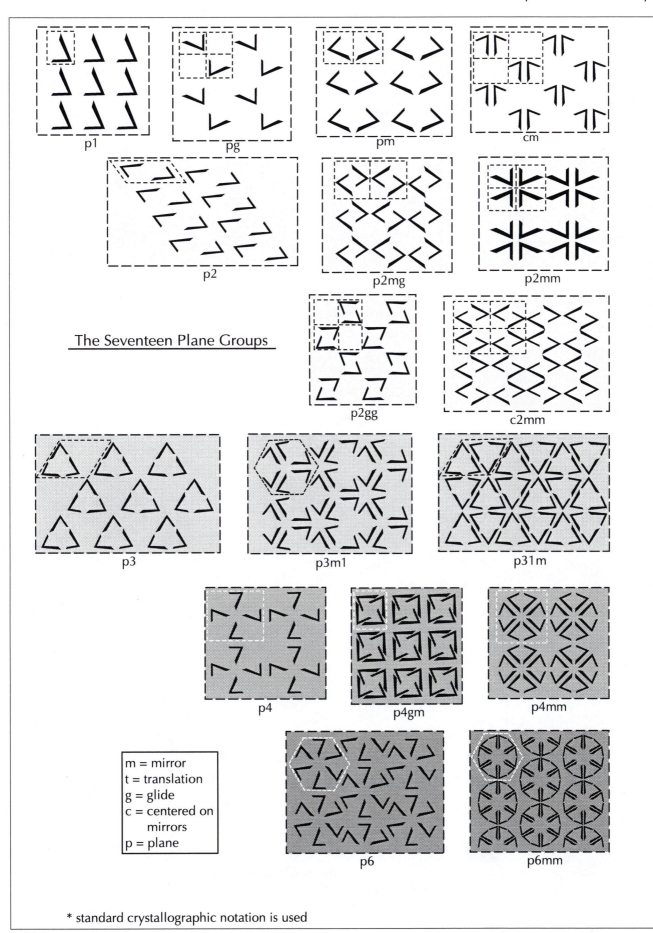

The Seventeen Plane Groups

p1 pg pm cm

p2 p2mg p2mm

p2gg c2mm

p3 p3m1 p31m

p4 p4gm p4mm

p6 p6mm

m = mirror
t = translation
g = glide
c = centered on
    mirrors
p = plane

* standard crystallographic notation is used

29

Each symmetry operation has an associated symmetry element. An element of symmetry is the implied geometric object about which the particular operations can occur. These are points, lines and planes. Although different, elements and operations are interdependent upon each other. These

Operation	Dimension	Element
Rotation	two	point (rotocenter)
	three	line (rotation axis)
Reflection	two	line (mirror line)
	three	plane (mirror plane)

are summarized in the chart on this page.

There is also a relationship betweeen the two kinds of symmetry operations. This relationship occurs in both two and three dimensions. The point of intersection of two axes of reflection (2-d), or two planes of reflection (3-d), is a point of rotation of the object. The angle of rotation needed to superimpose the object on itself is twice the measure of the angle between the axes or planes of reflection.

Symmetry Elements

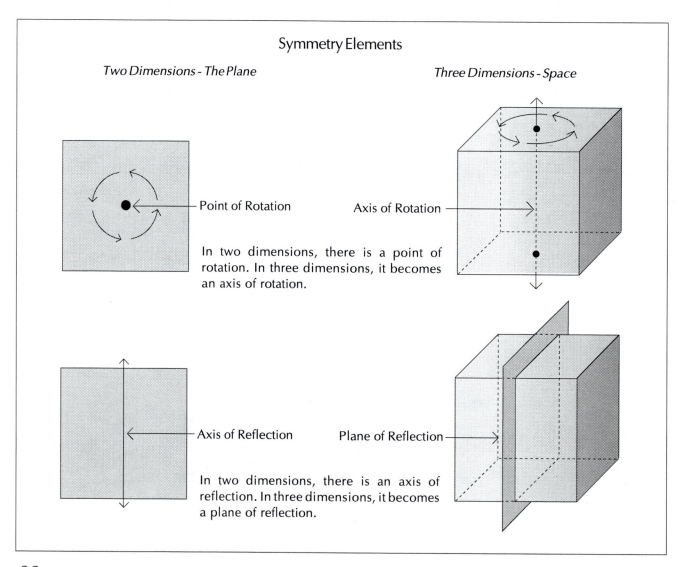

Two Dimensions - The Plane

Point of Rotation

In two dimensions, there is a point of rotation. In three dimensions, it becomes an axis of rotation.

Axis of Reflection

In two dimensions, there is an axis of reflection. In three dimensions, it becomes a plane of reflection.

Three Dimensions - Space

Axis of Rotation

Plane of Reflection

This page:
Sculptures and architectural details that display an essentially symmetric structure. Notice the subtle deviations from symmetry.

Left: Guardian Lion, Ringling Brothers Museum, Sarasota, Florida.

Top: Ram's Heads, Public sculpture, Canada.

Bottom: Fountain, City Hall, Santa Barbara, California.

Inherent Symmetries of the Square and the Cube

Operation: Rotation

Two Dimensions - the Plane
Element: Point of Rotation

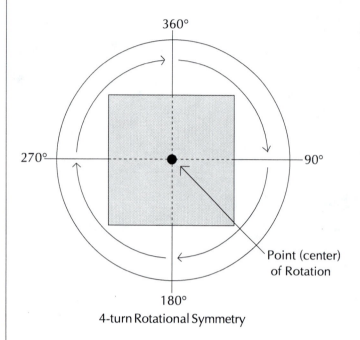

4-turn Rotational Symmetry

Two-dimensional rotation is the turning of an object about *a point in a plane* so as not to change the appearance of its orientation.

The number of times an object can be turned so that it becomes superimposable on itself within one complete revolution of 360° determines the type of rotational symmetry it exhibits. For example, an object that has 2-turn symmetry can be rotated 180° and 360° without changing its appearance. Notice that these are both multiples of 180°. An object that has 4-turn symmetry can be rotated 90°, 180°, 270° and 360° without changing its appearance. Notice that all of these are multiples of 90°.

* All of the two-dimensional objects that we explore in this book will have 1-turn symmetry.

Three Dimensions - Space
Element: Axis of Rotation

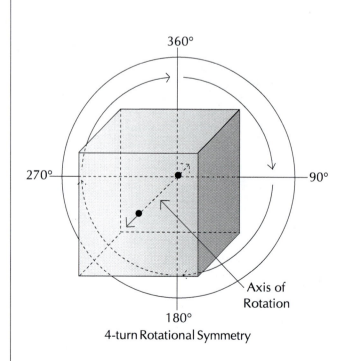

4-turn Rotational Symmetry

Three-dimensional rotation is the turning of an object about an *axis in space* so as not to change the appearance of its orientation.

Like the two-dimensional object, the number of times a three-dimensional object can be turned so that it becomes superimposable on itself within one complete revolution of 360° determines the type of rotational symmetry it exhibits. Therefore, an object that has 2-turn symmetry can be rotated 180° and 360° without changing its appearance. An object that has 4-turn symmetry can be rotated 90°, 180°, 270° and 360° without changing its appearance. Notice that when the square is used to construct the cube, the symmetries that are inherent in the square also become inherent in the cube.

* All of the three-dimensional objects that we explore in this book will also have 1-turn symmetry.

Operation: Reflection

Two Dimensions - the Plane
Element: Axis of Reflection

A two-dimensional object has symmetry of reflection if the axis of reflection divides it into two identical halves. This type of symmetry is sometimes referred to as mirror symmetry. If the object were actually cut in half along an axis of reflection and, the cut edge were placed touching the front of a mirror, the visual image would be that of the whole object.

Notice that the center of rotation is contained in the axis of reflection. All axes of reflection will pass through the center of rotation, however, a center of rotation is not always indicative that the object will have any axes of reflection.

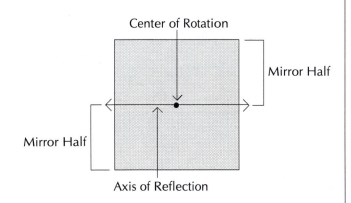

Three Dimensions - Space
Element: Plane of Reflection

As is with two dimensions, the three-dimensional object has symmetry of reflection if the plane of reflection divides it into two identical halves. Once again, if the object were actually cut in half along an axis of reflection, and the cut edge were placed touching the front of a mirror, the visual image would be that of the whole object.

Notice that the axis of rotation is cut by the plane of reflection. In this figure, all planes of reflection will bisect the axis of rotation, however, an axis of rotation is not always indicative that the object will have any planes of reflection.

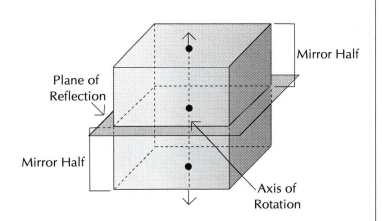

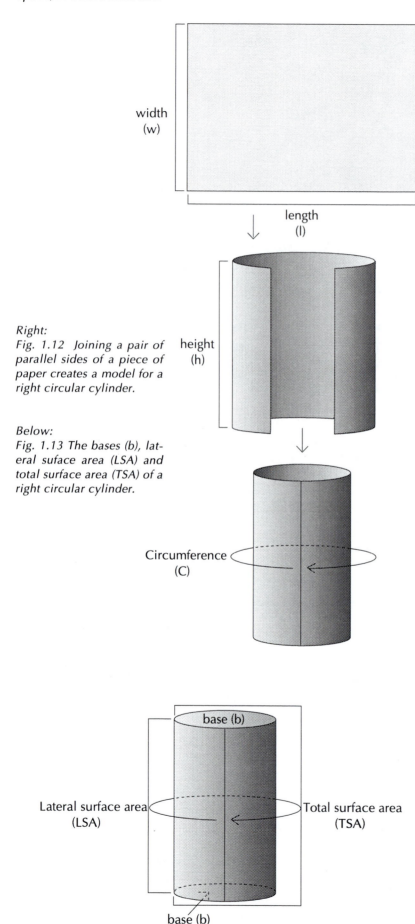

width
(w)

length
(l)

Right:
Fig. 1.12 Joining a pair of parallel sides of a piece of paper creates a model for a right circular cylinder.

height
(h)

Below:
Fig. 1.13 The bases (b), lateral suface area (LSA) and total surface area (TSA) of a right circular cylinder.

Circumference
(C)

base (b)

Lateral surface area
(LSA)

Total surface area
(TSA)

base (b)

The Right Circular Cylinder

Let us back up a moment to the unpleated plane. If we take our rectangular sheet of paper and roll it so that we can join a pair of parallel sides, we have a model that hints at one type of Euclidean solid, or three-dimensional figure. It is called the right circular cylinder; however, we will refer to it simply as the cylinder from this point on. Here, the width of the sheet of paper becomes the height of the cylinder, and its length becomes the circumference, or distance around the cylinder (Fig. 1.8).

Most people are familiar with this form. It is the one we find on the shelves of grocery stores filled with fruits, vegetables and dog food. Some of the common terms associated with this cylindrical form are tube, post, rod, pillar, column, drum, barrel, stalk or can, each with its own sense of size and use. A string can also be considered a cylinder.

While the cylinder that was constructed in Fig. 1.12 is open at either end, many cylinders completely enclose space, as in the example of a can. In this case, the disks on either end of the cylinder are called its bases. The height of the cylinder is the distance between these bases. The portion of the surface of the cylinder that lies between the bases and forms its circumference is called the lateral surface. When the areas of the bases are added to the lateral surface area their sum becomes the total surface area of the cylinder (Fig. 1.13).

The chart on the following page summarizes the symbols used in describing cyclinders. Since the base of a cylinder is a circle we include the following chart which defines geometric objects association with circles. Finally, the chart on page 28 gives the symmetries of a cylinder, as well as formulae for computing geometric quantities such as lateral surface area and volume for any specified cylinder. Remember to put in actual numbers when working with the equations.

Area (A)
The measure in square units of any bounded portion of the plane.

Base (b)
In a cylinder, the plane regions on either end.

Height (h)
In a cylinder, the distance between the bases.

Lateral surface area (LSA)
In a cylinder, the portion of the surface that lies between the bases.

Total surface area (TSA)
This includes the lateral surface area and the area of the base, or bases, of any three-dimensional figure.

Volume (V)
The measure, in cubic units, of any three-dimensional object.

The Circle

Circle
The set of all points in a plane at a given distance from a given point, which is referred to as the center of the circle. The circle is then named by its center. It is measured in 360°.

Radius (r)
A line segment from the center to a point on the circle. It can also be the number that designates the length of the line segment.

Chord
A line segment which has its endpoints on the circle.

Diameter (d)
A chord that passes through the center of the circle. It can also be the number that designates the length of the line segment.

Circumference (C)
The distance around the circle. This denotes a real number rather than a geometric figure.

Arc
The continuous unbroken part of the circle which lies between two points on a circle.

Tangent
A line that intersects or is tangent to the circle at exactly one point. This line is in the same plane as, but lies outside of, the circle.

$$\text{Circumference (C)} = 2\pi r$$
$$\text{Area (A)} = \pi r^2$$

Secant
A straight line that passes through and intersects the circle at two places.

Sector
A region in the interior of the circle bounded by two radii and the circle itself.

Quadrant
A sector that contains one quarter of the circle.

Symmetries and Formulae for a Right Circular Cylinder

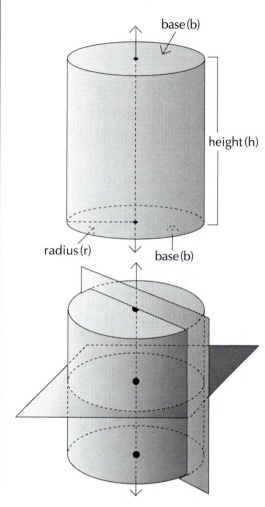

In each of the formulas below:
r= the radius of a base
h=the height of the cylinder
π=approximately 3.14

Lateral surface area: LSA=2πrh
The lateral surface area excludes the area of the two bases.

Total surface area: TSA=2πrh+2πr²
This formula adds the areas of the two bases to the lateral surface area.

Volume: V=πr²h
The area of the base x the height.

Rotational Symmetries: The cylinder has infinite-turn symmetry about an axis through the centers of both bases.

Symmetries of Reflection: Any plane that contains the axis of rotation of the cylinder is a plane of reflection. There are infinitely many of these. In addition, the plane that lies halfway between the bases, and is parallel to them, is a plane of reflection.

Now, let us give you an example of how to find the total surface area and the volume of a cylinder, using actual numbers. Our figure has a height of 12 units and each base has a radius of 3 units.

Approach:

1. Find the area of a single base.

   A=πr²

   A=3.14(3²)

   A=3.14(9)

   A=28.26 square units

2. Now find the lateral surface area of the cylinder.

   LSA=2πrh

   LSA=2[(3.14)(3)(12)]

   LSA=2(113.04)

   LSA=226.08 square units

3. Finally, find the total surface area of the cylinder.

   TSA=2πrh+2πr²

   TSA=226.08+2(28.26)

   TSA=226.08+56.52

   TSA=282.6 square units

Notice that the total surface area of the cylinder is nothing more than adding the area of the two bases to the lateral surface area.

1. Find the volume of the cylinder.

   V=πr²h

   V=(3.14)(3²)(12)

   V=(3.14)(9)(12)

   V=339.12 cubic units

This page:
The cylindrical form is suggested by many different kinds of architecture all over the world. Look at such structures as the Colosseum, the Column of Trajan, the Tower of Pisa and a Shaker barn.

37

Above:

Cylinders are wonderfully versatile shapes for solving certain design problems. Circular cylinders have greater volume for a given surface area, but rectangular solids are more advantageous when there is a need for close filling of space.

Consider creating a model for an architectural/sculptural outdoor environment which utilizes cylinders of various sizes, materials, colors, textures, etc.

What makes the cylindrical shape a useful one? Obviously, the answer depends on the particular design problem to be solved. For example, if a manufacturer wishes to create a metal container from a fixed amount of material, a little Calculus tells us that the circular cylinder will have greater volume than a rectangular solid. Therefore, the manufacturer can generate a more efficient package for the same amount of surface material if he or she produces cans rather than boxes.

If, however, the problem is to be able to store containers in the smallest amount of space, the rectangular solid is more efficient. It is a form that can pack space without leftover areas. Circular cylinders, on the other hand, while able to stack, cannot be closely packed with no empty spaces. If the problem is to design a container that has maximum volume for a given

surface area and will also pack space efficiently, Calculus proves that the cube is best suited for these purposes.

Another advantage of the circular cylinder is that it produces the most efficient distribution of heat. Its inherent streamlining cuts heat losses to a minimum. This is the reason we cook primarily in round pans rather than square ones.

Consider solid and hollow cylinders of equal length made of the same amount of material. The hollow one will have a greater diameter and can, therefore, support more weight than its solid counterpart. It is also more flexible, efficient, and resistant, and such shapes are abundant in the natural world. Circular cylinders make body shapes which have advantages for locomotion, and if the body is also flexible, the creature can roll up or bend around corners. A considerably large body can pass through a small space if cylindrical in form. Look at snakes, earthworms and caterpillars.

Hollow cylinders are useful for conducting liquids in and out of small spaces — think of veins, arteries, and soda straws. Again, hollow circular cylinders have the advantage over hollow rectangular solids. For the same perimeter or circumference, they will allow more material to pass through at once because of their greater volume.

Below:
Natural cylindrical forms. Perhaps you would like to research the biology and morphology of worms or snakes. How are they similar and how do they different? Why?

Above:
The megalith Stonehenge, as it stands today on the Salisbury Plain in England. In plan, it is circular in shape. In elevation, however, it suggests a cylinder.

Cylinder in Architecture: Stonehenge, England

Let us travel back in time about 5,000 years. While the ancient Egyptians were busy piling up huge stones in pyramidal forms, anonymous neolithic architects were erecting equally impressive upright stones in monuments we call megaliths. Some 50,000 of them have been found in western Europe and North Africa, all of which archaeologists agree were erected between 3500 and 1000 B.C. On the Salisbury Plain, about 80 miles southwest of London, England, stands one of the most famous of these megaliths — Stonehenge.

We look to astronomer Gerald Hawkins for some explanations. Associated with the Smithsonian Astrophysical Observatory, he spent several years in the early 1960's in an effort to unravel its mysteries. Although some of these may remain forever locked away, there are some facts that are known based on his research.

> To determine the anthropological reason for Stonehenge is impossible, and one can only speculate. The monument could certainly form a reliable calendar for predicting the seasons. It could also signal the danger periods for an eclipse of Sun or Moon. It could have formed a dramatic backdrop for watching the interchange between the Sun, which dominated the warmth of summer, and the Moon, which dominated the cold of winter.
>
> Gerald S. Hawkins
> Stonehenge Decoded

We now know that Stonehenge was used as an astronomical observatory. Its enormous uprights were placed to sight midsummer sunset, midwinter moonset, midwinter sunset, midsummer moonrise, and midwinter sunrise, respectively. Also, its entrance opens toward the midsummer sunrise. In addition to this, some researchers say that it is situated on a site that is considered to have a strong energy field, both magnetic and electric, and even today visitors often seem to be startled by the awesome presence of the place.

Stonehenge was built in three major stages by different groups of people between 1900 and 1500 B.C., and its appearance was altered radically during each stage. The order of construction of the various parts of the monument is not certain. However, the time of construction for the first phase can be pinpointed to 1900 B.C. using carbon dating of objects found during excavation.

In the first phase builders dug a huge circular ditch, and used the earth they removed to create banks on either side of it. The outer bank was only a couple of feet high, about eight feet wide, and formed a circle with a diameter of 380 feet. The inner bank, with its smaller diameter, however, was much larger, about six feet high and

twenty feet wide. There was a thirty-five foot opening to the northeast, facing the direction of the midsummer sunrise, which served as an entrance. These late Stone Age builders erected a coffin shaped megalith called the *heel stone* on the path to the entrance 100 feet outside the circle. The heel stone is made of sarsen, a kind of sandstone found in an area about twenty miles away.

It is also believed that the four *station stones* were erected at this time. If line segments were drawn connecting these four markers, a rectangle would appear. Gyorgy Doczi, in *The Power of Limits*, points out some of the golden connections at Stonehenge, one of which is the fact that this rectangle is a $\sqrt{5}$ Rectangle (Fig. 1.14).

Below:
Fig. 1.14 A $\sqrt{5}$ Rectangle is formed by joining the station stones which were erected during the first phase of building at Stonehenge. Notice that a $\sqrt{5}$ Rectangle is formed by the overlapping of two Golden Rectangles. Also during this first wave of construction fifty-six carefully spaced holes were dug in a circle just inside the outer bank. Discovered by John Aubrey 300 years ago, they now bear his name. It is unclear what the Aubrey holes were used for. Excavations reveal that they were filled both with chalk and human cremations.

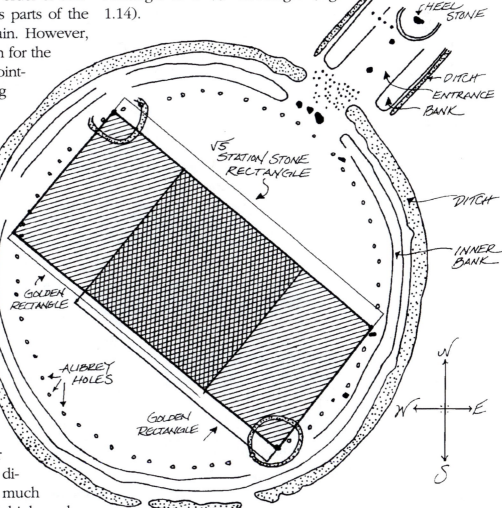

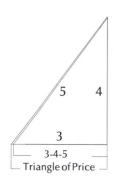

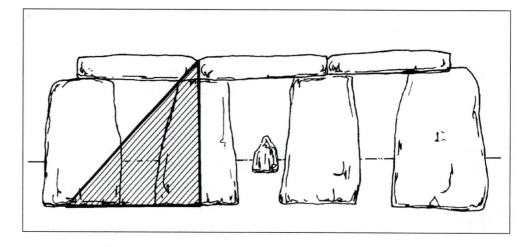

Above:
Fig. 1.15 The 3-4-5 Triangles formed by the uprights and lintels of the sarsen circle. The 3-4-5 Triangle approximates the golden proportion of the Triangle of Price, but uses whole numbers instead of an irrational relationship.

The second phase of building lasted from about 1750 to 1700 B.C., up until the end of the British Stone Age. During this time period two more concentric circles were erected in the center of this sacred space. These were constructed of bluestone, weighing up to five tons each. The entrance was widened by about twenty-five feet and a forty foot avenue was built connecting Stonehenge to the River Avon to accommodate the passage of these stones. The work of this phase was never completed, and in fact was taken down in the next stage of construction.

Four major elements were added to Stonehenge during the final building stage which began with the arrival of the Bronze Age in Britian. Two circles and two horseshoe shaped structures were built from different materials at different times, one inside the other. At the onset of this phase a group of five sarsen trilithons was erected to form a horseshoe with its opening to the northeast entrance of the original inner and outer circles. Trilithon is from the Greek meaning "three stone". The trilithons at Stonehenge are created by two uprights, weighing between forty-five and fifty tons, capped by a horizontal stone called a lintel.

At this time, a circle measuring 97' 4" in diameter, was erected around the horseshoe. Made of sarsen stone, it was constructed with thirty uprights capped with lintels, these being somewhat smaller than those in the horseshoe. The now familiar cylindrical shape of Stonehenge emerged.

Doczi again finds more interesting golden connections related to this final phase of building. He points out that if verticals are dropped at the seams of the lintels on top of the uprights in the sarsen circle, and diagonals drawn to form triangles (Fig. 1.15), the triangles are 3-4-5 Triangles. There is a very close relationship between the 3-4-5 Triangle and the Triangle of Price, which has golden ratio relationships.

The last addition was a circle of bluestone within the sarsen circle and a horseshoe of bluestone within the sarsen trilithon horseshoe (Fig. 1.16 on page 43). The use of bluestone was an amazing achievement, one that has been the focus of much speculation. This stone is found in the Prescelly Mountains of Pembrokeshire, hundreds of miles away from Stonehenge. Imagine not only the size of the work crew, but also the amount of time and effort that it

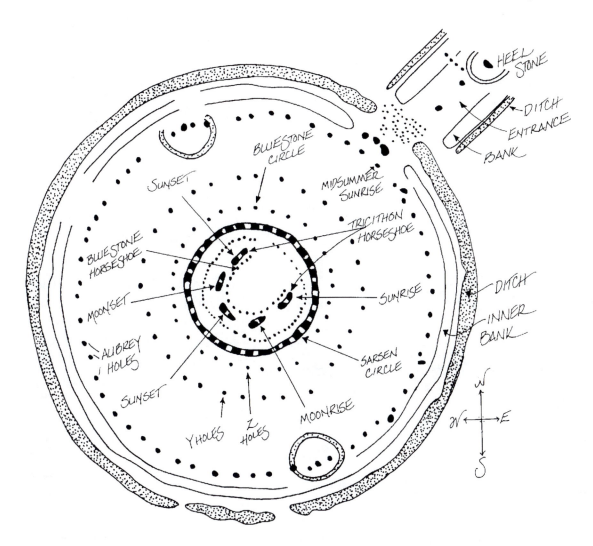

must have taken to move these huge boulders over land and water to get them to Stonhenge. Once there, the wonder remains as to how the stone was cut. Bluestone is so hard that even today, with the use of diamond drills, it takes many hours to bore a very short distance into this stone.

The builders of this phase were extremely sophisticated architects. All of the megaliths were hand worked. Lintels were secured by the mortise and tenon system, where grooves are created in one stone to accept ridges in another. It would seem that these people also wanted the uprights to appear perfectly vertical, since the technique called entasis was used to shape the stone so that there is a slight curvature toward the top to preserve the illusion of being straight up and down. You may recall that this was the same technique that the Greek builders used centuries later in creating the columns for the Parthenon.

Given the penchant for speed and expediency in our modern day society, can we understand what would drive a group of people to exert such energy, effort and time to a building project of this magnitude? Was it faith in continuity? Was it a belief in a purpose that was larger than an individual or a community and that lasted longer than a generation? One can only imagine what the answers to these questions might be. Perhaps the clue lies in the imagination.

Above:
Fig. 1.16   The results of the final building phase of Stonehenge. Notice a number of other holes were dug in two concentric circles between the Aubrey holes and the sarsen circle. The larger circle, called Y holes, contains thirty holes, and the smaller circle of Z holes contains twenty-nine. They are rather irregularly placed, were filled with chalk and rubble, and like the Aubrey holes, their use is not truly known. Some researchers believe, however, that they may have been used to chart the days in a month.

Noah was building an ark to survive the coming storm. We're building vessels for the storm we're already in.
A lunar module allows you to go to the moon and function. This model allows you to live on the earth and function.

Michael Reynolds
Architect

Earth Ships, USA

An interesting architectural use of the cylinder is found in the work of Michael Reynolds in Taos, New Mexico. As an architect and responsible citizen, he was concerned with both a housing shortage and the blight caused by the casual tossing of steel drink cans into the environment. In the early 1970's he developed a modular building block composed of eight steel cans (Fig. 1.17) which he used in the building of several homes.

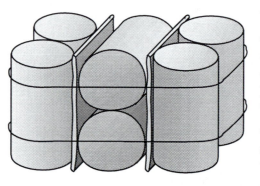

Left:
Fig. 1.17 Michael Reynolds' early building block made from eight metal drink cans. Notice that two of them have been flattened and placed vertically at each side of central pair.
Below:
Tire unit filled with earth, aluminum cans, and cement.

With time, his building units became a combination of used tires filled with packed earth and aluminum drink cans. This could be considered today's version of the old straw and clay adobe. A home might contain 800 - 900 old tires stuffed with a mixture of earth, aluminum cans, and lots of cement. These might be left unadorned or covered over. He calls his cre-

ations Earth Ships.

Mr. Reynolds' vision goes beyond architecture. He is interested in affordable housing, energy efficiency, ecological health, and self sufficiency. His earth ships are heated by the sun the energy of which is stored in the sculpted earth and tire walls. Sun powered photovoltaic cells provide electricity making the earth ship dweller independent from conventional power and utility companies. Mr. Reynolds' residences do not have standard plumbing, but rather have catch water roof systems to collect and filter runoff. A network of pipes transports used water back into the house. All wa-

ter, with the exception of sewerage, is recycled for use in indoor planters which are used to produce food that can be harvested year round. Sewers are not needed as Mr. Reynolds has invented solar composting toilets that reduce human waste to dust.

Reducing stress is another objective of this innovative architect. He feels that one way to liberate people from the stress of working at a job just to pay the mortgage is to offer them sound, affordable housing which they can build themselves, thus freeing them to do the things they really enjoy. It would seem that his venture is successful.

Above:

The "Can Castle", located in Taos, New Mexico. Administrative building for experimental architecture by Michael Reynolds. What is visible on the exterior by walls are the aluminum cans set in cement. This matrix functions both as structure and design. The object on the roof is the holding tank for water.

Designing on the Cylinder

In addition to the cylinder's usefulness as a structure for solving architectural problems, it also presents an interesting surface for pattern in other design areas. It is difficult, however, to work on a surface curved in three-dimensional space. Prototypes should be designed on easy-to-manage and inexpensive materials. Since the lateral surface of a cylinder is rectangular when opened up, it is easier to develop an armature, skeletal structure, for design using this planar figure. It is important to remember that the surface will look different in three dimensions and you must pay attention to what happens at a seam.

The most obvious design structure might be to break the rectangle into a series of bands. A less obvious design is that of the helix. The curve of the helix is not one that can be built spontaneously. It is generated by moving a point around and along a cylinder at a constant angle. Construction 5 on page 45 shows how to build a helix so that you can use it for your own design purposes. Construct your image on the rectangle first. Think about a pattern that fits the constraints of a particular ratio.

One of the most fascinating and important helical structures that we know is the double helix of DNA, found in the cells of animate forms. It carries the genetic information for the reproduction of life. It looks somewhat like a spiral staircase which uses the cylinder as an implied armature.

Such a configuration enables it to carry a great deal of information in a very small volume. The economy of materials, energy, and space, earmarks Nature's frugal housekeeping.

46

| Given a rectangular sheet of paper |

1. Begin at one corner of the paper (A) and, with your compass, mark off congruent segments along the width of the paper (B, C, D, E, F, G, H, and I). It does not matter if there is an unequal portion left over. If you want to construct a tight helix, make these units fairly small. Increase the size for a looser one.

2. Without changing the compass setting, repeat from corner J to mark off K, L, M, N, O, P, Q and R.

3. Lightly draw in $\overline{RI}$.

4. Draw $\overline{JB}$, $\overline{KC}$, $\overline{LD}$, $\overline{ME}$, $\overline{NF}$, $\overline{OG}$, $\overline{PH}$ and $\overline{QI}$.

5. Construct an angle congruent to ∠AJB using $\overline{RI}$. To begin, place the metal tip of the compass on J and cut an arc that intersects both sides of ∠AJB. Label these new points of intersection S and T. Without changing the setting, place the metal tip on R and cut an arc that intersects $\overline{RI}$. Label this new point of intersection U. Return to ∠AJB and place the metal tip on S and the pencil tip on T. Without changing settings, place the metal tip on U and cut an arc that intersects the one previously drawn. Draw a new line from R through the point where the two arcs intersect. Now, ∠IRV is congruent to ∠AJB.

6. Roll the paper into a cylinder and join so that the segments drawn in Step 4 match at their endpoints.

Now the diagonal line segments join to become continuous and form a helix.

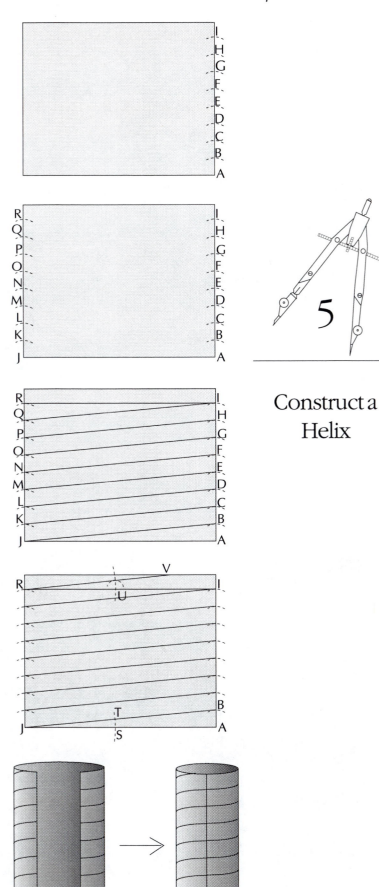

5

Construct a Helix

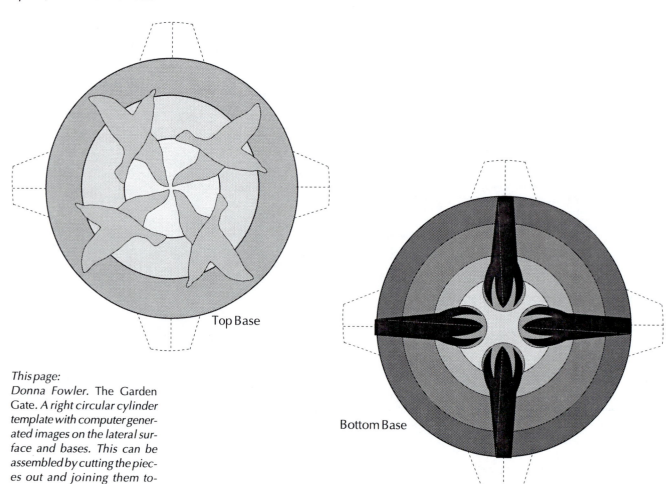

Top Base

Bottom Base

This page:
Donna Fowler. The Garden
Gate. *A right circular cylinder
template with computer generated images on the lateral surface and bases. This can be
assembled by cutting the pieces out and joining them together.*

Lateral Surface

This page:
Golden cylinders constructed of paper .These began
with a rectangle whose width
to length ratio is 1: 1.618.

Above left:
Donna Fowler. Completed
art work from computer generated images illustrated on
the previous page.

Above right:
Student works. (left to right)
Jackie Peters. Acrylic paint.
Bonnie Fernald. Cut paper
and marker with found elements. Ann MacLean. Col-
ored pencils.

Left:
Linda Maddox. Student
work. Technical pen and ink
and photocopied elements.

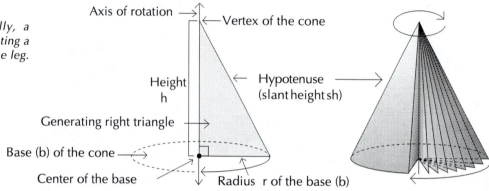

Right Top:
Fig. 1.18 A model of a cone can be formed by slitting a disk and overlapping two sectors.

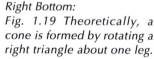

Right Bottom:
Fig. 1.19 Theoretically, a cone is formed by rotating a right triangle about one leg.

The Right Circular Cone

Another Euclidean solid that functions as one of the basic building units in the three-dimensional arts is the right circular cone, or, for the purposes of this text, the cone. Like the cylinder, this figure can also be quite simple to make. Instead of a rectangular piece of paper, however, this time we will begin with the circle. If we slit a circular disk along the radius vector at 0°, we can overlap sectors. Depending on the amount of overlap, the cone will have varying heights. For example, in Fig. 1.18, if sector A is fully overlapped by sector D, the cone will be of one height. If we overlap sectors B and A with sectors D and C, the cone will be of another height. It will be of a greater heigh and the circumference of the base will be smaller.

Since a circle has 360°, the overlap can be of any number of degrees within the 360°.

The cone is an object that can be generated by rotation. If you follow Fig. 1.19, you will see that this is done by rotating a right triangle in space about an axis lying along one leg of the triangle. This leg is the altitude of the triangle, and the height of the cone. The circular disk described by the leg perpendicular to the axis is the base. The endpoints of the leg lie along the rotation axis and lie at the center of the base and the vertex of the figure. The hypotenuse, or leg that is opposite the right angle of the triangle, becomes the slant height, or side length of the cone. The chart on page 51 gives the symmetries and formulae for a cone.

Symmetries and Formulae for a Cone

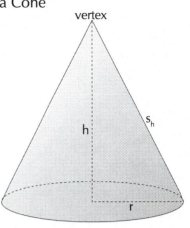

In each of the formulas below:
r=the radius of the base
h=the height of the cone
s_h=the slant height or side of the cone
π=approximately 3.14

Slant height: s_h= The determination of length requires the use of the Pythagorean Threorem

Lateral surface area: LSA = $\pi r s_h$
This does not include the area of the circular base.

Total surface area: TSA= $\pi r s_h + \pi r^2$
The lateral surface area + the area of the base.

Volume: V = $1/3\pi r^2 h$

Note that the volume of a cone is exactly one-third the volume of a cylinder with the same base and height.

Rotational Symmetries: The cone has infinite-turn symmetry about a rotation axis through the base and the vertex.

Reflection Symmetries: Any plane that contains the axis of rotation of the cone is a plane of reflection. There are infinitely many of these.

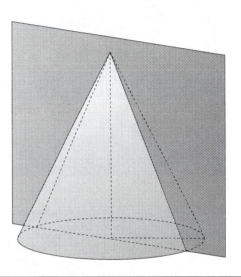

Left:
Student work. Virginia Wadland. Collage approach to developing the basic forms of three dimensions on the two-dimensional surface. These are the cone, cylinder, sphere and cube. Pencil and torn paper. Tones of pencil on sheets of paper were torn and pasted onto the surface of another paper.
Set up a group of geometric shapes and try the exercise for yourself.

The Right Triangle

Since the right circular cone is generated by a right triangle, and since the right triangle is a very important figure in geometry and trigonometry, we would like to take a short side trip to say a little bit more about it. Chapter 2 is devoted entirely to the triangle, right, equilateral and scalene.

A right triangle is one containing a right, or 90°, angle. Because two of its sides are perpendicular, it serves as a building block for many two and three-dimensional geometric objects. In particular, right triangles are used for finding the areas of polygons, the lateral and total surface areas of right circular cones, right pyramids, and particular polyhedra. It is also used as an aid in the calculation of the volume of many three-dimensional objects. It has great practical value to architects, surveyors, carpenters, engineers, navigators and astronomers, to name a few.

The most well known property of a right triangle is associated with the name of Pythagoras, an early Greek mystic, philosopher and geometer, who was thought to be born on the island of Samos in the Fifth Century B.C. Though many other cultures knew the properties of right triangles, it was he that proved their relationships. The proof he established held for all right triangles. His was the first abstract, generalized proof based on deductive, rather than inductive, reasoning. Deduction is the method used by mathematicians still. The Pythagorean Proposition is also known as the 47th proposition of Euclid as well as being called the "Carpenter's Theorem." It belongs to a family of equations called Diophantine.

Throughout his lifetime, Pythagoras was to absorb the ideas of a great variety of cultures which were all integrated into his teachings. As a young man, he travelled to Egypt where he spent many years studying under the tutelage of the Egyptian priests. When that country was invaded by the Persians, it is thought that he was captured and taken to Babylonia where he stayed for a number of years until he was able to return home to Greece at middle age. Some scholars say that at sixty years old, he met and married a beautiful young woman during a peaceful time in an otherwise most turbulent life. After being persecuted for his political beliefs, he lived in exile until he died at age ninety-nine.

The Pythagorean Theorem can be proved in several ways. Over the centuries, hundreds of different proofs of this theorem have been given including one by James A. Garfield, one of the presidents of the United States. What about the math skills of all the other presidents?

Since our concern is primarily with space, what involves us here is the geometric aspects of this proof. Even with that, there are limitless ways to go about proving this theorem using geometry. You, too, can also try to find another way of proving this.

The Pythagorean Theorem states a remarkable relationship between the sides of a right triangle. If a right triangle has sides of lengths designated as a, b, and c, where c is opposite the right angle, then $a^2 + b^2 = c^2$. This means that if squares are placed on the sides of the triangle, the sum of the squares on sides a and b would be equal to the number of squares on side c, the hypotenuse.

The triangle in the chart on the next page is called a 3-4-5 right triangle. In fact, a triangle constructed with side lengths of 3, 4, and 5 will contain a right angle opposite the side of length 5. The Egyptians used this fact when they constructed their carpenter's tools from pegs, ropes and knots in the form of a 3-4-5 triangle. The minimum number of 13 evenly spaced knots in a rope allows one to enclose an area in the shape of a right triangle. The problem with ropes, however, is that they stretch, especially when effected by humidity. Now, in Egypt that would not be a problem, but in England it would. Somewhere in history, the ropes became rigid pieces of wood. In the 20th Century, the triangle is made out of plastic.

If we know any two sides of a right triangle, we can use the algebraic relationship, as stated above, to find the remaining side. Suppose we know that the hypotenuse, c, equals 17 units and that one side, or leg, of the triangle is 15. We can name either a or b 15 and put the numbers into the formula:

$$a^2 + 15^2 = 17^2$$
$$a^2 + 225 = 289$$
$$a^2 = 289 - 225$$
$$a^2 = 64$$
$$a = 8$$

On page 55, we show you three examples from a series of works in which the artist explores the visual aspects of the geometric proof of the Pythagorean Theorem by the 12th century Hindu mathematician, Bhaskara. Perhaps, you would like to research another variation and do your own visual exploration.

This page:
The 3-4-5- triangle is a member of an infinite family of right triangles that have whole numbers for sides. Can you construct the following members? 5-12-13; 7-24-25; 9-40-41; 11-60-61. Do you notice a pattern appearing? Could you continue generating other members of this series?

The Pythagorean Theorem

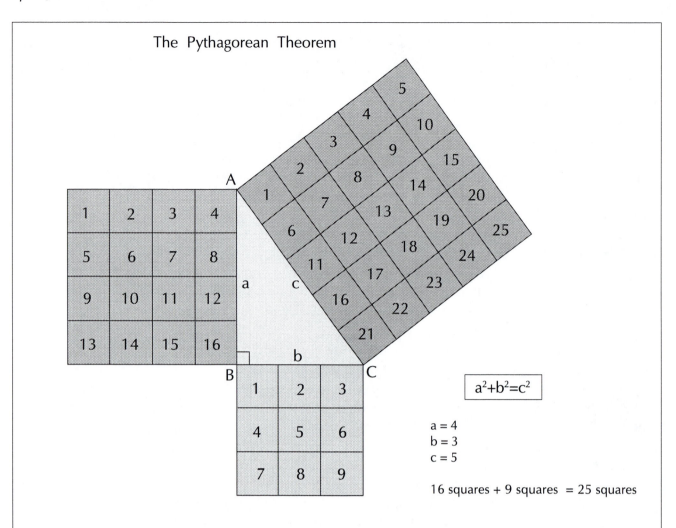

$$a^2+b^2=c^2$$

a = 4
b = 3
c = 5

16 squares + 9 squares = 25 squares

Find edge lengths, given the real number information for $\triangle ABC$.

$a^2=c^2-b^2$

$a^2=5^2-3^2$
$a^2=25-9$
$a^2=16$
$a=4$

To find side a:

or

$a=\sqrt{c^2-b^2}$

$a=\sqrt{5^2-3^2}$
$a=\sqrt{25-9}$
$a=\sqrt{16}$
$a=4$

$b^2=c^2-a^2$

$b^2=5^2-4^2$
$b^2=25-16$
$b^2=9$
$b=3$

To find side b:

or

$b=\sqrt{c^2-a^2}$

$b=\sqrt{5^2-4^2}$
$b=\sqrt{25-16}$
$b=\sqrt{9}$
$b=3$

$c^2=a^2+b^2$

$c^2=4^2+3^2$
$c^2=16+9$
$c^2=25$
$c=5$

To find side c:

or

$c=\sqrt{a^2+b^2}$

$c=\sqrt{4^2+3^2}$
$c=\sqrt{16+9}$
$c=\sqrt{25}$
$c=5$

This page: Rochelle Newman. Three artistic variations on Bhaskara's proof of the Pythagorean Theorem. Acrylic paint on illustration board. The originals of these are in color. Bhaskara was a Hindu mathematician born in 1114. In his proof, he used four right triangles in the square of the hypotenuse leaving a square in the middle whose side equals the difference between the two sides of the right triangle. These are then rearranged.

Designing with the Cone

For design purposes, there is an advantage to overlaying a polar grid on a circle of the desired size. The grid allows for more accurate placement of the design elements. In this way design structures can be drawn onto the surface while it is still flat. If we slit the circle along the 0° radius vector, it is very easy to overlap the edges to exactly the desired number of degrees. When the overlap angle has been calculated in accordance with the design elements, most of the overlapped angle can be removed and the new sides joined to form the cone. For example, in Fig. 1.20, we would have three complete design elements if the overlap angle is 90°, and two complete design elements if the overlap angle is 180°. If, however, the overlap angle is 270°, only one design element remains.

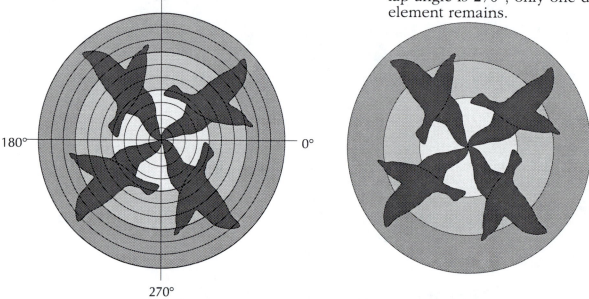

Above:
Fig. 1.20 The circular disc for a right circular cone with, and without, a polar grid overlaid. Cones can be constructed by slitting on the 0° radius vector and overlapping the edges by the desired angle.

Right:
Three different cones cut from this same pattern.

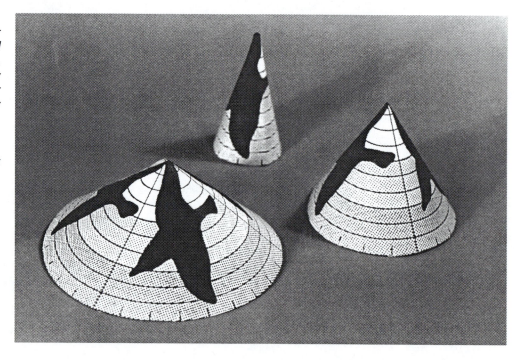

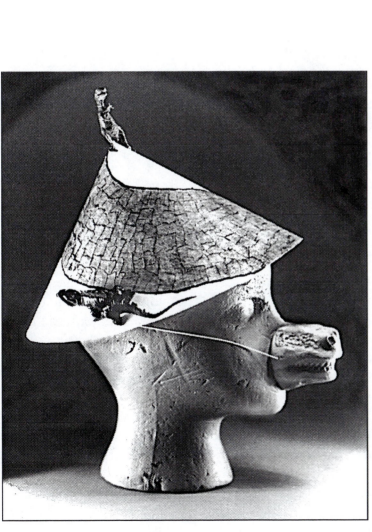

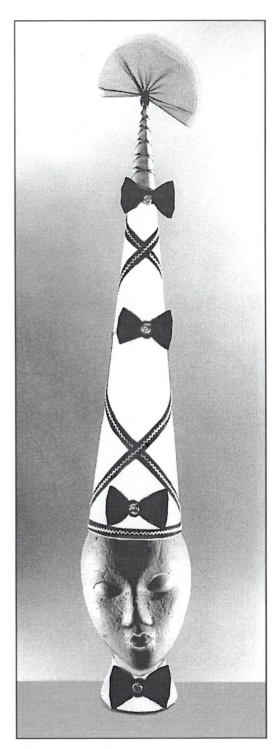

This page:
When planning a party,
play on the pliable plane,
putting pretty patterns on
your party particulars.

These facing pages: Nature's architectural diversity is displayed in the many types of seashells that house members of the mollusc family.

Magnificient sculpture, elegant architecture and affordable housing are all rolled up, in the form of a seashell, around one small soft bodied animal. This creature belongs to the mollusc family and fossil shells tell us that its members have been around and evolving for millions of years. The study of seashells, outer covering and inner life, is the science of malacology. Shells can be as small as peas or as large as four feet in length. Like snowflakes, both in number and variety, no two seashells are exactly alike. They come smooth and rough, spiny and contained, patterned and plain, dun colored and brilliant. They have been used as money, musical instruments, body ornaments, and symbols of fertility and religion. As artists, we can learn much about design from them in relation to color, pattern, and, for this particular book, structure and form.

The mollusc is not involved in real estate transactions. Yet the animal

needs a larger and larger house as it matures. Therefore, ever the handyman, it is continually in the process of building additions to the one it already owns. Shells fit around the animal and grow by accretion. Some molluscs, like bivalves, such as the delicious clam and scallop, prefer a more open floor plan in their homes. The size of their great rooms increase along with the size of their bodies. Others, like the much displayed nautilus, like to add on new rooms while sealing off the old ones. The homes of these gastropods become spiral in shape. If the animal remained the same size, the resulting house would be much like a tube rolled up. Since it gets larger, its shell also continually gets larger, and the resulting form is like a coiled cone. This conical form is common to all those molluscs whose houses appear to have a spiral shape, regardless of the different types of architectural details displayed.

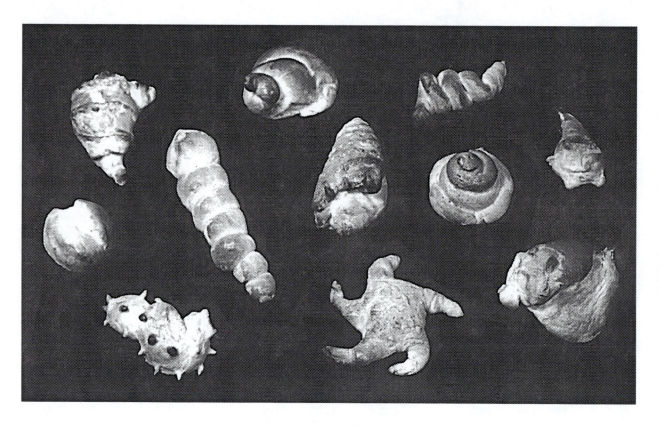

Above:
Ann MacLean. Bread dough
seashells.

Bread Dough Seashell Sculpture

Bread dough is a delicious medium for creating models of seashells. Mistakes and successes are equally tasty! The following is a recipe for soft pretzels, and will make roughly thirty-two of them. It is up to you to determine how many seashells you can create with one batch.

2 cups warm water

2 pkgs. active dry yeast

$\frac{1}{2}$ cup sugar

2 tsp. salt

$\frac{1}{2}$ stick softened margarine

1 egg

$6\frac{1}{2}$ to $7\frac{1}{2}$ cups flour

Dissolve the yeast in water in a large bowl and add the sugar, salt, margarine, egg and 3 cups of flour. Beat until smooth. Continue to add flour until dough becomes stiff. Cover tightly and refrigerate for 2 to 24 hours.

Turn the dough onto a lightly floured board, and divide it into manageable pieces. To create sculptures, mold the pieces of dough and brush them with a mixture of egg yolk and 2 Tbsp. of water. Sprinkle them with coarse salt, and let them rise in a warm place for about 25 minutes until the dough has doubled in size. Then bake them at 400° F for about 15 minutes or until done. Cool them on wire racks.

Bon appetit!

Or on a rainy or hot day, a single sheet of material can be slit and folded into a hat that will repel either the rain or too much sun. Because of its simplicity, stability and the aforementioned water shedding property the cone has held an important place throughout history as an architectural form. We have discovered, however, that the very best use of the cone is one that is both functional and biodegradable. That is to fill it with one's favorite flavor of ice cream and to eat it with pleasure.

Above:
The cone as a structure for design in hats and houses.

61

Problems

1. Select at least four different shaped circular cylindrical containers from your pantry shelf. For each, measure the radius and height and compute the total surface area and the volume. By comparing volume and surface area, determine which of the containers is the most efficient.

2. The height of a circular cylinder is 16 cm. and the circumference of each base is 10 cm.
    a. Find the lateral surface area of the cylinder.
    b. Find the total surface area (use 3.14 for π).
    c. Find the volume.

3. A storage tank in the shape of a circular cylinder has a height of 25 m. and a radius of 9 m. If one gallon of paint covers 400 square meters, how much paint would you need to paint the tank on all surfaces except the bottom?

4. Using Construction 5 on page 31, construct two different helices.
    a. Make one with a wide wrap and left-handed.
    b. Make one with a very tight wrap and right-handed.
These could become the basis for a project.

5. A silo is in the shape of a cylinder with a conical top. If the cylinder has a diameter of 12 m. and a height of 20 m., and the cone has a height of 8 m., what is the grain capacity of the silo?

6. Construct a Golden cone from a Triangle of Price given the height of 1.27, the radius of 1, and the slant height of 1.62.
    a. Find the volume of the cone.
    b. Find the lateral surface area.
    c. Find the total surface area.

7. Given a piece of paper, arch and crenellate a fanfold with either acute or obtuse angles.

8. Pleat a plane in which you have the following sequences:
    a. M, M, V, V
    b. M, V, V, M, V, V
    c. M, V, M, skip, M, V, M

9. Using the slitting techniques described on pages 22 and 23, do a slitting sampler that uses the following formats as opposed to the rectangular examples.
    a. Use a square format.
    b. Use a pentagonal format.
    c. Use a circular format.
    d. Use a triangular format.

Projects

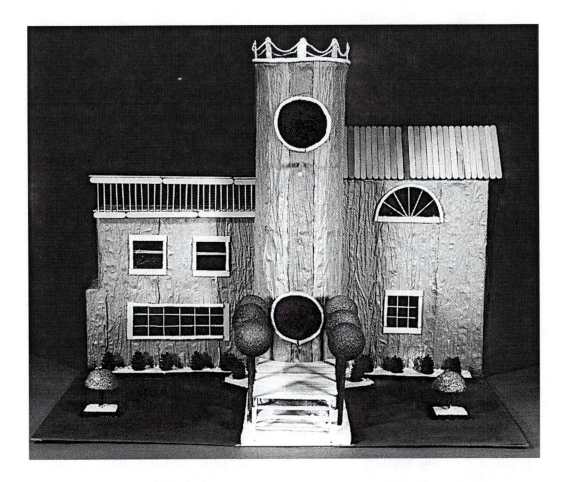

1.   Create a Golden Cylinder, one whose circumference to height ratio is 1.1618 (Ø). Begin by drawing a Golden Rectangle (1:1.1618) which will be the lateral surface. Construct two circular bases whose circumference is the same as the length of the rectangle. The radius of the circles will be the length of the rectangle divided by 2π. Leave tabs for joining. Develop one surface pattern for the bases, and a complementary one for the lateral surface. Be concerned with: the overall color structure, the fact that the finished piece will have a seam on the lateral surface, and that the joining needs to be an integral part of the design solution.

2.   Develop a fantasy birdhouse built of recycled cylindrical and conical forms.

3.   Design a pattern on a rectangle that could be transferred to a circular cylinder to create either a cookie-cutter rolling pin or a paint

Above:
Student work. Kirk Hansbury. Fantasy birdhouse from recycled and found materials, such as, popsicle sticks, styrofoam balls, and cardboard.

roller for patterning walls.

4. Use a fan fold and variations thereof to create a modular unit. Make multiples of the unit and join to create one of the following:
   a. Rapunzel's tower,
   b. Sleeping Beauty's castle, or
   c. the house that Jack built.

5. Using any one or a combination of any manipulations of the plane described in this chapter, develop a unit from a sheet of 8.5" x 11" paper . Duplicate at least five times and create a modular sculpture. Do not add color, but rely solely on the play of light and shadow across the form for interest.

6. Using felt or other fabric and slitting techniques, create a costume that would suggest chain mail armour for King Arthur's knights or a diaphanous garment for Oberon in *A Midsummer Night's Dream*.

7. Create a fancy parasol from a conical shape.

8. Design a party hat from a conical form and pattern it.

9. Create a fantasy shell in clay or bread dough, and give it an appropriate environment.

10. Using empty tin or aluminum cans, a pair of metal snips, and your imagination, create a sculptural form.

11. Research the body patterns found on snakes. Use one of them that appeals to you as the basis for a black and white design structure to be used on a circular cylindrical container. Try a color variation.

12. Do an architectural rendering of a fantasy shell house for a Victorian or post-modern gastropod or mollusc or choose another architectural period.

13. Research the engineering of the "pop-up" book. Design and execute a single page for a book of fairy tales or myths.

14. Research the sculptural works of 20th Century artists. Then, using cardboard cylinders found around the house, create a scale model for an outdoor sculpture based on the work of a particular artist of this century.

15. Research the function and form of the fan in Oriental cultures. Design and execute one based on a particular example from your research but add a personal touch.

16. Find a packaged item and redesign the package into one that is more efficient or solves a particular design problem of your choice.

Further Reading

Alexander, Daniel E. *Graphical Geometry*. Dubuque, Iowa: Kendall/Hunt Publishing Company, 1983.

Cundy, H. Martin and A. P. Rollett. *Mathematical Models*. Oxford and New York: Oxford University Press, 1961.

Doczi, Gyorgy. *The Power of Limits*. Boulder and London: Shambala, 1981.

Hilbert, D. and Cohn-Vossen, S. *Geometry and the Imagination*. New York: Chelsea Publishing Company, 1952.

Gardner, Martin. *Penrose Tiles to Trapdoor Ciphers*. New York: W. H. Freeman and Company, 1989.

Hawkins, Gerald S. in collaboration with John B. White. *Stonehenge Decoded*. New York: Dell Publishing Co., Inc., 1965.

Kasahara, Kunhiko. *Origami Omnibus*. New York: Japan Publications, 1988.

Olson, Alton T. *Mathematics through Paper Folding*. Reston, Virginia: National Council of Teachers of Mathematics, 1977.

Row, T. Sundara. *Geometric Exercises in Paper Folding*. New York: Dover Publications, Inc., 1966.

2 A Triangular Affair

The hydrogen atom—the simplest of all atoms consisting of only one proton and one electron—is the building stone of the universe. In the nuclear furnaces of the stars, hydrogen is transformed into the hundred-odd elements that make up the universe including our planet, its water and air, rocks, plants and animals, man himself, and everything created by man.

Andreas Feininger
The Anatomy of Nature

Even the most complex of substances is created from finite combinations of a finite number of elements. Thus, atoms can be considered the basic building blocks for natural materials. Chemists can both analyze and synthesize substances by understanding how the elements come together to form the compounds. The periodic table (Fig. 2.1) catalogs the logical structure of 103 natural chemical elements by giving us an order for them.

We often give children building blocks in order to enhance their development on a number of levels. The modularity of the blocks allows for pleasure in manipulating the constituent parts. These playful structures enhance a child's perception of mass and volume while teaching the natural constraints of space.

This page:
Fig. 2.1 The periodic table of chemical elements.

Left:
Detail of the hydrogen block of the periodic table.

Bottom:
The complete periodic table. In 1869, the Russian chemist, Dimitri Mendelyeev, developed the table for the chemical elements. They are arranged in order of their atomic weights, number of protons, beginning with hydrogen.

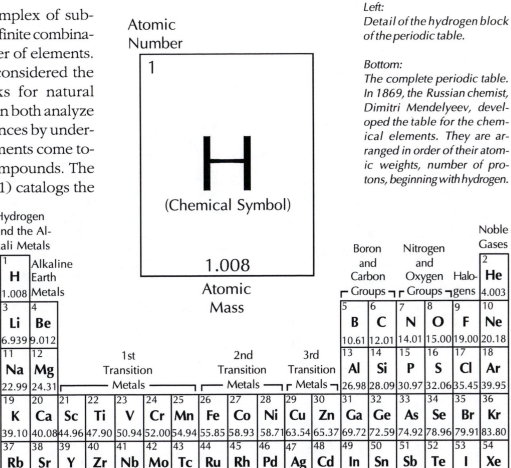

Atomic Number

| 1 |
| H |
| (Chemical Symbol) |
| 1.008 |

Atomic Mass

Vital Statistics of the Triangle

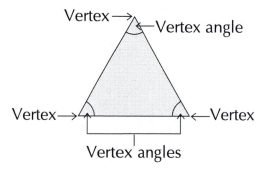

All triangles have three sides, three vertices, and three angles, often referred to as vertex angles.

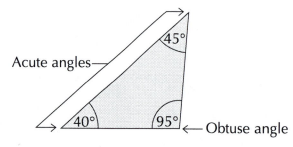

If the angle measures between 0° and 90°, it is called acute. If it measures between 90° and 180°, it is called obtuse.

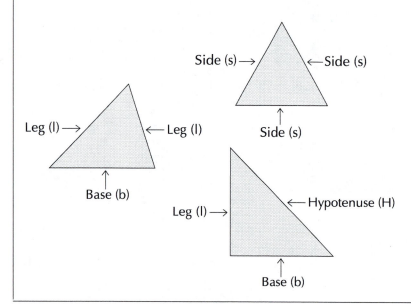

The term hypotenuse is only used as the side opposite the 90° angle in a right triangle.

Base is used when one side of a triangle is in special relationship to the other two--usually the other two sides are equal and the remaining side is called the base.

Throughout this text we will look at families of three-dimensional geometric building units of various types. The ancestors of all of these structures are the two-dimensional polygons. The angle at which two sides meet is called the vertex angle. Polygons can be either convex or concave. A polygon is convex if a line segment joining any two points of the polygon lies entirely within the polygon. For the most part, we will focus on convex polygons.

Perhaps you noticed, as you folded the models of the previous chapter, how often the triangle appeared, and how it lent strength to the paper structure. In this chapter, the focus is on forms that incorporate the triangle. It is the polygon with the fewest

An altitude of a triangle is a line drawn from a vertex perpendicular to the opposite side (sometimes called the base of a triangle)

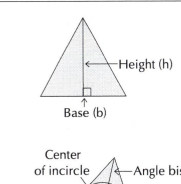

Height (h)

Base (b)

An angle bisector cuts a vertex angle in half.

The three angle bisectors meet at a point in the center of the triangle. The incircle of the triangle is the circle drawn with the common intersection point as center. The incircle is tangent to each side of the triangle at the point where the angle bisector and the side of the triangle intersect.

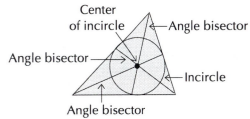

Center of incircle — Angle bisector

Angle bisector

Incircle

Angle bisector

The perpendicular bisector of a side of a triangle is a line through the midpoint of the side, at right angles to the side. The perpendicular bisector of the three sides of a triangle meet at a common point. The circumcircle of the triangle is the circle drawn with this point as center and radius equal to the distance from the center to one of the vertices. The circumcircle will pass through all three vertices of the triangle.

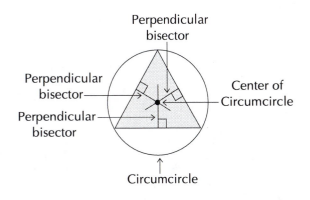

Perpendicular bisector

Perpendicular bisector

Center of Circumcircle

Perpendicular bisector

Circumcircle

*The equilateral triangle is a special case. The center of the circumcircle need not fall within the triangle.

The perimeter (P) of a triangle is the total length of the sides. If all lengths were congruent, they would be assigned the same letter.

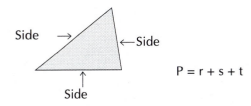

Side

Side

Side

$P = r + s + t$

To obtain the area of a triangle, multiply the altitude of a triangle by its base and divide by 2.

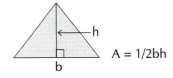

h

b

$A = 1/2bh$

possible number of sides that will enclose space, and it is also the most stable of all these figures. The chart at the top of these facing pages describes some of the triangle's vital statistics, while the chart on page 70 offers procedures to find both the angle bisectors and perpendicular bisectors of the sides of an equilateral triangle since this chapter focuses on this particular family member. The chart on page 71 presents some of the Triangle Family members, and the charts on pages 72 and 73 give some basic triangle subdivisions, as well as some external groupings of them, that can be used for purposes of surface design. What other ways can you discover for subdividing areas?

Procedure to Find Angle and Perpendicular Bisectors of the Equilateral Triangle

Angle Bisector

Step 1

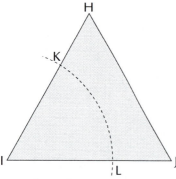

Placing the metal tip of your compass on I, cut an arc that intersects both $\overline{IH}$ and $\overline{IJ}$. Label the point of intersection on $\overline{IH}$, K, and the point of intersection on $\overline{IJ}$, L.

Step 2

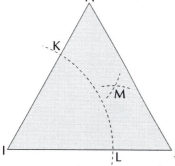

Placing the metal tip on K, use your compass to measure slightly more than half the distance between K and L, and cut an arc. Keeping the same compass setting, place the metal tip on L, and cut an arc that intersects the one just drawn. Label this point of intersection M.

Step 3

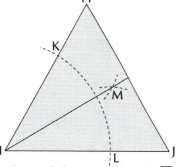

To complete the angle bisector, draw in $\overline{IM}$, extending it to intersect the side of the triangle.

Perpendicular Bisector

Step 1

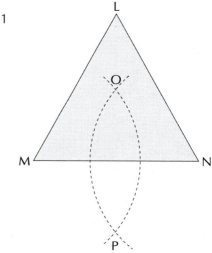

Placing the metal tip of your compass on M, open it to more than half the distance between M and N, and cut an arc that intersects $\overline{MN}$. Now, without disturbing the compass setting, place the metal tip on N and cut an arc that intersects the one just drawn. Notice that this arc intersects the previous one at two places. Label the points of intersection O and P.

Step 2

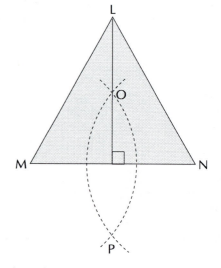

To complete the perpendicular bisector, line your straightedge up with O and P, and draw the line OP.

*Angle bisectors and perpendicular bisectors are not usually the same. They are here because we are using the equilateral triangle.

Triangle Family Membership

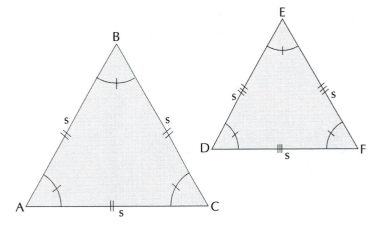

The Equilateral Triangle Family

The Equilateral Triangle is from a finite family of triangles all having the same shape. An equilateral triangle has three equal sides and three equal angles. Since the angle sum of a Euclidean triangle is 180°, each angle of an equilateral triangle measures 60°. Because all the sides are congruent and all the angle are congruent, an equilateral triangle is called a regular triangle. Notice that the two triangles to the right are similar.

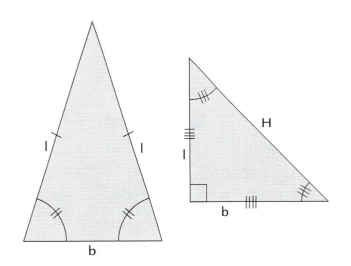

The Isosceles Triangle Family

The Isosceles Triangle family has triangles of infinitely many different shapes. All of its individuals have two equal sides . The equal sides are called the legs of the triangle and the remaining side is called the base. If you refer back to the chart on page 7 you will see one of this family's well known members. It is the Golden Triangle with its angles of 36°, 72°, 72°.
When the Isosceles Triangle appears as a 45°, 45°, 90° Right Triangle, however, we usually call the base the hypotenuse.

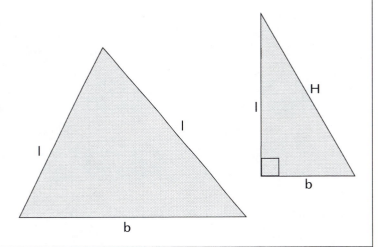

The Scalene Triangle Family

The Scalene Triangle family also has infinitely many differently shaped triangles. All the sides of a scalene triangle have different lengths and all its angles have different degree measures.This group spawns a right triangle that is one half of the Equilateral Triangle, and the architect's best friend. It is the 30°, 60°, 90° Right Triangle.

Some Basic Design Armatures of the Triangle
(Internal Subdivisions)

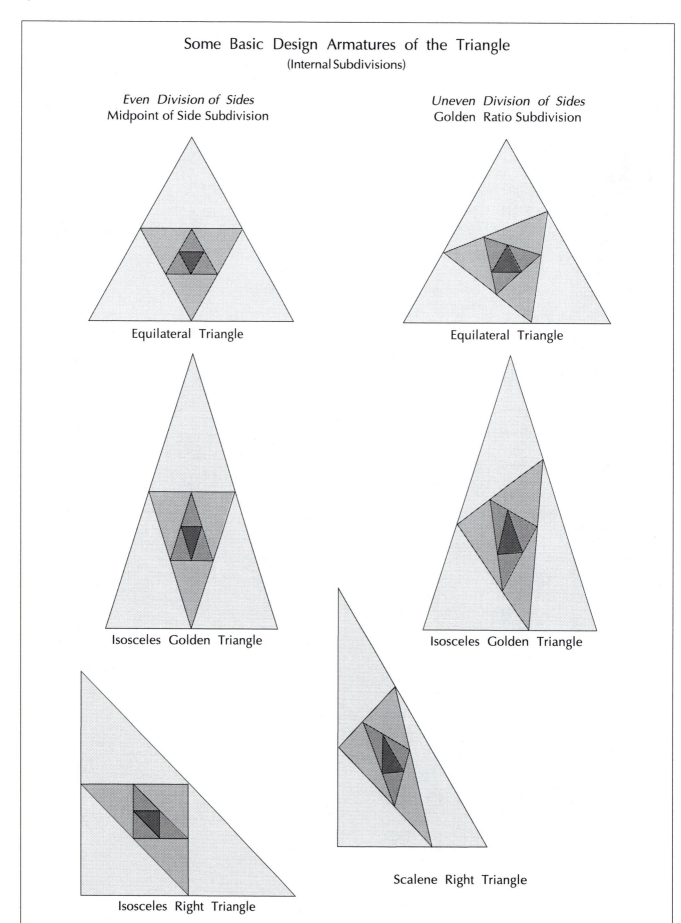

Even Division of Sides
Midpoint of Side Subdivision

Uneven Division of Sides
Golden Ratio Subdivision

Equilateral Triangle

Equilateral Triangle

Isosceles Golden Triangle

Isosceles Golden Triangle

Isosceles Right Triangle

Scalene Right Triangle

Some Basic Design Structures Using the Triangle
(External Groupings)

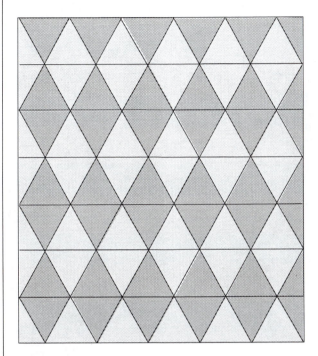

Equilateral Triangle

Isosceles Golden Triangle

Isosceles Right Triangle

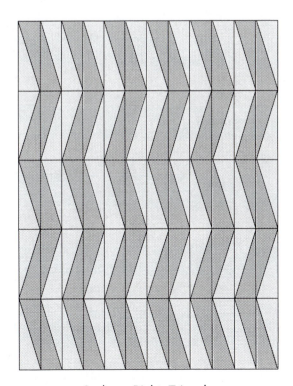

Scalene Right Triangle

These facing pages: Naturally formed triangular structures. Notice the Vallela vallela swimming on the surface of the water.

As you have seen, the triangle is a wonderful design element that can be used by artists and nature alike. In nature an implied triangle frames many different flowers and fruits, and the facial and body structures of certain animals. Of course, here the beauty of the triangle is purely a by-product. It is for its other attributes that it functions in natural design. Foremost among these, no doubt, is its stability.

The ocean is a rich source of triangular structures as most fish have fins of this shape. In the August, 1987, *Discover* magazine article, "Jellyfish Aren't Out to Get Us", author Shannon Brownlee describes another sea creature that is suggestive of a single triangle. It is the jellyfish, *Valella valella*, sometimes referred to as the *by-the-wind sailor*. It appears that the sail attached to the top of its two inch wide rhomboidal body propels it along. However, it is actually a combination of body structure, water drag, and sail position that contribute to the mobility of this little water animal.

According to Brownlee, the sail of the Valella valella is unique in both its form and position. It is *S*-shaped and triangular, running diagonally across the body asymmetrically to the major axis. The structure and position of this appendage make it rigid

regardless of wind direction. Its flat body structure forces Valella valella to spin when wind and water current work in opposite directions. When wind and water drag are from the same direction, the little creature moves gracefully along in a sideways drift.

The author states that the direction that the Valella valella sails is also affected by the way it uses its tentacles. It has the ability to retract or extend them, using them much like rudders. It never moves into the wind as would a normal sailing vessel, but rather sails at angles up to 60° from a downwind direction.

The sail is canted to the right or the left rendering the Valella valella either right-handed or left-handed. Biologists believe that this enables these small wonders to populate oceans in both the Northern Hemisphere, where wind currents travel in a clockwise direction, and the Southern Hemisphere, where a counter-clockwise heading is the rule. One of the interesting questions for biologists is, "Who begets whom?" Does each sailor give rise to only its own kind, right-handed or left-handed? Are they destined to swim in the same circles forever? Or can one particular type produce offsprings of both like and opposite handedness? Are there other ocean creatures with this same propensity?

Vital Statistics of a Polyhedron Using the Tetrahedron*

*Like the equilateral triangle, the tetrahedron is a special case

interfacial angle

vertex

Faces

A polyhedron is a three-dimensional form that completely encloses a volume of space. Each different polyhedron is made up of a particular number and type of polygons whose surfaces become the faces of the form. Like its polygonal faces, the polyhedron can be either convex or concave. In order to be able to enclose space without gaps, the polygons forming the figure must have matching edges with equal lengths. A minimum of four polygons is required to make a polyhedron.

Edges

When two polygons come together to form the side of a polyhedron, there is an internal angle that is formed between the two adjacent faces. This is called the interfacial, or sometimes, dihedral, angle. Since dihedral can often refer to two-dimensional tilings, we have chosen to use interfacial.

An interfacial angle is the angle that you would see if you sliced through an edge with a plane perpendicular to that edge.

Different polyhedra have different interfacial angles. A skeletal polyhedron may be described and constructed by edges only.

Vertices

When three or more polygons come together, the point at which their vertex angles meet is called a vertex of the polyhedron. Every polyhedron has its own particular number of vertices.

The three-dimensional figures composed of triangular faces that we look at in this chapter, are examples of polyhedra. A polyhedron may be defined as a three-dimensional solid bounded by polygons. Polyhedra may also be classified according to whether they are concave or convex. Some of the characteristics of polyhedra are inherited from their ancestor polygons which may be likened to the "elementary particles" of physics. Poly-

Vertex Nets and Vertex Orders

A vertex net is the set of numbers that describes the type and number of polygons that come together at the vertices of a polyhedron. For example, 3-3-3 indicates that three triangles meet at a vertex.

The order of numbers in a vertex net describes the positions of different kinds of polygons around a vertex..The individual numbers refer to the number of sides on a polygonal face which forms the vertex. (4 indicates a square, 5 a pentagon, etc) As a group, these numbers describe the particular combination of polygons at the vertex. For example, 3-4-3-4 indicates that there is a triangle, and then a square, and then a triangle, and then another square at each vertex. The numbers of a vertex net can be read in a clockwise or counterclockwise direction, beginning at any position.

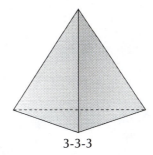

3-3-3

Vertex net

The vertex net of 3-3-3 tells us that three triangles meet at every vertex of this figure.

The vertex net is where the four polygons touch.

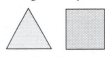

3-4-3-4
or
4-3-4-3

The vertex nets of 3-4-3-4 and 4-3-4-3 describe the same vertex; however, only one would be used at a time. Either way, they describe an alternation between triangles and squares at each vertex.

Below is a shorthand notation that indicates only the polygons in a particular type of polyhedron.

Polyhedra Typing

The various combinations of polygons and vertices that a polyhedron might have give rise to specific types of polyhedra. For example, if a polyhedron is constructed from only one type of regular polygon and its vertices are all congruent, it is said to be a regular polyhedron. If a polyhedron is constructed from two different types of regular polygons, and its vertices are congruent, it is said to be semiregular. See the chart to the right.

Regular Polyhedra	*Semiregular Polyhedra*
3-3-3 The polyhedron has: One kind of regular polygonal faces, and Congruent vertices	3-4-3-4 The polyhedron has: Two (+) kinds of regular polygonal faces, and Congruent vertices
Vertically Regular Polyhedra	*Nonregular Polyhedra*
3-3-3 3-3-3-3 The polyhedron has: One kind of regular polygonal faces, and Two (+) kinds of vertex nets	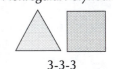 3-3-3 3-4-3-4 The polyhedron has: Two (+) kinds of regular polygonal faces, and Two (+) vertex nets

gons come together in particular ways to build a more complex unit. These, in turn, become the blocks that combine into the packing and stacking of components that will be discussed in Chapter 5. There are constraints of space that dictate which ones and how many can come together to make a packing unit. Do you think that there is a relationship between what polygons can come together and which polyhedra group? Could you prove this mathematically?

Rochelle Newman. Models. Polyhedra in which art, math, and technology are combined. The pattern on the single triangular face is a computer generated image based on the "Sierpinski Triangle". Notice that the design armature is built by the division of midpoints of edges. Here, multiples of this triangle are used to create the pictured polyhedra.

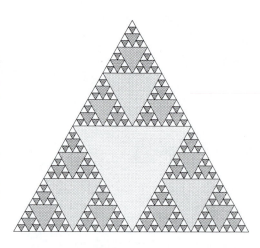

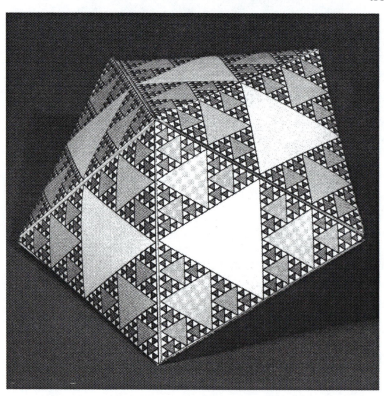

As we begin our exploration of polyhedra, keep in mind that there are many ways to approach the study of these forms. Each involves looking for common characteristics. We are going to conduct a search for forms that adhere to certain sets of rules. Since we are concerned with the needs of the artist as well as the mathematician, our approach will give emphasis to the visual.

For the purposes of mathematical investigation, one need only consider the vertices and edges of figures, which act as a skeletal framework with the faces being implied. For the artist, however, the faces provide surfaces for unending design potential, thus presenting yet another group of questions and another type of fascinating activity.

Basic construction techniques for forms in three dimensions build upon skills and concepts that begin with the two-dimensional surface. By adding the element of depth, complications occur which require more patience, more practice, and more care in order to produce a quality product. After determining the use of the object, the following factors must be taken into consideration: the type and characteristics of the materials chosen; the size and mass of the finished object in regards to its care and storage; the accuracy of the tools used in construction; and the precision of craftsmanship involved in the details of the surfaces and edges. Now, after having said all this, please let us tell you of the great pleasure and challenges involved. A carefully constructed polyhedron with a beautiful face is a wonderful sight to behold!

Our approach will be to begin with a single equilateral triangle. We will then add more equilateral triangles, one at a time, keeping them edge-to-edge and in a single row. Our goal will be to find out how many of them are needed to enclose space.

In order to facilitate your understanding of the process, it is helpful to have some physical models. The simplest way to obtain a row of equilateral triangles is to cut them from isometric grid paper in which the grid is triangular to begin with (Fig. 2.2). The lengths of the sides of the triangles should be at least an inch long so that they can be easily manipulated. If your grid paper has smaller units, remember that you can increase the size of the triangles using multiples of the units.

An isometric dot array, with its alternating rows of dots (Fig. 2.3), would work equally well for drawing triangles in a row. It also offers the advantage of allowing you to easily draw equilateral triangles with different length sides. With either kind of grid paper, it is fairly simple to draw triangles whose side lengths will be comfortable to work with. Once

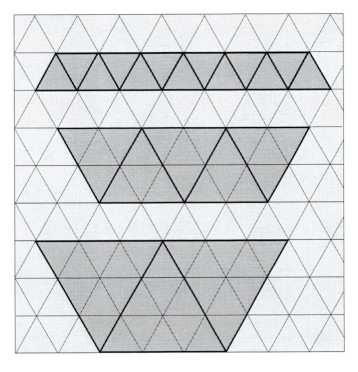

Top:
Fig. 2.2 Isometric grid paper provides a useful guide for the construction and subsequent cutting out of rows of equilateral triangles. Triangles with convenient side lengths can be obtained by using multiples of the triangular units.

Bottom:
Fig. 2.3 An isometric dot array offers the same advantages as the grid paper.

drawn, the triangles should be cut out so that you can manipulate them for your own exploration. If neither kind of grid paper is available, Constructions 6 and 7 on pages 80 and 81 show you how you can make your own rows of triangles.

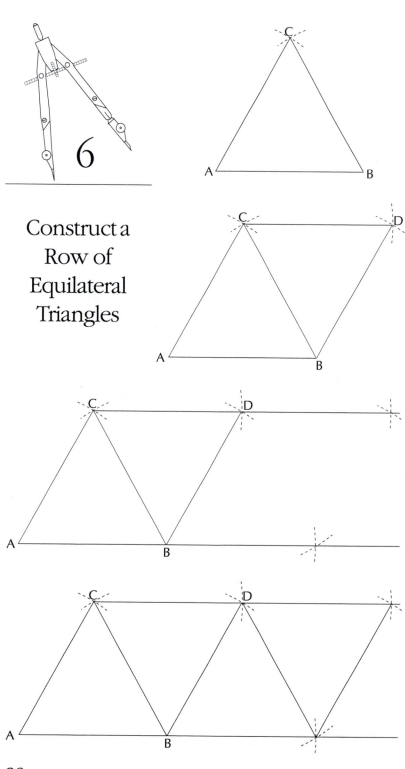

Given side $\overline{AB}$

1. Open the compass to measure AB and with the metal tip first on A and then on B, cut a pair of intersecting arcs on one side of $\overline{AB}$. Label the point of intersection C.

2. Draw $\overline{AC}$ and $\overline{CB}$.

3. Without changing the compass setting, and with the metal point first on B and then on C, cut a pair of intersecting arcs on the side of $\overline{CB}$ opposite A. Label the point of intersection D. Draw $\overline{CD}$ and $\overline{DB}$.

4. Extend $\overrightarrow{CD}$ and $\overrightarrow{AB}$ as far as needed to accommodate the length of the row of equilateral triangles you want.

5. Without changing the compass setting, mark off congruent segments on $\overrightarrow{AB}$, beginning by putting the metal tip on B. Extend as far as desired.

6. Repeat on $\overrightarrow{CD}$, beginning at D.

7. Continue drawing segments between points of intersection on the two rays in the pattern established by $\overline{AC}$, $\overline{CB}$ and $\overline{DB}$.

Now you have constructed a row of four equilateral triangles.

6

Construct a Row of Equilateral Triangles

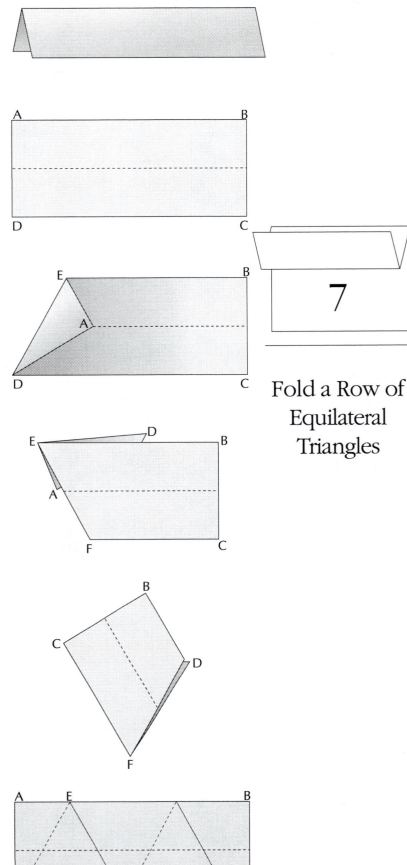

Chapter 2 A Triangular Affair

Given a long, rectangular strip of paper

1. Fold the strip in half lengthwise. It does not matter whether this fold appears as a mountain or a valley. Open and flatten out the piece of paper. Label the rectangle ABCD.

2. Fold vertex **A** over so that it rests on the fold completed in Step 1 and ΔADE is formed.

3. Fold the strip (in a mountain fold) along $\overline{AE}$ through to the other edge of the paper strip. Label the end of this new fold F.

4. For the next triangle, do not open the mountain fold from Step 3. Valley fold the strip along $\overline{DF}$ being careful to match up edges of the paper.

5. Continue to fold the strip along the side of the most recently folded triangle. Keep the previously folded parts on the outside so that the bulk does not interfere with the accuracy of your folds. This will result in alternate mountain and valley folds. Work carefully as it is easy to develop inaccuracies that will get magnified as you progress along the strip. Continue until you have folded the desired number of triangles.

Now when you open and flatten the piece of paper you will see that you have folded a row of equilateral triangles.

7

Fold a Row of Equilateral Triangles

81

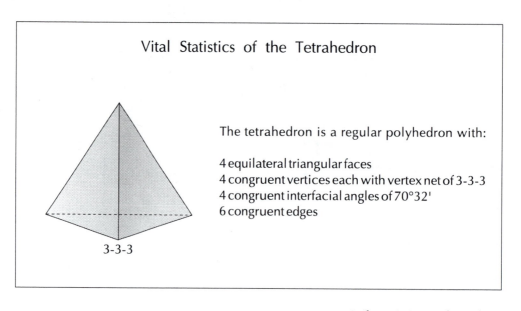

Vital Statistics of the Tetrahedron

The tetrahedron is a regular polyhedron with:

4 equilateral triangular faces
4 congruent vertices each with vertex net of 3-3-3
4 congruent interfacial angles of 70°32'
6 congruent edges

3-3-3

The Tetrahedron

We already know that it takes a minimum of four faces to make a polyhedron, so let us consider what happens if we have fewer than four triangles in a row. A single triangle will not stand on its own nor will it enclose space. A row of two or three triangles (Fig. 2.4 A and B), however, can be folded so as to stand on edge, and in so doing, define space. A row of three triangles, when folded along edges, can also be made to appear to enclose space as with a folding screen.

With four triangles in a row (Fig. 2.4 C), however, we can fold the polyhedron, called the tetrahedron, whose vital statistics can be found in the chart at the top of this page. Because of its triangular faces, it is an extremely stable figure. Its structure fascinated men of science, such as Alexander Graham Bell, the inventor of the telephone, who spent a great deal of his time investigating its properties. He built tetrahedral kites and discovered that they had lightness, strength, and rigidity, and could be combined easily to produce larger structures.

Right and below:
Fig. 2.4 A, B and C Triangles all in a row.

A and B. A row of two or three triangles can be made to stand on edge even though it cannot be folded to completely enclose space. They are suggestive of a folding screen.

C. When there are four triangles in a row, however, they can be folded to make a tetrahedron which fully encloses space.

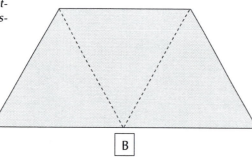

A

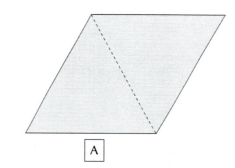

B

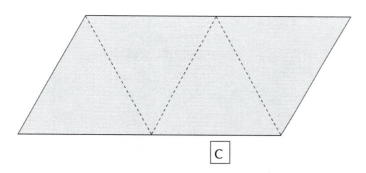

C

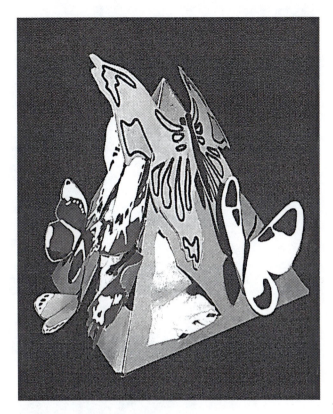

This page:
Tetrahedral structures embedded within art.

Left:
Student work. Mark Mc-Grade. Butterfly transformation on a tetrahedron. Acrylic paint on paper.

Below:
Student work. Eugene Bourassa. tetrahedral sculpture made from twigs.

Research the sculptural work of the English artist Andy Goldsworthy for inspiration on working with natural materials and forms in an elegant and eloquent manner. Sensitivity to what lies without and within is part of what art is all about.

Right:
A building with a triangularly capped tower. Seattle, Washington.

Below:
Detail of triangular bridge trusses on a bridge in Portsmouth, New Hampshire. Perhaps you would like to research the design of bridges or do a photographic essay on bridges in your community.

Now, let us construct the model of a tetrahedron. This can be done in a variety of ways, all of which begin with the construction of polygonal pattern pieces. We shall call pattern pieces without glue tabs, nets. When glue tabs are added, they will be called templates. If you begin with a paper pattern, you can either use acetate in the photocopier or you can lay a piece over your pattern and trace directly onto it with a permanent marker. If you construct your pattern pieces on the computer, there are special clear acetates for printers.

Define the edges of the polygon with a solid dark line. Define what will become glue tabs with a finer, dashed line. Mark the center of the polygonal face with a black dot. To find the center of a regular polygon, either bisect two adjacent angles, two adjacent sides, or an angle and an adjacent side (Fig. 2.5). Any pair of these bisectors will meet in the center. Mark the midpoint of the edges with a short black line perpendicular to each edge. Then, finally, mark each vertex with an arc. Fig. 2.6 gives an example of a template with the center, the midpoints of edges, and the vertices all marked.

Score the dark solid lines with a pointed instrument (like the metal tip of your compass) on the unprinted side of the acetate. If you score on the printed side you may scratch off the marker or toner. Cut the pieces out on the inside of the finer dashed line so that none of the edge is visible when finished. The tabs will not need to match each other exactly or be perfectly shaped. You will be able to staple the pieces together on the outside of the model, and you will find these transparent tabs are unobtrusive.

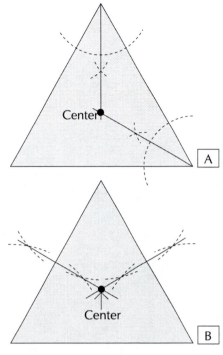

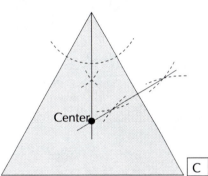

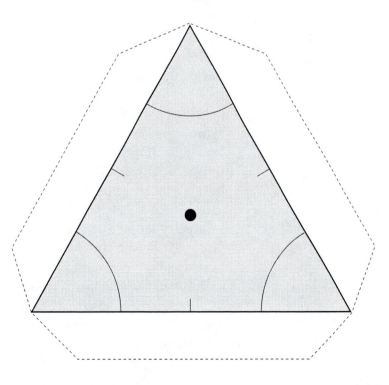

Left:
Fig. 2.5 Three different ways to find the center of a regular polygon. Again we have used the equilater triangle.

A. By finding the intersection of two adjacent angle bisectors

B. By finding the intersection of the perpendicular bisectors of two adjacent sides

C. By finding the intersection of an angle bisector and an perpendicular bisector of the adjacent side.

Below:
Fig. 2.6 The template for a tetrahedron model. The center of the polygon, the midpoints of its sides and the vertices have all been marked.

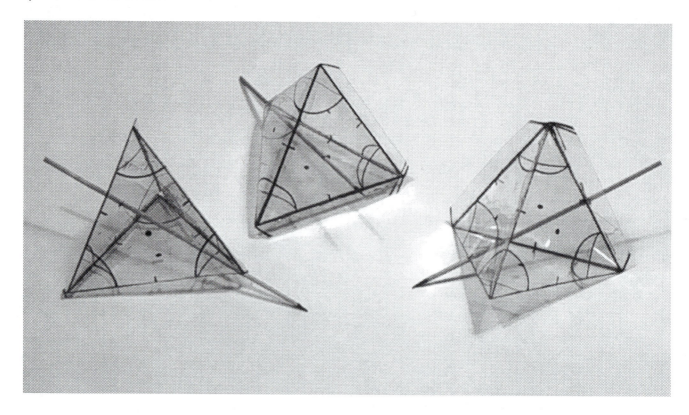

Looking for Symmetry in All the Right Places

Above:
Rochelle Newman. Clear acetate models with small wooden rods.
Faces, edges, and vertices are all logical places to begin the search for symmetries in any polyhedron. Acetate models facilitate the search. Wooden rods are used to locate the axes.
Notice where these rods enter and exit the form.

After you have built your model, and before looking for its symmetries, you need to pierce the centers of faces, midpoints of edges, and its vertices so that a thin rod, such as a wooden skewer, may be passed through the figure as an imagined axis of rotation. These axes help to determine the rotational symmetries when pushed through the figure. They also provide something to physically grasp as you begin to turn your mode, in order to look for the types of rotational symmetry it contains. Since the operation of rotation is physically performable, it might be easier to begin your search for symmetries by first looking for axes of rotation. You can then move on to looking for planes of reflection in your search for reflectional, or mirror,

symmetry. Remember that you must always consider faces, edges, and vertices.

Symmetry is the search for an orderly arrangement that does not change through various transformations. It provides us humans with a degree of comfort in a world that appears chaotic. Symmetry becomes the yardstick by which to measure the degrees of asymmetry. Scientists today find both aspects of reality inextricably linked. In chaotic states, there are pockets of order. In ordered events, there are disorderly disturbances. Contemporary physicists are investigating the primal building blocks of matter which they call elementary particles. These are found within the nucleus of the chemical atoms. These scientists are looking to see where there is

symmetry and where there is not.

To this point we have examined relatively simple three-dimensional figures for symmetry. (Remember the cylinder and cone from Chapter 1.) In these cases it has been a fairly straightforward task to observe the figure and determine where the symmetries occur. Polyhedra, however, come in many different forms, many of which are fairly complicated. Before we come to the point where we want to take a look at any particular symmetries, it might be helpful to consider a general strategy. Let us start with some basic questions.

1. Do I understand what the symmetry operations are?
2. Do I understand what the symmetry elements are?
3. How do I know what to look for?
4. Are there rules for finding the symmetries?

5. Does learning about symmetry require the use of intellect, hands, eyes, intuitions or feelings?
6. Does knowing require experience?

There are different ways of knowing and they involve the use of different faculties. We can know through our hands with tactile and kinesthetic experience, our hearts with intuitive insights, and our heads through rational and logical thinking. Because very few of us have the ability to picture in our minds a complete model of a concept, one that we can mentally take apart or observe from all sides, we must employ all of the above ways of knowing in order to find answers. Left and right brain thinking become complements in the search for answers. Each enhances the other.

Above:
Rochelle Newman. Model of five interlocking tetrahedra. Acrylic paint on a smooth bristol paper.

How would you approach looking for the symmetries of this form?

Can you discover other models that have interlocking tetrahedra?

Space, Polyhedra and Symmetry

The existence of a polyhedron is the result of the constraints of three-dimensional space. These constrains limit not only how polygons come tgether to frm polyhedra, but also, how many of them are needed and what kinds can be combined. The faces of a polyhedron must completely enclose a volume of space without gaps. Every vertex of a polyhedron must have angles that measure less than 360°, or else the vertex would be planar, or two dimensional.

The inherent symmetries of a polyhedron are separate from, and are not affected by, its orientation in space. There are logical places to look in order to find the different types of symmetries in a particular polyhedron. We suggest that you use the following hierarchy. First look for axes of rotation. Begin at the center of rotation of all of the polygonal faces. Then, continue on to the midpoint of all edges. Finally, search at the vertices. What have you discovered? Look for planes of reflections next. Begin with the axis of reflection of each of the polygonal faces. Continue on to the line through the midpoint of two opposite edges on a polygonal face. Then, search at the vertices. True axes of rotation will enter and exit the polyhedron *only* at specfic locations. The points of entry are: the center of rotation in a face, the midpoint of an edge, or at a vertex.

The axes will exit the form at the center of rotation in a face, the midpoint of an edge, or a vertex. Some of the various combinations of entrances and exits can be as follows: center of rotation in a face/vertex; midpoint of an edge/midpoint of an edge; vertex/vertex. The angle which an axis of rotation forms with a face, an edge, or a vertex is very specific. When there are axes of rotation through faces, all of these will be at right angles to the face containing the center of rotation. When there are axes of rotation through edges, all of these will be at right angles to the edge, and will lie in the plane that bisects the interfacial angle. When there are axes of rotation through vertices, all of these will enter or exist through the apex of the vertex.

Above:
An edge and vertex view of the sculpture by Isamu Noguchi that is shown on the previous page.

When looking for the reflection, or mirror planes, it is important to remember that they will enter and exit at the axis of reflection of a polygonal face, the midpoint of an edge, or an entire edge. If the intersection is not an axis of reflection in a face, the midpoint of an edge, or an entire edge, you need not do any further investigation. There is no plane of reflection here. When the axis of reflection of a face and a complete edge are intersected by the implied plane of reflection, the vertex will also be involved. As you imagine the plane, look to see if the two halves into which it cuts the polyhedron, are mirror images of one another. If they are, then there is a plane of reflection. If the polyhedron is not split into mirror halves, then there is no plane of reflection. The position and angle at which planes of reflection will intersect the figure are also very specific. They are as follows: A plane of reflection through a face will be perpendicular to the face and pass through the mirror line of that face. The reflection, or mirror plane, passes, or will bisect, the interfacial angle of a complete edge. Any plane of reflection passing through a vertex will already have been found when searching for the planes of reflection in faces and edges. Entrance and exit locations of the

This page:
Top:
Painted large scale metal outdooor structure in Burns Park, Denver, Colorado.
Artist unknown.
Bottom:
Large scale metal outdoor sculpture in downtown Zeckendorf Plaza, Denver, Colorado. Artist unknown.
Notice the stacking of the tetrahedra which transforms a simple unit into a complex form.

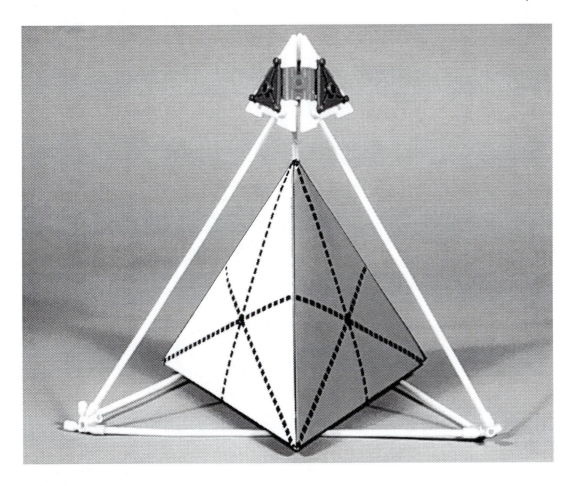

Above:
Rochelle Newman. Model.
Paper tetrahedron set inside
a skeletal tetrahedron made
of sticks and rubber connec-
tors, capped with a plastic
tetrahedron. The graphic
tape lines mark vertices, midpoints of faces, and mid-
points of edges.

axes of rotation and planes of reflection are intimately linked. You must
be certain that when entering and
exiting the figure, all axes and planes
are siumultaneously at their proper
90° angles and/or bisecting the interfacial angle at all places. Remember
to check for mirror halves where
planes of reflection might be and the
same kind of symmetry at either end
of an axis of rotation. In addition to
this, axes and planes must be considered as single entities with entrances
and exits, and as such, can only be
counted once. For example, an axis
may enter a face and exit a vertex,
but it does not get counted twice.
Rather, it is counted as a single axis
that enters and exits through a face
and a vertex.

The symmetries of the polygonal
faces *might* lead to symmetries of

the polyhedron, but there are not
guarantees that theywill. If we cannot find any symmetry in any of the
polygonal faces, however, there will
be *no other* places to look for symmetries in the polyhedron. Mathematically we say that the existence of
symmetries in the faces, edges, and
vertices is a *necessary* but not *sufficient* condition for the existence of
symmetries in the polyhedron.

On the next few pages we have
included illustrations to help you
find the symmetry of the tetrahedron. The chart on pages 92 and 93
illustrates how you can use your
acetate model to look for the rotational symmetries of the tetrahedron.
The chart on pages 94 and 95
illustrates the symmetries of the
tetrahedron.

Rotational Symmetry Search of the Tetrahedron

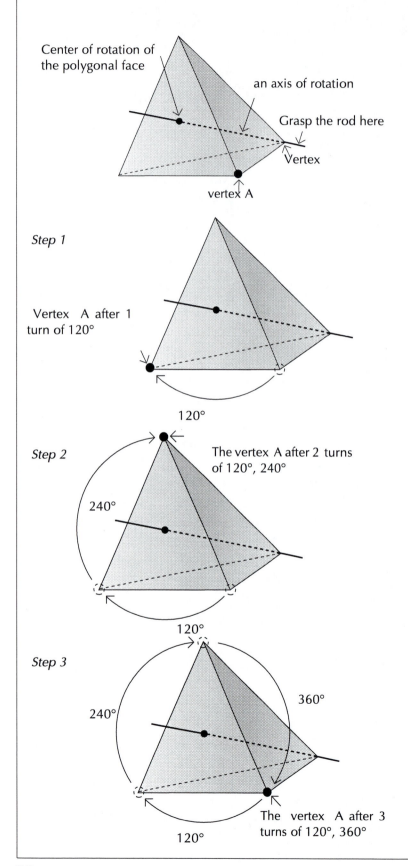

Center of rotation of the polygonal face

an axis of rotation

Grasp the rod here

Vertex

vertex A

Step 1

Vertex A after 1 turn of 120°

120°

Step 2

240°

The vertex A after 2 turns of 120°, 240°

120°

Step 3

240°

360°

The vertex A after 3 turns of 120°, 360°

120°

Looking at Faces and Vertices

Make a model. Hold it so that you can look directly at a face. Insert the rod through the rotation center of the face, and push it through the vertex that is opposite that face. The rod will be perpendicular to the face and it will pass through the apex of the vertex. It will function as an axis of rotation for the polyhedron. Notice that we have labelled vertex A so that you can follow the change of position of the tetrahedron.

Step 1
We now turn the tetrahedron about the rod to discover what kind of rotational symmetry is present at the faces and vertices. We find the first turn by rotating vertex A in a clockwise direction until the figure becomes superimposable on itself.

After turning 120°, the tetrahedron is superimposed on itself, with the identity vertex in a new position. Because this face is a regular polygon, we now know that all subsequent turns about it will be in increments of 120°.

Step 2
From its new location, rotate vertex A in a clockwise direction for another 120° to complete the second turn of this rotation.

After turning 240°, the figure is superimposed on itself once again. Notice that vertex A is again in a new position.

Step 3
Complete the third turn by once again rotating vertex A for the final 120°.

After turning the tetrahedron 3 turns about the axis, vertex A, is now superimposed on its original position, so the axis is an axis of three turn rotational symmetry. Since there are four faces and four vertices which share the intimate relationship of these axes of rotation, the tetrahedron has four 3-turn axes.

Looking at Edges

We will now search for a rotation axis through the midpoints of two edges. This time, hold your model so that you can look directly at an edge. Insert the rod so that it pierces the midpoint of that edge, and continue to push until it exits through the midpoint of the opposite, but nonparallel edge. As you can see, the rod lies in the planes that bisect the interfacial angles of the edges. After checking the symmetry at both ends and finding them to be the same, we can conclude that this rod will also function as an axis of rotation. Once again, we use a marked vertex, B, to determine the degree of rotational symmetry .

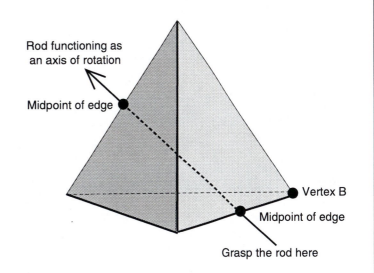

Step 1
We begin by rotating the vertex B in a clockwise direction until the tetrahedron becomes superimposed on itself.

After being turned 180° in a clockwise direction, , the figure is superimposed on itself. With the vertex B, 180° away from its original position. Because the tetrahedron is a regular polyhedron, we now know that all subsequent turns at this axis will be in increments of 180°.

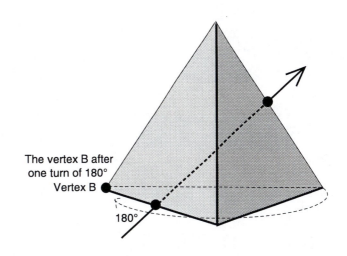

Step 2
We complete the second and final turn of this rotation by rotating the vertex   B through another 180°.

Since we have rotated though 360° the vertex B and the figure are now both superimposed on their original positions. Although the tetrahedron has six edges, each 2-turn roation axes passes through a pair of edges so there are three such axes. We say that the tetrahedron has three 2-turn axes. Thus the rod through the midpoints of these edges is a two-turn rotation axis.

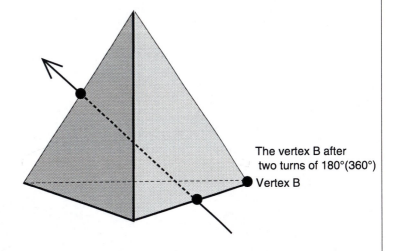

Symmetries of the Tetrahedron

Operation: Rotation
Element: Axis of Rotation

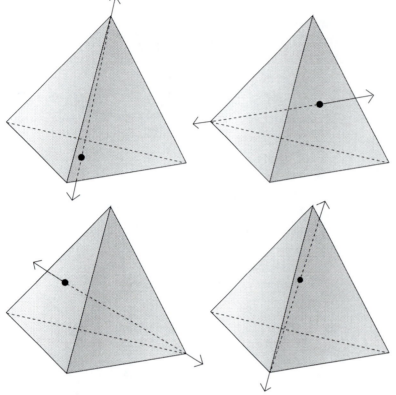

Centers of Rotation in Faces and Vertices

As you have already seen, some of the axes of rotation pass through a vertex and the center of rotation of the opposite face. There is a total of four vertices and four faces Therefore, the tetrahedron has four 3-turn rotation axes..

Midpoints of Edges

Some of the axes of rotation pass through the midpoints of opposite but nonparallel edges. There is a total of six edges (three pairs of opposite edges) and, therefore, the tetrahedron has three 2-turn rotation axes.

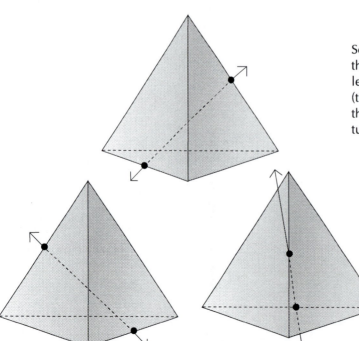

A single view of the tetrahedron with a plane of reflection

Reflection in Faces, Midpoints of Edges and Entire Edges

Notice that each plane of reflection, mirror plane, slices through the whole polyhedron and has a specific location. There are three mirror planes for each face. (See the axes of reflection in the single face.) Each one passes through a mirror line of the face and the edge opposite that face. Since the tetrahedron has four faces, there is a total of 12 planes of reflection.

Twelve planes of reflection plus twelve rotational symmetries equals a total of 24 symmetries.

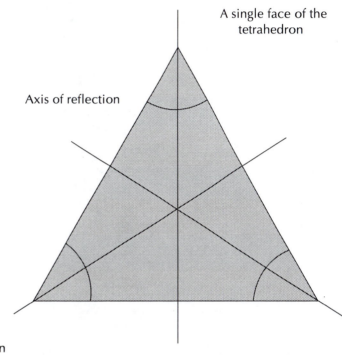

A single face of the tetrahedron

Axis of reflection

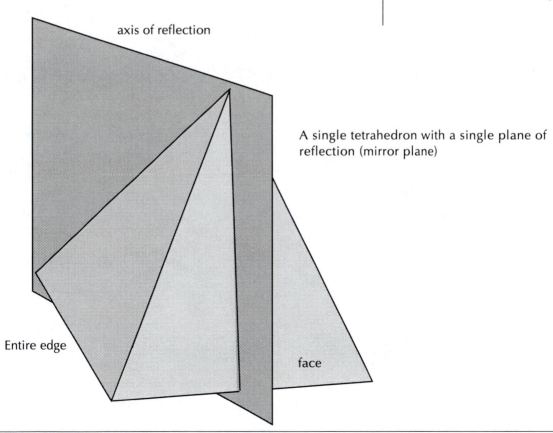

axis of reflection

A single tetrahedron with a single plane of reflection (mirror plane)

Entire edge

face

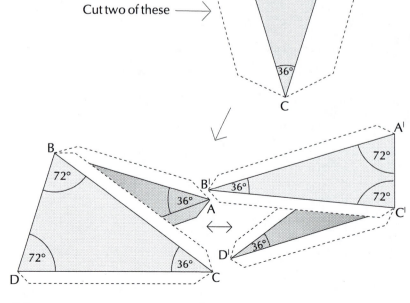

36°

72°　72°
72°　72°
36°　　36°

36°

72°　72°　72°　72°

Above:
Fig 2.7 A single template for a nonregular tetrahedron with congruent Golden faces.

Right and below:
Fig. 2.8 A two unit template can also be used to construct a nonregular tetrahedron.

A

36°

72°　72°
D　　　B
72°　72°

36°

C

Cut two of these ⟶

B

72°

A

72°

D

72°　36°

C

A'

72°

B'　36°

72°

C'

36°

D'

The Nonregular Tetrahedron

The tetrahedron is a wonderfully versatile form that can also be constructed from triangles other than equilateral ones. For example, we might want to use isosceles triangles, in this case Golden Triangles with angles of 72°, 72° and 36°. The template must be changed from one with four equilateral triangles to one with four congruent Golden Triangles (Fig. 2.7).

Score and mountain fold all line segments making up the triangles, and then glue the tabs together. When working on a model of a polyhedron that will be more elegant than the clear acetate ones, the glue tabs will be on the inside and, therefore, will not be seen. This type of model is easiest to put together if you glue two tabs together at a time and wait until they dry before moving on to the next pair. It takes a little longer this way, but the figure will stay together better and be a lot less frustrating to work on. A pin can be inserted into a corner in order to pull the vertices together before the glue has set. A tacky white glue works well on paper.

Another way to construct a nonregular tetrahedra from congruent isosceles triangles involves the use of a two unit template. Once again, we have chosen the Golden Triangle. Here, the triangles are joined in base-to-base pairs, with each pair making up one unit. Two units will be needed to complete the tetrahedron, each one fitting leg-to-leg with the other one (Fig. 2.8).

Make sure that you have included the glue tabs before proceeding. Cut the pieces out and then mountain

As a "constructivist" sculptor, I find the triangle a fascination, both as a polygon and as the planes of a tetrahedron. The strength of the triangle inherent in its rigidity seems to me to carry over visually as a portrayal of its structural strength.

When the edges of four triangles form a tetrahedron, the result is a construction which does not relate to quadrilateral orientation. This in turn produces unexpected visual delights and is extremely strong.

With rare exception, my work is totally related to tetrahedrons and triangles.

Arthur Silverman

Above:
Arthur Silverman. Aluminum Trio. Matte aluminum. 16' x 3' x 6'. 1986. Three nonregular tetrahedra joined at the midpoints of edges.

Photo courtesy of the artist.

fold all of the line segments of the triangles. Glue them together matching A to A¹, B to B¹, C to C¹ and D to D¹.

A unit of two congruent triangles of any type can also be coupled with a unit of two congruent isosceles triangles to form a non-regular tetrahedron. A single template can be used here. In this case, it is a little easier to fit the faces together correctly if a two unit template is used. Construction 8 on pages 98 and 99 shows you how to make a non-regular tetrahedron.

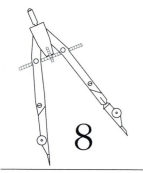

8

Construct a Nonregular Tetrahedron

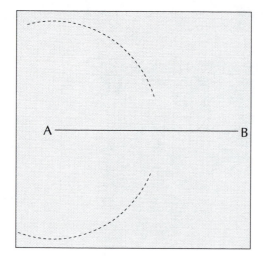

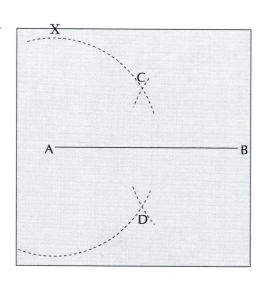

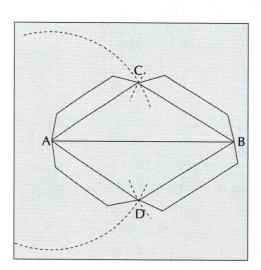

Given a piece of paper suitable for building models

(*You will be constructing two figures on the paper, so give yourself room.*)

Initial Construction
(Unit A)

1. Draw a line segment and label it $\overline{AB}$. The length of this segment is arbitrary, but it will become one edge of the tetrahedron so choose the length to best suit your purposes.

2. Open the compass to more than half the length of $\overline{AB}$, and cut arcs on both sides of $\overline{AB}$. These arcs determine another edge length of the tetrahedron.

3. At the point of the greatest distance, marked x, between arcs drawn in the previous step, open the compass to measure more than half the distance between the two. Without changing the setting, put the metal tip on B and cut arcs that intersect those drawn in the previous step. Label the points of intersection C and D.

4. Draw $\overline{AC}$, $\overline{AD}$, $\overline{BC}$ and $\overline{BD}$. Add glue tabs. Notice that you have two pairs of congruent lengths.

5. Erase all extraneous markings.

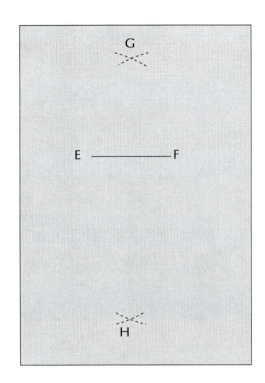

(Unit B)

1. One another part of the paper, draw a segment that measures less than the distance from C to D. Label it $\overline{EF}$. $\overline{EF}$ will determine the remaining edge of the tetrahedron. The longer $\overline{EF}$ is , the flatter the tetrahedron will be.

2. Open the compass to measure $\overline{AC}$. With the metal tip first on E and then on F, cut a pair of intersecting arcs on the same side of $\overline{EF}$. Label the point of intersection G.

3. Open the compass to measure $\overline{BC}$. With the metal tip first on E and then on F, cut a pair of intersecting arcs on the opposite side of $\overline{EF}$ from those cut in the previous step. Label the point of intersection H.

4. Draw $\overline{EG}$, $\overline{FG}$, $\overline{EF}$ and $\overline{FH}$. Add glue tabs.

5. Erase all extraneous markings.

Assembly

1. Cut out the two units. Mountain fold all line segments making up the triangles.

2. Glue the two pieces together so that C matches E, A matches G, D matches F, and B matches H.

Now you have constructed a non-regular tetrahedron.

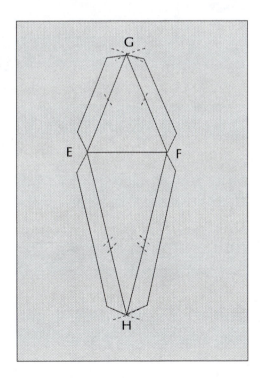

This page:
Arthur Silverman. Sculptures with tetrahedral and triangular elements.

Top:
Dance Steps. Matte aluminum. 44" x 92" x 48". 1991. The fluid curvature is the result of the relationship between the elongated triangles.

Bottom:
Bay Hill Fan. Matte aluminum. 11' x 4'6" x 2'9". 1987. Three tetrahedra standing on edge and joined at their vertices describe two negative triangular spaces.

Photos courtesy of the artist.

By now it is probably clear that with an understanding of just the tetrahedron, you can have a wonderful time playing for a very long time. Sculptor Arthur Silverman, whose work is pictured on this page and elsewhere in this chapter, has done just that. He has devoted a major part of his professional artistic life to creating sculptures from both triangular and tetrahedral forms, theme and variation.

Architecture of Nature

Throughout this exploration of forms with triangular components, we have seen that the tetrahedron is truly a basic building unit in the three-dimensional geometric world. Interestingly enough, it is also a basic building unit of the natural world which includes both organic and inorganic substances. Before we can understand how tetrahedral formation occurs, however, we must take a detour to briefly discuss the atomic physics of an atom, one of the most fundamental building units of the chemical and physical realm.

As curious creatures, we often seek understanding through questioning the, "who, what, why, where, when, and how," of our existence. If you can recall the game that we played as children which asked the question, "Is it animal, vegetable, or mineral?", you will have the essence of the classifications of organic and inorganic chemistry. While it is accurate to say that all animals and vegetables belong to the organic realm, it would be inaccurate to say that the only substances belonging to the inorganic classification are minerals.

Above:
Animal, vegetable, or mineral?
Objects found in the organic and inorganic realms.

Although nature does not discriminate between the individual elements used in either organic or inorganic, there is a great deal of difference in the results when combinations of two or more elements are brought together. That they do differ is obvious even to the understanding of a child, who suely knows there is a difference between a person and Mt. Everest. Based upon this distinction, the question of, "How do they differ?", also seems to be apparent at a surface level. One of the most obvious answers is, the person is living and the mountain is not. Herein lies what is commonly thought to be the split between organic and inorganic chemistry. Interestingly enough, however, what is commonly thought to be a fracture turns out to be a continuum. Scientists move back and forth between the disciplines of these realms because at the molecular level, there is no difference between them.

The answers to many of the questions referring to how they differ are somewhat difficult to answer and must first be researched and discovered in science laboratories and then learned in classrooms. For example, organic substances frequently exist as liquids or gases due to their low melting and boiling points, while many inorganic substances can be found as solids in rocks and minerals. Also, many organic substances do not dissolve easily in water and

are inflammable in air, while many inorganic substances do not dissolve in water and do not ignite easily in air. Many inorganic mixtures can also conduct electricity.

There are 103 naturally occurring elements which are listed in the periodic table. These are the basic building units of natural chemistry, whose scientists seek to explain such things as, the formation of a snowflake, and the burning of a flame. These 103 elements are also the basic building units that combine in various ways to make hundreds of thousands and perhaps even more substances present in f the natural world. Only 25,000 of them, however, are classified as inorganic. Oxygen (O), the most abundant element in existence can be found in a vast array of combinations with other elements in both the organic and inorganic domains. After oxygen, silicon (Si) is the predominent element of the inorganic domain, while the carbon atom (C), is found in *all* of the elemental mixtures in the organic realm. Here, a vast majority of substances are formed from only a few elements: carbon (C), hydrogen (H), oxygen (O) and nitrogen (N). If you refer back to the periodic chart on page 67, you will notice that all of these are found in the beginning of the table.

Dimitri Mendelyeev organized the table so that the vertical columns displayed similar characteristics,

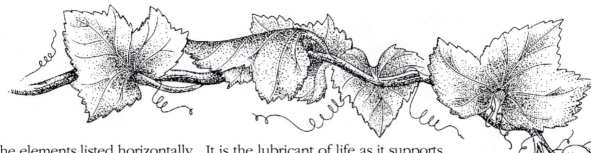

while the elements listed horizontally changed gradually from left to right. These similarities and differences are due to the electronic configurations of the outer shells of the atoms. Metals are listed on the left side, while non-metals are on the right.

A great deal of organic chemistry is devoted to the different shapes and arrangements that can occur when carbon atoms are combined with other carbon atoms, and with other elements as well. Different arrangements of carbon and hydrogen atoms can lead to striking differences in the properties of substances. The study of the different structures that can be formed by the particular arrangement of the atoms within crystals (crystallography) is found in the realm of inorganic chemistry.

There is a vital interplay among the substances common to these separate branches of science. It is an interdependency so great, that if the balance between the two is interrupted, so too, is life itself, a matter that we must all come to grips with if we are to survive as a species. Plants produce oxygen, which is inorganic, in addition to supplying the largest amount of organic mixtures necessary for the nourishment of the living kingdom. Minerals supply the trace elements that allow the enzymes to be produced that are essential to the survival of plant life, and also those substances that support the material needs of humankind. It is water, however, that is our most precious natural resource.

It is the lubricant of life as it supports plant, animal, and planet simultaneously.

In this section we will explore the basic concepts of atomic architecture. We will focus upon the organic kingdom as we look at methane (CH_4), the simplest of carbon-based molecules, and water (H_2O), the most abundant substance on earth. You will discover that although these are unique mixtures, methane always has implied tetrahedral structure and if the conditions are just right, so too can water. In subsequent chapters we will explore both the inorganic kingdom, through the wonderful patterns and symmetrical structures of crystals, and the kingdom of living organisms through the biological structure of the cell.

By touching lightly upon these subjects, we seek to support the hypothesis that there is an undeniable need for the union of art, math, and nature. Nature is a magnificent piece of work that is in perpetual motion. Its origin has been the topic of discussion and wonder since the beginning of human consciousness. Scientists use mathematics as the tool by which to quantify nature in an effort to define and ultimately make use of its findings. Art seeks to create understanding as it composes and makes manifest the results of the previous description. Mathematics and science seek to analyze experience while art attempts to synthesize experience.

Atomic Structure

Above:
Student work. Ellen Rutgers. The Dancing Adams.
Pen, ink and markers.
So much is packed inside an atom. An atom has a nucleus heart surrounded by a cloud of electrons. In relative terms, the distance between the nucleus and the electron cloud is great; therefore, the control by the nucleus over the electrons is weak. This weakness is what allows the chemical and physical interactions to take place.

Let us begin our exploration with the mystery and wonder of a single atom. The chemical symbol of each atom can be found in the periodic chart on page 67. The word atom comes from the Greek word, atomos, meaning indivisible. Until modern times it was believed to be a solid, inseparable unit. Today, however, advances in technology have changed our understanding of the structure and composition of the atom.

To date, scientists are certain that an atom is not truly a solid, but rather, it is a composite single unit with a diameter of approximately one hundred millionth of a centimeter. It has both subnuclear and subatomic parts, some bearing a positive electrical charge, some a negative charge, and some being neutral with no electrical charge at all. These minute particles of matter are mostly arranged in a symmetrical manner that is governed by electrical forces. Attractive forces hold atoms together, while repulsive forces prevent bonding. It is not surprising that the concept of the complementarity of the universe, positive and negative, is also displayed as the very thing that an atom relies upon for its cohesive structure, the positive and negative charges within.

In the early part of this century it was believed that an atom had a nucleus, or core, that consisted of two different types of primary units called protons and neutrons. These nucleons, as the protons and neutrons are referred to collectively, have approximately the same size, but differ in their electrical charges. The protons are positive, while the neutrons are electrically neutral.

Current atomic theory, however, suggests that nucleons are neither the smallest nor the only elements present within the nucleus. Rather,

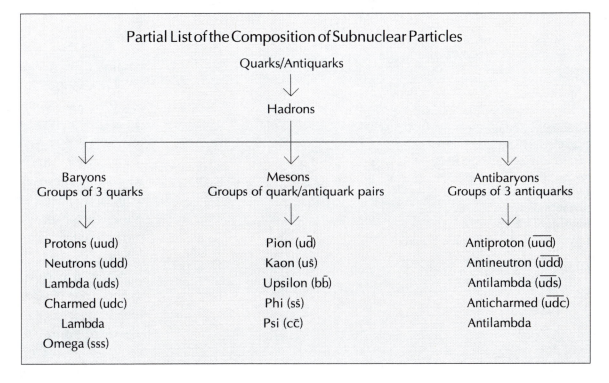

Fundamental Subnuclear Particles			
Quarks		**Antiquarks**	
Flavor/Symbol	Electrical Charge	Flavor/Symbol	Electrical Charge
Up (u)	+2/3	Antiup (ū)	-2/3
Down (d)	-1/3	Antidown (d̄)	+1/3
Charmed (c)	+2/3	Anticharmed (c̄)	-2/3
Strange (s)	-1/3	Antistrange (s̄)	+1/3
Truth (t)	+2/3	Antitruth (t̄)	-2/3
Beauty (b)	-1/3	Antibeauty (b̄)	+1/3

Partial List of the Composition of Subnuclear Particles

Quarks/Antiquarks
↓
Hadrons

Baryons Groups of 3 quarks	Mesons Groups of quark/antiquark pairs	Antibaryons Groups of 3 antiquarks
Protons (uud)	Pion (ud̄)	Antiproton (u̅u̅d̅)
Neutrons (udd)	Kaon (us̄)	Antineutron (u̅d̅d̅)
Lambda (uds)	Upsilon (bb̄)	Antilambda (u̅d̅s̅)
Charmed (udc)	Phi (ss̄)	Anticharmed (u̅d̅c̅)
Lambda	Psi (cc̄)	Antilambda
Omega (sss)		

there are more fundamental particles called quarks and antiquarks that combine to form baryons, mesons, and antibaryons which then combine to form hadrons. These then become the units that group together to form the elements within the nucleus. The top chart on this page gives the names and polarities of some the quarks and antiquarks that are known to date, while the bottom chart presents a partial list of their groupings. It is theorized that the nucleus is bound into a cohesive unit by an interplay among the electrical charges of these units.

Groups of up to two hundred and twenty nucleons can cluster together to form a single nucleus. One of the largest stable nuclei is that of bismuth (Bi), a metallic white substance. It has a group of 209 nucleons, 83 of which are protons and 126 are neutrons. The neutron/proton ratio is approximately equal for those elements with atomic numbers up to about 20. This ratio increases, however, for the larger elements. On the whole, the nucleus bears a positive electrical charge.

Above:

Notice that scientists, although serious about what they do, are playful in naming what they "see".
Humans name things in order to communicate with each other. The assumption is that all parties in a communication loop understand the meanings assigned.
Each discipline has its own special language that participants must learn in order to share ideas.

The other components of the atom are outside the nucleus and are called electrons. An electron has a negative electrical charge and is about 1/2,000 the mass of a nucleon. The current understanding of how electrons are located in atoms comes from some rather complicated mathematics of wave mechanics, based upon concepts such as the Uncertainty Principle and the wave nature of particles. The Uncertainty Principle states that we cannot know both the position and energy of a particle at the same time with any certainty. If the position is known, the energy is not, and vice versa. Orbital theory puts forth the premise that there are regions, or orbitals, around an atom in which there is a high probability of finding an electron. Two electrons with opposite spins can go in each orbital.

The shapes of these regions, or orbitals, are quite interesting, as they are what give the atoms their three-dimensional forms. The simplest orbital is that of an *s-orbital*, which is a spherical region centered at the nucleus. The next kind of orbitals are *p-orbitals*, shaped like a figure-8 centered on the nucleus. There are three p-orbitals, one for each direction in three dimensions along the x, y and z axes of the Cartesian coordinate plane.

Although there are several different types of orbitals, the chart on this page only illustrates what the s and p-orbitals look like. It is the location and position of the p-orbitals in particular molecular bonds that result in implied triangular and tetrahedral configuration. It is for this reason that we are illuminating only these orbitals.

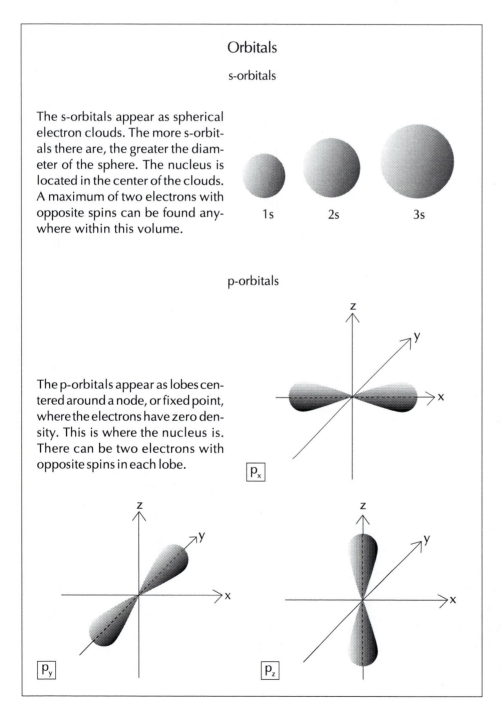

Orbitals

s-orbitals

The s-orbitals appear as spherical electron clouds. The more s-orbitals there are, the greater the diameter of the sphere. The nucleus is located in the center of the clouds. A maximum of two electrons with opposite spins can be found anywhere within this volume.

1s 2s 3s

p-orbitals

The p-orbitals appear as lobes centered around a node, or fixed point, where the electrons have zero density. This is where the nucleus is. There can be two electrons with opposite spins in each lobe.

p_x

p_y

p_z

In all but one case, there are always an equal number of protons and electrons in a neutral atom. This appears as the atomic number of each element in the periodic chart (see Fig. 2.1 on page 67). The hydrogen atom, however, is the exception. It is unique in that it has one proton, no neutrons, and one electron that spins in an s-orbital.

Although electrons prefer to be in the lowest possible energy state, this is not always the case. From time to time they become excited by the absorption of energy, and move to the next energy level. The different energy states of an atom can be thought of as orbitals with different radii. The radii are fixed, or quantized, a consequence of the wave nature of the electrons. There are only certain numbers of wave cycles that can form a continuous wave around a nucleus. The top chart on this page illustrates an example of one that will work and one that will not.

At each level, energy is absorbed as light, or photons, which are related to the color spectrum. The colors that are not absorbed by the molecules are what we perceive as the color of the substance . For example, if the molecules in an object absorb all colors except blue, then the object appears blue when light is shined on it. Light is emitted when a molecule or atom emits a particular energy. An example is when sodium atoms, excited by the heat in a flame, emit photons with energy that corresponds to yellow light. If you can imagine, for just a moment, that the hydrogen atom is a balloon, then the analogy illustrated in the bottom chart on this page describes the process by which energy is absorbed and color is emitted.

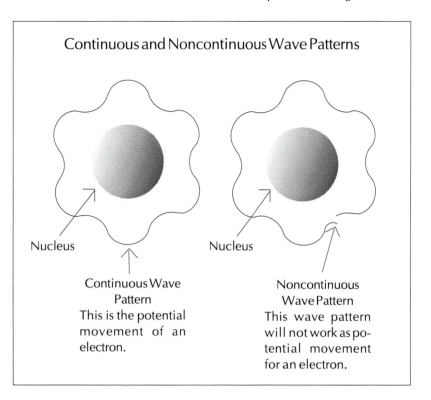

Continuous and Noncontinuous Wave Patterns

Nucleus

Nucleus

Continuous Wave Pattern
This is the potential movement of an electron.

Noncontinuous Wave Pattern
This wave pattern will not work as potential movement for an electron.

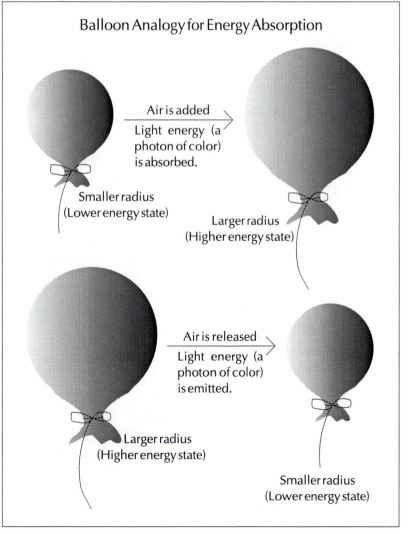

Balloon Analogy for Energy Absorption

Air is added
Light energy (a photon of color) is absorbed.

Smaller radius (Lower energy state)

Larger radius (Higher energy state)

Air is released
Light energy (a photon of color) is emitted.

Larger radius (Higher energy state)

Smaller radius (Lower energy state)

Molecular Concerto: The Interatomic Bond

When two or more atoms come into close proximity , they can join forces to become what is called a molecule. A molecule is the smallest indivisible unit that can retain the characteristics of a larger amount of the material called a chemical compound. Often these combinations of elements are recognized by their molecular formulas, such as CH_4, the description for methane gas.

There are additional ways in which to represent chemical compounds as the chart on this page illustrates. Here, methane is noted in six different ways, each having its own particular use. In all cases, however, we receive the same information, and that is, the constituent parts of a molecule of methane are: one carbon atom (C) and four hydrogen atoms (H_4).

Molecular bonding is a complex process which involves a number of factors. One of the first to be considered is the valence, or specified number of bonds, that an atom can make. This number is primarily determined by the electrons in the outermost orbit, or shell, as it is sometimes called, and is commonly referred to as the valence orbital. If this orbital is full, the atom will not readily bond with any other atoms, and conversely, if it is not, there is a potential for bonding. For example, hydrogen has a valence of one and is said to be monovalent, the result of a single electron in its only orbital. Carbon has a potential valence of four due to the number of electrons in its valence orbital. It, therefore, can join in four places.

The type of bonding that can occur between and amongst atoms is greatly dependent upon the electronegativity of neighboring atoms. The electronegativity number of each individual atom expresses its potential to either "give" or "take" electrons during the bonding process. This number is a combined measure of ionization energies, or the power needed if one atom is to give off electrons, and electron affinities, or the amount of energy gained once an electron has been taken. Those atoms that have a tendency to give electrons

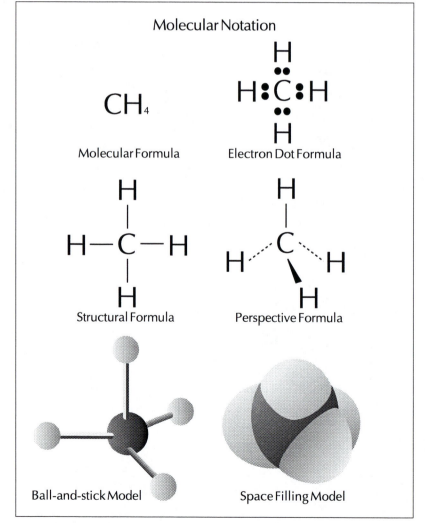

Molecular Notation

CH_4

Molecular Formula

Electron Dot Formula

Structural Formula

Perspective Formula

Ball-and-stick Model

Space Filling Model

are said to be electropositive, and those atoms that have a tendency to take electrons are said to be electronegative.

When the difference in electronegativity between the two atoms is small, these two elements can enter into what is called a covalent bond. This type bond involves only those atoms that have the tendency to take electrons from neighboring atoms. Because the energy necessary to do so is approximately equal in both atoms, there is a mutual sharing of these electrons. While the negative forces of the shared electrons become strongly attracted to both nuclei, it is the repulsive forces between the positive charge of the nuclei that determines how near to each other the merging atoms will come. The interplay between electrical forces that makes this bond a particularly strong and stable one. When this process is complete, the atomic orbitals are combined and a new molecular orbital is formed. Fig. 2.9 illustrates what happens when two atoms with s-orbitals merge.

When two approximately equal electronegative atoms with s-orbitals and p-orbitals approach each other, they have the ability to combine in a special way to form very diferent molecular orbitals that are called hybrid orbitals. It is this type of merging that results in molecular orbitals that give us geometric shapes. If one s-orbital combines with one p-orbital, the result is hybrid orbitals that are called sp, and these form linear bonds. If one s-orbital combines with two p-orbitals, the result is three sp² orbitals, that form planar bonds that are arranged as an equilateral triangle 120° apart. Finally, if one s-orbital combines with three p-orbitals, the

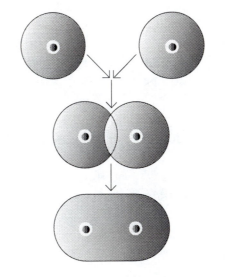

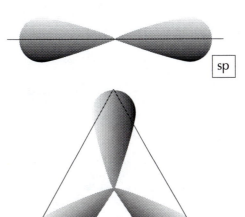

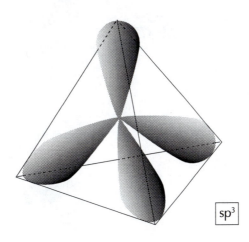

result is four sp³ orbitals that are oriented in a tetrahedral form. Fig. 2.10 illustrates the formation of these hybrid orbitals. These can then overlap with other s-orbital atoms to form covalent bonds.

Left:
Fig. 2.9 The process of the covalent bond.

Top:
Two s-orbital, electronegative atoms approach each other.

Center:
The positive charge of the nuclei attract the negative charge of the bonding electrons and their atomic orbitals overlap.

Bottom:
Because both nuclei have a positive charge they begin to repel each other and nearness is established, making this bond stable and strong.

Left and below:
Fig. 2.10 The three sp orbital hybrids.

Top:
The combining of one s-orbital and two p-orbitals results in a linear bond.

Center:
The combining of one s-orbital and three p-orbitals results in a triangular bond.

Bottom:
The combining of one s-orbital and four p-orbitals results in a tetrahedral bond.

Below:
Fig. 2.11 The methane molecule bonding process.

A. Hydrogen and carbon atoms begin to merge.

B. One of the 2s electrons is excited into the 2p$_z$ state.

C. The 2s and three 2p orbitals combine to make four sp^3 orbitals.

D. The four hydrogens covalently bond with the unpaired sp^3 electrons.

We will now consider the structure of methane (CH$_4$), the simplest of carbon-based organic molecules. It is the essential component of natural gas, and can be found seeping through cracks in the earth's crust. It is produced when vegetable matter begins to decompose in the absence of oxygen. Although odorless itself, when methane mixes with the unusual odor of decomposing vegetation in a swampy area, it is sometimes referred to as marsh gas. While stable in-and-of-itself, methane is highly flammable and has the potential to be explosive when it collides with other types of molecules in closely confined areas. For this reason it is often deadly when found in coal mines.

Fig. 2.11 illustrates the methane bonding process. Referring back to the periodic chart on page 67, we see that the neutral carbon atom has six protons, and so, six electrons. We already know that the hydrogen atom has only one electron. Describing this process has its own language which is not always easy to understand. We give the following as an example.

The notation of the electronic structure of the full orbital names of the carbon atom is:

$$1s^2\ 2s^2\ 2p_x^{\ 1}\ 2p_y^{\ 1}$$

Essentially, what this means is that the carbon atom has two electrons in a 1s orbital, two in a 2s orbital, and one each in a 2p$_x$ and 2p$_y$ orbital. The notation for each of the four isolated hydrogen atoms is:

$$1s^1$$

This tells us that hydrogen has only one electron in a 1s orbital.

When these five atoms meet there is a change in the configuration of the carbon. First, one of the 2s electrons is excited into a 2p$_z$ state. The electronic notation for the carbon atom now becomes $1s^2\ 2s^1\ 2p_x^{\ 1}\ 2p_y^{\ 1}\ 2p_z^{\ 1}$. After this occurs, the remaining 2s orbital and the now three 2p orbitals combine to form an sp^3 tetrahedral hybrid. Now, the four hydrogen atoms with their single electrons are free to bond with the unpaired electrons in each of the four lobes of the carbon atom. Because the hydrogen and carbon atoms are close in electronegativity, covalent bonds will strongly link them together.

Methane Molecule
4 hydrogen atoms + 1 carbon atom

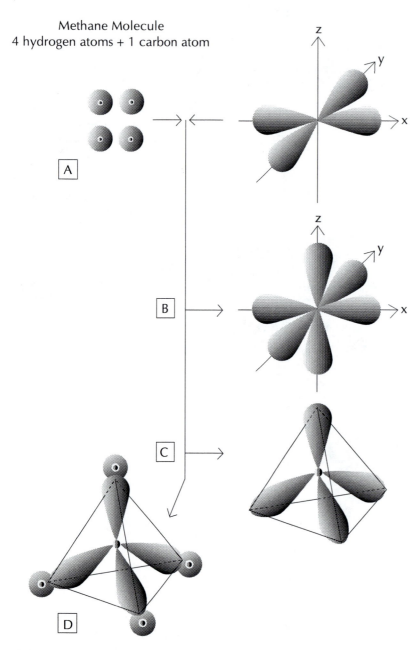

Although different in its chemical composition, water (H_2O), also has a molecular structure that is derived from the tetrahedron. Its form differs from methane, however, in that its orbitals are not as closely aligned to the vertices of the tetrahedron because of repulsion. While a single molecule of water is bound by covalent bonds, it clusters into larger groupings with hydrogen bonds. These are particularly strong bonds. They occur because the hydrogen nucleus does not attract the small, electronegative oxygen atom very strongly, and the hydrogen atom is left with a significant positive charge that can be attracted to another molecule.

When heat is applied to water, the heat is absorbed as kinetic energy. Although the individual water molecules do not change, their relationship to each other does. Even a small elevation in the temperature of water send its atoms "dancing". At 100° C (212° F) water boils, agitating the molecules. An enormous expansion takes place and density is diminished as some of the molecules escape in a vapor (Fig. 2.12). Steam then condenses into a liquid. Water is most dense in the liquid state at room temperature. Less heat means a more stable condition. Molecules dance about freely sometimes colliding with each other and occasionally even bounce off the walls of the container (Fig. 2.13). At 0° C (32° F) water becomes a solid. There is not much change in volume, but there is a significant change in character. As movement slows down, molecules just quiver as they settle into a more definite arrangement. Because ice has somewhat less density than the liquid, it floats (Fig. 2.14).

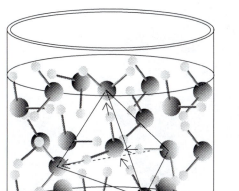

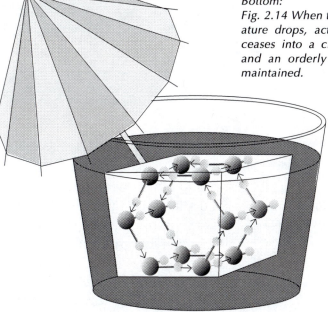

This page:
Have a drink on us!

Top:
Essentially, a chemical reaction is the rearrangement of atoms.
Fig. 2.12 In a heated state, water molecules do the jitterbug, crack apart, and escape as water vapor.

Center:
Fig 2.13 When tepid, the molecules slow down and they dance the rumba. Water molecules attract each other and on rare occasions they can even cluster into tetrahedral formation.
Bottom:
Fig. 2.14 When the temperature drops, action nearly ceases into a close 2-step and an orderly pattern is maintained.

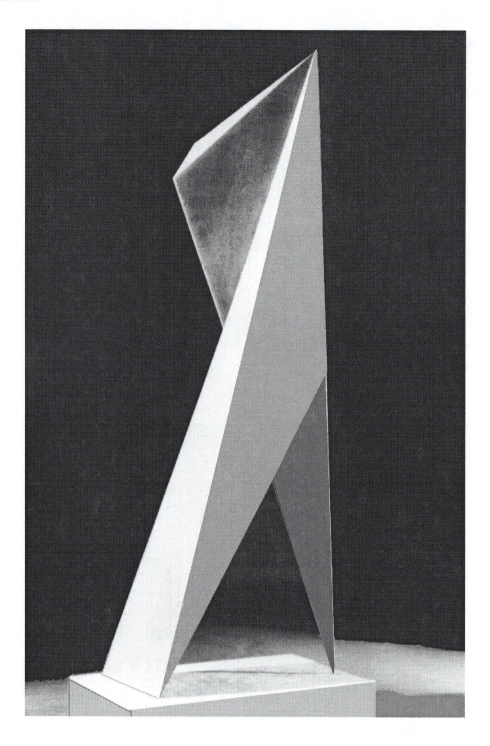

Above:
Arthur Silverman. Striding Form in Cor-ten. Corten steel. 6'8" x 29" x 18". 1976. Two joined tetrahedra, one standing on an edge and one on a vertex.

By now, it has become obvious that an in-depth discussion of chemistry and physics would take volumes of books, and space. We hope, however, to have whetted your appetite for further research and understanding in a search to find other connections between ourselves and our planet and our universe. These same atoms dance through all of it. In the human search for truth in all aspects of our lives, perhaps one thing is certain, there is no absolute Truth in any arena of investigation. Therefore, the quest is ever ongoing. Each person, each generation, each age should be open to new possibilities in any human endeavor.

Above:
A cob of corn is a natural form that has kernels arranged in a helical manner.

The Tetrahelix

We conclude this chapter with a form that can be found in the natural world, but can also be used for artistic purposes. It is called a tetrahelix, and it is constructed from tetrahedra joined in a helical manner. In Chapter 1, we introduced the helix as a linear structure on a one-dimensional structure on a cylindrical surface. Here, we reintroduce the helix in tetrahedral form. This gives us a structure that can go on indefinitely in three dimensions. According to Peter Pearce, this form is economical at several levels (see Further Readings). Such a column is extremely stable and strong because of its triangular faces. It also has fewer components for a given length. It is a structure that has also been explored in detail by Buckminster Fuller, whose work will be discussed in greater detail in Chapter 4.

113

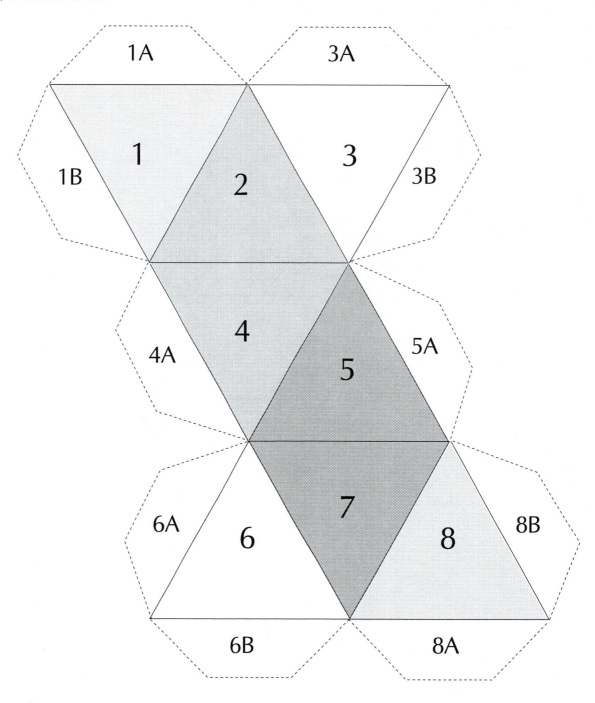

By joining two of the single templates from page 82 (Fig. 2.4B), we obtain a new template for the building of the tetrahelix (Fig. 2.15). Although there is more than one way in which these templates can be glued together to enclose space, there is only one way that will give the needed unit for the tetrahelix. Glue tabs have been numbered to aid in this process. There are also different ways in which the finished units can be joined to each other. Again, there is only one way that will result in a tetrahelix. Faces have also been numbered in order to clarify their positions. Instructions for building the units and the tetrahelix are given on the facing page. Can you discover other forms that can be obtained if the order in either the unit or the joining of the units is altered?

Template Assembly

Begin construction by assembling the individual units. This is done by gluing the tabs together in the following order:

1. Tab 1A to tab 3A
2. Tab 3B to tab 5A
3. Tab 8B to tab 1B
4. Tab 4A to tab 6A
5. Tab 6B to tab 8A

In Fig. 2.16, you will see three views of the completed unit.

Tetrahelix Assembly

Always bond face 6 of one unit to face 3 of the next unit. In so doing,

Face 2 is adjacent to face 4
Face 1 is adjacent to face 8
Face 5 is adjacent to face 7

In the completed tetrahelix you will notice that there are three distinct rows which form continuous patterns. They are:

1. 1,8; 1,8; 1,8...
2. 2,4; 2,4; 2,4...
3. 5,7; 5,7; 5,7...

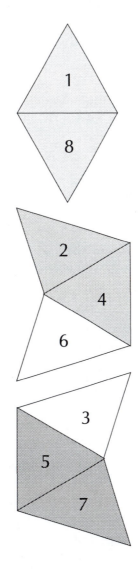

Above:
Rochelle Newman. Model of tetrahelix. Paper and acrylic paint. Different tones of gray have been used on the faces to emphasize the twisting of the object.
Use a fast setting or tacky glue. Rubber bands help as binders around units until drying is complete. Be patient. These bounce around while you are putting them together.

Left:
Fig. 2.16 Three views of the template unit needed for the construction of the tetrahelix.

Problems

1. Research the life and education of Dimitri Mendelyeev. How did he become interested in the development of the periodic table?

2. Develop a basic design armature for a right triangle that uses a combination of simple and Golden Ratio divisions.

3. Develop a grouping of triangles using more than one type. An example is, a grouping that uses scalene and isosceles triangles. First develop a row and then repeat this row any number of times until a bounded planar surface is covered.

4. Construct a paper model of a tetrahedron whose faces are isosceles triangles with vertex angles of 25°.

5. Research the family of carbon molecules. Build toothpick and gumdrop models of some.

6. Research triangular forms found in marine life. How many different types of triangles are rep-

resented. Document your research by illustrating these aquatic critters. Use black and white or color.

7. Develop two different non-regular tetrahedra.

8. Can you find variations on the tetrahelical structure that uses other than the equilateral triangle?

9. Research the topic of the "Big Bang" theory of the origin of the Universe. Why is nuclear physics part of this investigation? Use written and visual documentation.

10. Research the tetrahedral structure found in silicates (SiO_2). Where can they be found? Document these substances by constructing gumdrop and toothpick models of their structures.

11. Research the chemical composition of either ice cream, or chocolate, or both. What, if any, are the likenesses or differences in the chemical compositions of these delightful delectibles.

Projects

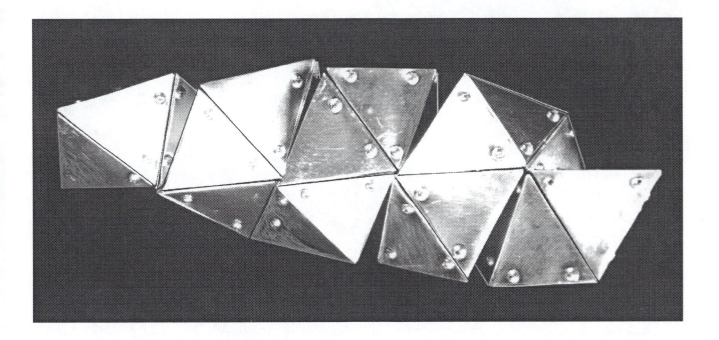

1. Using tissue paper, adhesive and strong, lightweight struts, create a kite built on a tetrahedra structure.

2. Using a graduated group of triangles, develop a sculptural model that spirals. Think of it as a small scale model that could be executed for a public site. Paying attention to scale, create an environment for your model using collage, drawings, photos, etc.

3. Using the structure of the tetrahedron, design and execute a model for a totem pole that pays homage to the butterfly. Research the symbolism as well as the form of this creature. Or use another creature of your choice.

4. Research the subject of shark and fish fins. Why are they the sizes and shapes they are? Use your research as the basis for developing a prototype for a windsurfing board.

Above:
Student work. Bob Dumas. Variation on the tetrahelix using aluminum and screws.

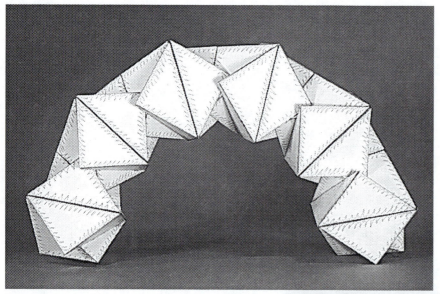

Above:
Student work. Immer Cook. Two views of stacked right angle tetrahedra to form an arch. Line drawing on paper that has been photocopied the requisite number of times. Units are then given tabs, cut out, and assembled.

Can you develop a template for a tetrahedron that uses right triangles? This is not as easy as it sounds. Here is a chance to work through a problem mathematically first. Then, translate your solution into art.

5. Make a set of triangles with notched sides or vertices so that they will fit together without adhesive. Develop a modular sculpture, and do something distinctive to each face.

6. Using several different types of triangles, develop a free-form sculpture-in-the-round.

7. Build a column of tetrahedra. Collage or draw natural images onto the surface as a statement of reverence for Nature.

8. Do a drawing of a fantasy cityscape in which the structures use triangles. Use your choice of black and white or color.

9. Research the structure of DNA. Using what you have learned, create a sculpture that echoes its principles.

10. Do a series of drawings moving from the representational to the abstract based on the helical structure of corn.

11. Do research on the positive and negative charges of protons and electrons Apply your research to create a sculptural form.

12. Develop an architectural form with interior and exterior views based on the molecular structure of methane.

Further Reading

Blackwell, William, A.I.A. *Geometry in Architecture*. New York: John Wiley and Sons, 1984.

Brownlee, Shannon. "Jellyfish Aren't Out to Get Us." <u>Discover Magazine</u>. August 1987: page 5+

Cotterill, Rodney. *The Cambridge Guide to the Material World*. Cambridge and New York: Cambridge University Press, 1985.

Coxeter, H. S. M. *Regular Polytopes*. New York: Dover Publications, Inc., 1973.

Cundy, H. Martin and A. P. Rollett. *Mathematical Models*. Oxford and New York: Oxford University Press, 1961.

Goldberg, Steven A. *Pholdit*. Hayward, California: Activity Resources Company, Inc., 1972.

Holden, Alan. *shapes, space and symmetry*. New York: Columbia University Press, 1971.

Migdalski, Edward C. and George S. Fichter. *Fishes of the World*. New York: Greenwich House, 1983.

Pearce, Peter and Susan Pearce. *Polyhedra Primer*. New York: Van Nostrand Reinhold Company, 1978.

Pugh, Anthony. *Polyhedra a visual approach*. Palo Alto, California: Dale Seymour Publications, 1990.

3 Cubes and Company

Above:
Canadian urban architecture that is suggestive of cubic modularity found in the city of Edmonton, Canada.

It is now time to focus our attention on building units with rectangular rather than triangular faces. These are the ones we are probably the most familiar with, and the kind that most likely come to mind if we stop to think about modular construction. It is easy to see why the rectangular solids are a natural choice for stacking, but why and when did they become the choice for the finished structures as well? When humans moved from caves to constructed shelters, they first used impermanent materials such as grasses, animal skins, twigs, tree limbs, and bones to keep out hostile forces. Materials like these are easy to form into structures with sloping sides such as conical or pyramidal forms or lean-tos erected against natural formations.

Did using more permanent materials foster a change in the shapes of human-made structures? Did stone cleave more easily along parallel and perpendicular planes, or was it easier to stack them to form upright walls? Did the ancient Egyptian concern, with vertical and horizontal in their paintings and sculpture, carry over to a similar concern in temple architecture? Did humans begin to require structures with greater volume-to-floor space ratios as they became collectors of goods? Did they want more head room or more appropriate surfaces for displaying their artworks? Did the requisite engineering techniques appear on the scene before shapes began to change or because of the change?

Whatever the reason or reasons, the rectangular solid had become an architectural standard, at least until the Twentieth Century. The rectangular solid is certainly no less evident in three-dimensional geometry. It is one of a larger family of six-sided polyhedra known as hexahedra, those composed of six faces, which will be the focus of this chapter.

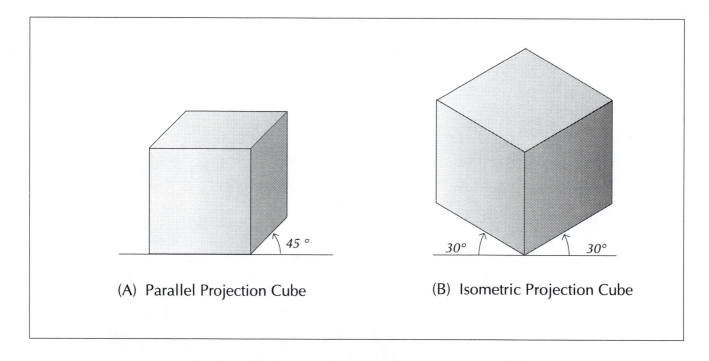

(A) Parallel Projection Cube   (B) Isometric Projection Cube

Above:
Fig 3.1 The cube drawn in perspective.

A. The cube drawn in parallel projection.

B. The cube drawn in isometric projection.

There are other ways to draw the cube besides these. You might like to investigate the subject.

The most conceptually uncomplicated of these forms is the cube with its six congruent square faces. Like the square, its two-dimensional counterpart, the cube acts as a basis for a great many other figures. Operations can be performed on this unit which will alter its appearance and change its inherent characteristics. Before we explore these operations, however, let us first examine how we will visually represent this three-dimensional figure.

Because a book is designed on a two-dimensional surface, and this particular book deals with three dimensions, we shall have to represent our forms by their two-dimensional projections. There are many ways in which our perceptions will accept a drawing as an actual three-dimensional object, but we will limit ourselves to parallel projection and isometric projection as seen in Fig. 3.1. These two systems are commonly used for architectural renderings and draftsperson's drawings.

These blueprints, as they are often called, require a great deal of accuracy. Sometimes they are made with the use of a computer and a CAD program, and sometimes they are rendered by hand with the use of tools, such as architectural triangles, compass, straightedge, protractor, T-square, and, finally, an eraser. As a result, these drawings are more dependent upon a logical systematic approach in their final steps than a spontaneous and immediate freehand drawing. This is not to say that the beginning stages of the process, the rough thumbnail sketches, do not spring forth from the same intuitive centers.

In both projection systems, three faces of the figure can be seen at the same time, and all verticals remain vertical. Under the isometric system, an image is constructed so that all actual lengths are preserved. In the parallel system, one face is parallel to the picture plane and the lines that appear tomove away from the viewer are constructed at an angle.

Any angle may be used, but we have chosen 45°. The effect of depth distortion is corrected in this case by halving the actual length of any receding lines. For example, when drawing a cube, the receding lines would be half as long as the sides of the undistorted square face. You might like to experiment with changing the angle to 30° or 15° in order to see how the shape of the figure is transformed. Try doing a drawing like the one depicted on this page. You would need to do some research into linear perspective as well. Begin by looking at the paintings, drawings, and prints of artists of the Italian and Northern Renaissance.

On page 124, we offer one way to draw a cube in parallel projection and on page 125 we show the way to draw a cube in isometric projection.

Usually, one system at a time appears in a single drawing so that the structure of the image is consistent and, therefore, easier to "read". The assignment for the drawing depicted on this page was to create a unified composition using different and contradictory space systems for representing three-dimensional events on a two-dimensional surface. Can you notic the different kinds of projection seen here? What kinds of feelings about depth does the artist create in you?

Above:
Student work. Eva McAvoy.
Colored pencil on paper.
The drawing is given unity by the use of neutral tones throughout.
Notice that size change and placement on the picture plane helps to give the illusion of deep space.

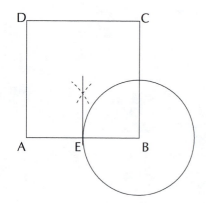

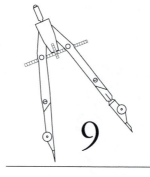

9

Construct a Parallel Projection of a Cube

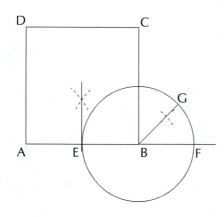

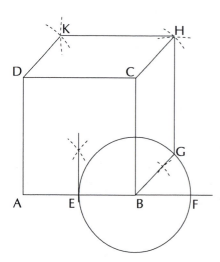

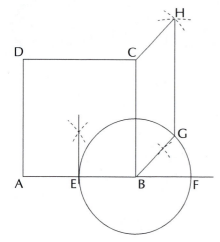

Given square ABCD

1. Find the perpendicular bisector of $\overline{AB}$. Label its midpoint E.

2. Construct a circle centered at B with radius $\overline{BE}$. (Only the upper half of the circle is actually needed.)

3. Extend $\overrightarrow{AB}$ so that it intersects the other side of circle B. Label the point of intersection F.

4. Bisect ∠CBF, and extend the bisector just to circle B. Label the point of intersection G.

5. Open the compass to measure BG, place the metal tip on C, and cut an arc in the exterior of ABCD. Open the compass to measure BC, place the metal tip on G, and cut an arc that intersects the one just drawn. Label the point of intersection H.

6. Draw $\overline{CH}$ and $\overline{GH}$.

7. Open the compass to measure CH, place the metal tip on D, and cut an arc in the interior of ∠DCH. Open the compass to measure DC, place the metal tip on H, and cut an arc that intersects the one just drawn. Label the point of intersection K.

8. Draw $\overline{DK}$ and $\overline{HK}$.

Now ABGHKD represents a cube in parallel projection.

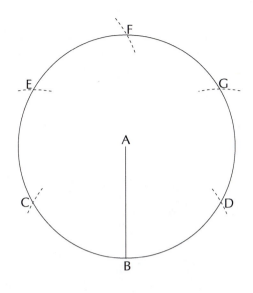

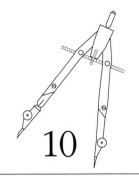

10

Construct an Isometric Projection of a Cube

Given a circle with radius $\overline{AB}$

1. Open the compass to measure AB. Without changing the setting, place the metal tip on B and cut an arc in circle A on either side of B. Label the points of intersection C and D.

2. Without changing the compass setting, place the metal tip on C and cut another arc in circle A. Label the point of intersection E.

3. Once again, without changing the compass setting, place the metal tip on E and cut another arc in circle A. Label the point of intersection F.

4. Finally, without changing the compass setting, place the metal tip on F and cut another arc in circle A. Label the point of intersection F.

5. Draw $\overline{BC}$, $\overline{CE}$, $\overline{EF}$, $\overline{FG}$ and $\overline{GD}$.

7. Draw $\overline{AE}$ and $\overline{AG}$.

Now BCEFGD represents a cube in isometric projection.

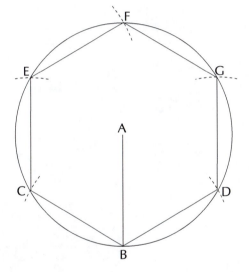

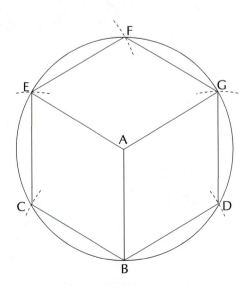

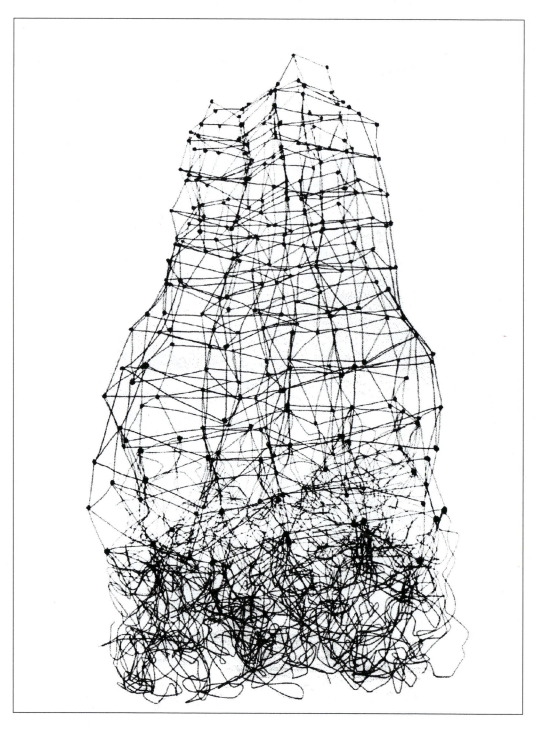

Above:
Wendy Waxman. Get Set.
Wire sculpture 42" x 27" x
28". 1991.

Now let us look at some ways to actually construct a cube in 3-space. It would seem that one of the simplest would be to utilize the concept of vertices and edges, and construct what we might call a skeletal cube. Let us begin with the humble materials of drinking straws and paper clips, and see what happens. Cut the straws into twelve congruent lengths for the edges. Join twenty-four paper clips together in groups of three for the vertices. For each group of three, insert one paper clip into each of the three edges (straws) that come together at a vertex.

After you have assembled this figure and attempted to set it on a flat surface, you will notice that it is a truly unstable piece of work! It seems to

require some type of internal support or rigidity at the vertices. This figure might be considered the "bones" of the polyhedron. However, unlike some natural forms, it lacks the musculature to take advantage of its jointed structure, and it collapses unless the vertices are rigid.

The reason the straw cube will not support itself is due, in part, to the materials, but in greater part to the basic instability of the square that forms the face. Many polyhedra can be constructed using the straw and paper clip technique, but most of them would collapse because of the potential instability of the polygonal faces. This weakness can be counteracted, however, if the polygonal faces are broken down into constituent triangles and struts are used to brace their sides.

While the straw cube can be considered a conceptual skeleton, it must be recognized that the difference between conceptualization and physical reality is often insurmountable.

We see Nature in its physical manifestation. Humans impose concepts in order to begin to understand these structures found in the natural world. The trick is to build models in which concept and physicality mesh.

In the case of the cube, we need only to be careful to take the instability of the square into consideration as we try to make the concept physical, and use appropriate materials and techniques. The acetate model described in the last chapter works very well. Another technique for building skeletal polyhedra is to insert toothpicks into gumdrops, as the vertices. A word of warning — because delicious, the vertices tend to get eaten quickly. In dry weather these will get hard but when the humidity increases, the gumdrops soften and the structure collapses. This quick construction technique is useful, however, to aid in the exploration of polyhedral forms or to create studies for more elaborate projects, such as models of chemical bonds or geodesic architectural or sculptural structures.

Above:
Skeletal models can be constructed from toothpicks and gumdrops, straws and paper clips, or acetate. When straws and paper clips are used, some models will be stable and others will not.
The new polymer clays now available might make the job easier. These come in a variety of colors and when baked quickly in toaster or convection ovens, they become hard. The toothpicks can be left in while they are baking.

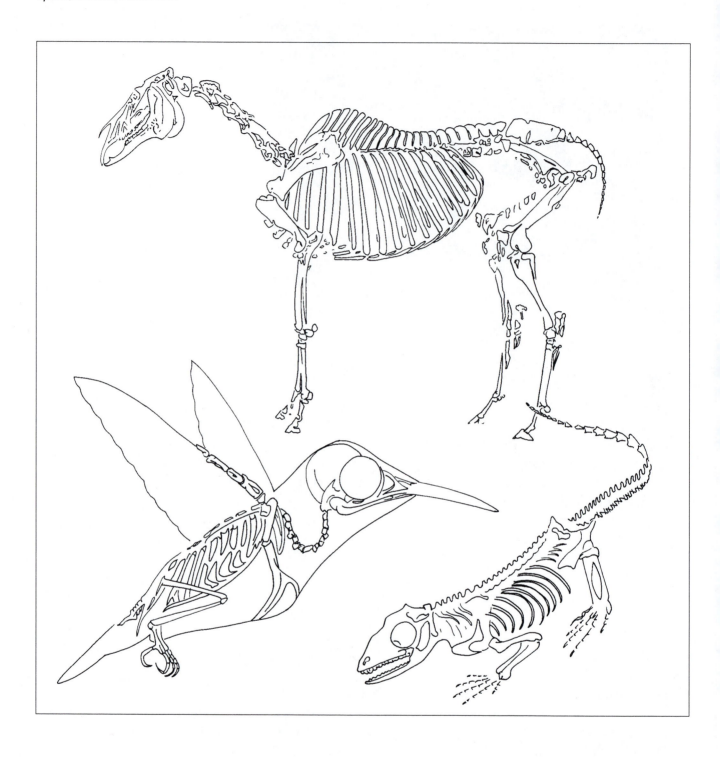

This page:
The skeleton of an animal provides the same framework for structure as does the system of vertices and edges in a polyhedron.

Bones have an inherent sculptural quality which, in its pure and elemental form, is akin to the best in modern abstract sculpture. They are fundamental in the truest sense of the word, combining maximum strength with minimum weight and expenditure of material.

Andreas Feininger
The Anatomy of Nature

Left:
When the tetrahedron sits inside the cube, it lends the same type of support that bones do to the body. Tooth-pick and gumdrop model.

Below:
Fig. 3.2 An example of stacking solid tetrahedra inside a skeletal cube.

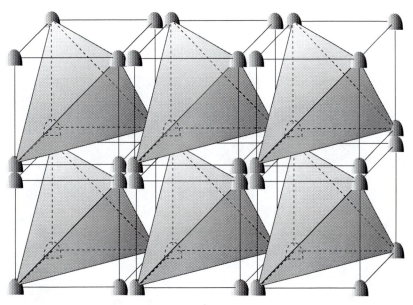

Interestingly enough, when a skeletal tetrahedron sits inside a cube, it acts as the bone-like structure that gives the cube stability. The $\sqrt{2}$ diagonals of the cube become the unit 1 side lengths of the tetrahedron. When these two polyhedra are combined in this way, the edges of the tetrahedron are said to triangulate the faces of the cube. We will discuss the concept of triangulation in greater detail in Chapter 4.

Would an internal tetrahedron give stability to the cube so that they can work together in a sculptural and architectural system? Try building a model to see. Fig. 3.2 illustrates the stacking of modular units that consist of a solid tetrahedra inside a skeletal cube. The overall appearance of this stacking somewhat resembles the space frame, or lattice, of a crystal which is built of layer upon layer upon layer of atoms.

These facing pages:
These are just a few of Nature's creatures. Notice how she integrates skeletal armatures, bilateral symmetry, and surface pattern into distinctive and magnificent variations. Nature provides habitats for all manner of creatures in all sizes and shapes. Each species has a basic body plan and that plan defines much of what happens within it. The mode of existence, whether it be air, land or sea, determines the design.

Size is the most important organizing principle for any animal. It relates to the effect of forces such as gravity, temperature, water pressure, light, humidity, the availability of food, the number and proximity of predators, mates, etc. Larger size brings with it the possibility of a greater ability for internal specialization. With greater size, there is a need for a system for circulating body fluid. the animal also requires a supporting skeleton that will carry its weight and bulk.

A large object has more volume in relation to its surface than a small object. Thus, the increase in volume necessitates an increase in surface area by introducing complications such as hair, branching elements, lengthening and hollowing out of forms.

Every zebra can be identified by the pattern of its stripes. While particular patterns identify different species, the stripes on each zebra are unique to each individual. What about those of tigers or cows? Would the same hold true for them?

If the vertices and edges of a polyhedron can be thought of as the bones of the structure, then the interiors of the polygonal faces may be likened to the skin. As soon as a structure has a surface, the possibilities for design become endless. Materials alone offer a myriad of choices. Think of all the different types of surface patterns exhibited by the huge

You might like to research the connections between patterns of one species and those of another.

Or you might like to consider the question of the relationship between mathematics and patterns found on animals, insects, butterflies, flowers. What do these all have in common?

Or an even larger question to investigate would be "what is the relationship between atomic patterns, chemical patterns, biological patterns, and artistic patterns? This question might keep you awake for a few nights. What accounts for the similarities among patterns and what accounts for the differences?

Scientists who study the origins of the Universe say that "we are made of stardust". What does that statement suggest to you? How would you go about researching the facts that would support this statement?

array of living creatures on this planet. If we also think of ways to deliberately embellish this surface: make-up, tattoos, scarification, pleating, slitting, embossing, painting, etc., we begin to get an inkling of the excitement in store when the mathematical perfection of polyhedral forms is coupled with the endless variety of artistic expression.

Consider a face of the cube. This is a versatile form for an artist whether or not it is part of a polyhedron. Even if multiples of just a single square region,

with notches at vertices and midpoints (Fig. 3.3) are used, sculptural forms can be obtained by arranging the units in many different ways. No adhesives are necessary because the notches allow the units to be integrated. Bristol board offers a strong but relatively lightweight structure. Patterns can also be added to the unit face prior to assembly.

The importance and versatility of the square have not changed. Numbers, as well as having quantitative properties, have symbolic associations for certain cultures. The numbers from one to ten had special meanings for the early civilizations of Sumaria, Babylonia and Egypt. For the Egyptians, the number four was sacred. It signified the four winds, the four cardinal directions of north, south, east, and west, and the four corners of the world. For the Egyptians, the sky rested on four pillars. The square, therefore, was the geometric expression of this number and it was explored extensively in the construction of the great pyramids which were built upon square bases. Six square faces joined, as in Fig. 3.4 on page 133, form a template which, when folded up, will produce a cube whose vital statistics are given in the chart on this page. Notice that the centers of rotation of the faces, the midpoints of edges, and the vertices have been marked.

If you copy this template onto clear acetate you can employ the process described in the search for symmetry in Chapter 2. You will be able to locate all of the symmetries of this figure if you apply the directions to the cube instead of the tetrahedron. After doing so, you can compare your findings with the chart on pages 134 and 135.

> *Other polygons can be notched and assembled in a similar manner.*

Right:
Fig. 3.3 Slit square modular unit.

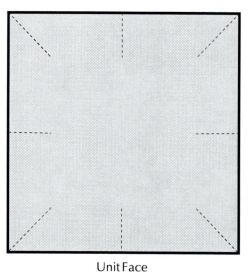

Unit Face

Vital Statistics of the Cube

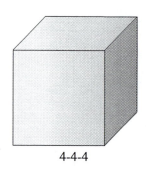

4-4-4

The cube is a regular polyhedron with:

6 square faces
8 congruent vertices with a vertex net of 4-4-4
12 congruent interfacial angles of 90°
12 congruent edges

The variety of our world which lies so richly at hand is a modular variety; matter is modular. Its molecules fulfill the most precise of stereotypes free from interesting variations of the craftsman's hand or the furnace heat. Their number alone, and the motions and interactions of those myriads weaves the intricacies of reality.

Philip Morrison
Physicist

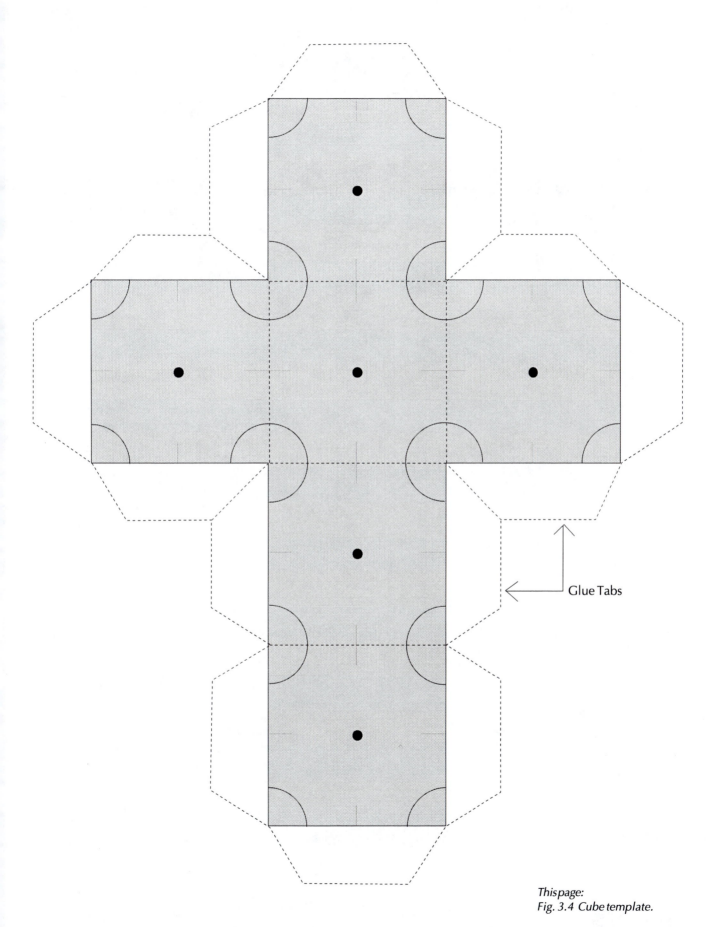

Glue Tabs

This page:
Fig. 3.4 Cube template.

Symmetries of the Cube

Operation: Rotation
Element: Axis of Rotation

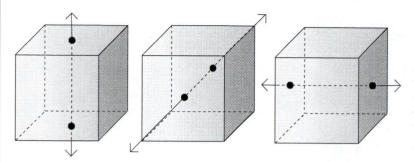

Rotation Axes Through Faces

An axis of four-turn rotation intersects the center of a pair of opposite faces. One-fourth of a complete 360° turn brings the cube into coincidence with itself. There are three pairs of opposite faces and, therefore, three 4-turn axes.

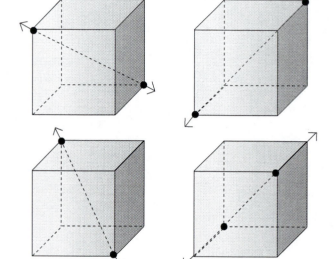

Rotation Axes Through Vertices

An axis of 3-turn rotation intersects a pair of opposite vertices. One-third of a complete 360° turn brings the cube into exact correspondence with its original position. There are four pairs of opposite vertices and, therefore, four 3-turn axes.

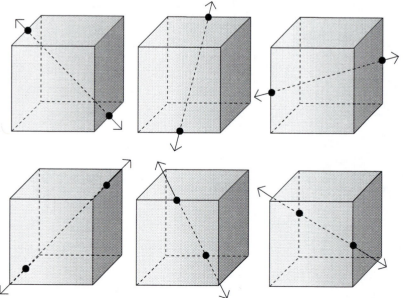

Roation Axes Through Midpoints of Edges

An axis of 2-turn rotation intersects the midpoints of a pair of diagonally opposite edges. One-half of a complete 360° turn brings the cube into coincidence with itself. There are six pairs of opposite edges and, therefore, six 2-turn axes.

Operation: Reflection
Element: Mirror Plane (Plane of Reflection)

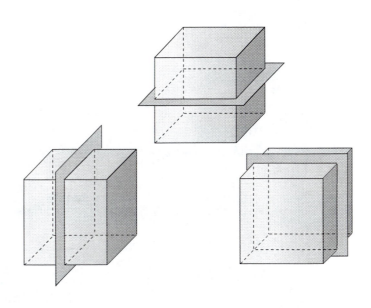

Mirror Planes Through Midpoints of Edges

A mirror plane bisects a pair of opposite faces and passes through the midpoints of four edges. There are three pairs of opposite faces and, therefore, three mirror planes through faces and midpoints of edges.

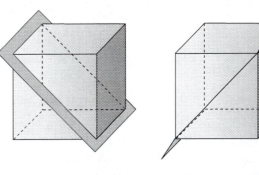

Mirror Planes Through Two Diagonally Opposite Edges

A mirror plane contains an opposite pair of edges. There are six pairs of opposite edges and, therefore, six mirror planes through diagonally opposite edges.

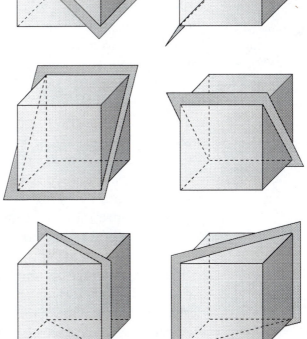

The Peek-a-Boo Cube

Up to this point, we have dealt with the surfaces of the cube, but there are things that can be done in the interior as well. Some of the faces can be cut open to allow light to pass through from face to face, making an internal design. Here, we use the cube template as the jumping off place for variations of interior structure. As you can see, in Fig. 3.5 on page 137, some panels have to be added to the original template.

For demonstration, we have chosen to use a subdivision of the square as our design element. You, however, may choose to use the template as a guide only, developing your own design on it. If you do so, the design elements must be on faces 1, 2, 3 and 6. This will give you two faces on the interior of the cube and two faces on the exterior. You might also want to enlarge the template to make it easier to manipulate.

If you are going to use our design element, copy the template in Fig. 3.5 directly onto bristol paper so that it will have enough rigidity to hold up to the construction. If you are creating your own design, you may want to copy the template onto less expensive copier paper first. In this way, you can preserve the outline, and the design can be covered before copying the template onto bristol paper. Once the template is on heavier paper, with or without design elements, you can move on to pages 138 and 139 for instructions as to how to complete the peek-a-boo cube. There are also some hints and suggestions if you are developing your own design.

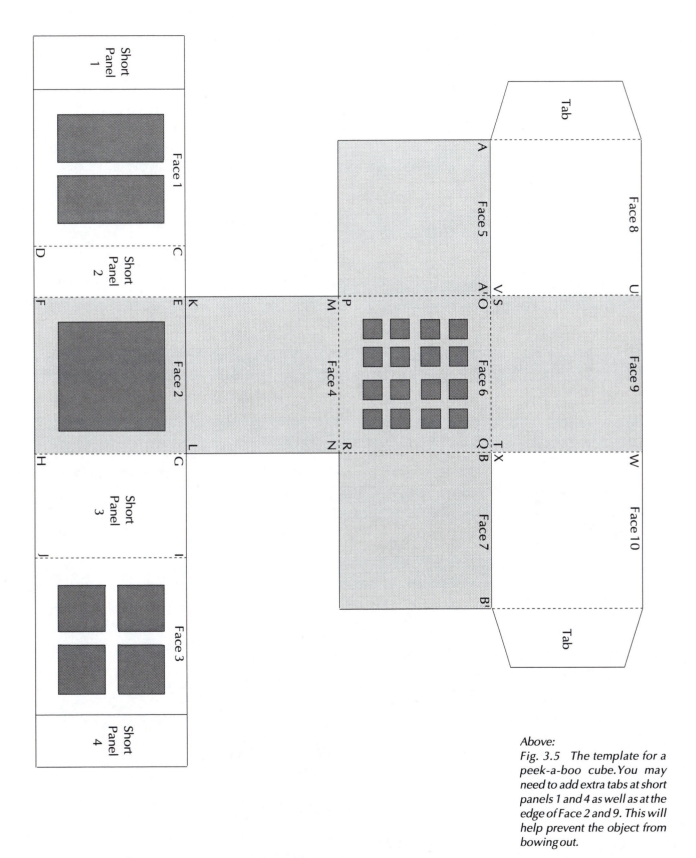

Above:
Fig. 3.5   The template for a peek-a-boo cube. You may need to add extra tabs at short panels 1 and 4 as well as at the edge of Face 2 and 9. This will help prevent the object from bowing out.

These facing pages:
Fig. 3.6 Illustration of template preparation and assembly of peek-a-boo cube.

Template Preparation
1, 2, 3, 4 and 5

Cube Assembly
1

Cube Assembly
2

Template Preparation

1. If you are using your own design, now is the time to mark it on the template. While the structure is deceptively simple, the design variables are not . Design is essentially a problem solving activity. The problem presented here, is to integrate four faces that will let light penetrate through the cube, provide interesting area break-up, and have an overall sense of unity. Too much variation on each face will only cause overall confusion. Therefore, there must be a subtle balance between the size of the elements, their orientation , the ratio of open to closed areas, and color variation, if it is used.

2. Working from the center out, remove the dark gray design elements on faces 1, 2, 3 and 6. Be certain not to bend any faces or break any connections.

3. Score and mountain fold along the two solid lines at the short panels 1 and 4.

4. Score and valley fold the remaining dashed lines.

5. Set the template on a flat surface for support while folding. The side of the template with the markings on it becomes the inside of the cube.

Cube Assembly

1. Fold short panel 2 up at EF, and fold face 1 down at CD, so that it is parallel to face 2. Then, run a bead of tacky glue next to the crease at IJ.

2. Fold short panel 3 up at GH, and fold face 3 down at IJ, so that it is now parallel to faces 1 and 2. Fit the edge of short panel 1 up to the

crease at IJ and into the bead of glue. Let it set before continuing on.

3. Fold this unit (faces 1, 2 and 3) up at KL so that it is perpendicular to face 4. Then, run a bead of glue just inside the crease at OP.

4. Fold the unit up at MN so that face 4 is perpendicular to face 6, and faces 1, 2, 3 and 6 are all parallel to each other. The edge of short panel 2 should rest in the bead of glue at the crease at OP. Let it set before continuing on.

5. Put a dot of glue at the center of the top edge of face 5. Fold face 5 up at OP so that it rests against the unit, and is perpendicular to face 6. Let the glue set.

6. Put a dot of glue at the center of the top edge of face 7. Fold face 7 up at QR so that it rests against the other side of the unit, and is also perpendicular to face 6. Let the glue set.

7. Fold the unit up at ST so that face 6 perpendicular to face 9.

8. Fold face 8 up at UV, and slide the tab under face 4.

9. To finish the cube, fold face 10 up at WX, and slide the tab under face 4 once again.

10. When the assembly of the peek-a-boo cube has been completed, the outside surfaces can be further manipulated in any number of ways. Color can be added or perhaps a design in black and white.

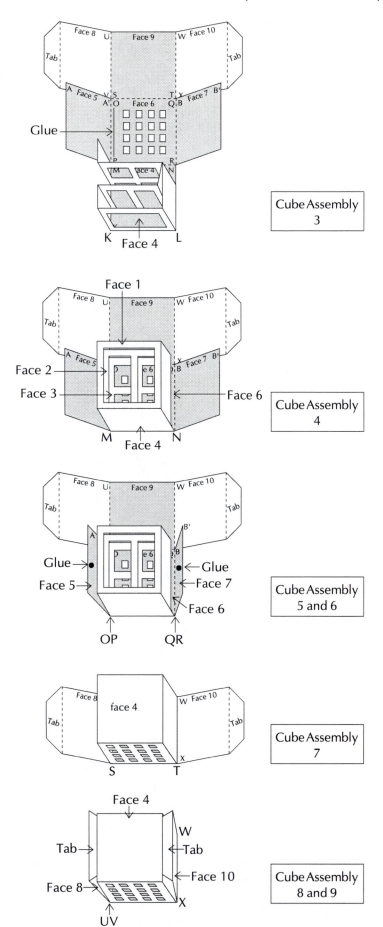

Cube Assembly 3

Cube Assembly 4

Cube Assembly 5 and 6

Cube Assembly 7

Cube Assembly 8 and 9

Polyhedra Transformations

Skew

To replace all square faces with congruent rhombic ones. This operation will change the planar orientation of adjacent faces while retaining the property that opposite pairs of faces are parallel.

Slice

To cut a cube with parallel planes. This operation dissects the cube.

Truncate

To slice across the vertices creating a polygonal face.

Stretch

To elongate all the faces of a cube that lie between a pair of parallel faces.

Transformations of the Cube

Operations can be performed on any part of the cube (or any other polyhedron) to transform its appearance. These manipulations can be done to its faces, its vertices, and its edges. Parts can be taken away, added, shifted, or deformed in order to construct new units that might preserve some of the essential qualities of the original polyhedron, and change others. In Chapter 5, we will look at some standard mathematical transformations of polyhedra. For art purposes, however, there are some other operations that we will introduce here. These include skewing, slicing, and stretching, and truncating. The definitions for these operations are given in the chart on this page.

Obviously, when building models or using cube transformations for artworks, the choice of materials should be directly linked to the type of transformation. For example, chamfering can be handled nicely with paper whereas slicing would better lend itself to a solid material such as clay or wood. Skewing is possible if a model of a cube is skeletal with flexible

vertices. Stretching can be accomplished more easily by determining what the figure will look like before attempting to construct it.

Keep in mind that a change in size will affect the stability of the structure. The larger an object, the more gravitational forces are felt and the weaker it will be. If a large cube and a small cube are hollow and made of the same material, the large cube will be flimsier than the small one. If the cubes are solid, than an increase in size increases the tendency toward breaking apart. You may need to experiment with different sizes to determine which is the most satisfactory for the material you choose.

On the next several pages we will look at some specific examples of these transformations. Instructions are given in certain cases to help you construct paper models to serve as jumping-off points for your own creative explorations. Please remember that sizes may be changed for your convenience as long as all lengths are changed proportionally.

Facial Transformations of the Cube

One of the most direct ways to alter the cube is to transform the plane surfaces of the faces. In Chapter 2 we used a variation on the "Sierpinski Triangle" to embellish the face of a triangle. Here, we use a variation of the "Sierpinski Sponge" to transform the faces of a cube. Fractal subdivisions provide visual excitement and connections to phenomena in the natural world.

Fractal patterns are the result of an algorithm, or mathematical rule being used in a recursive manner, repeated as many times as necessary to obtain the desired complexity. The fractal illustrated on this page in Fig. 3.7 begins with a square initiator. The initiator is the figure upon which the transformations will take place. In the second generation we see the generator. The generator sets the rule that describes what will be done to the initiator. In this case, it is to remove the middle square of area 1/9 of the original. This pattern differs from a true fractal in that it incorporates gray tonal changes as the process develops. Subsequent generations replace each of the eight remaining implied squares with a scaled down copy of the generator.

Square Initiator

Generator
Second Generation

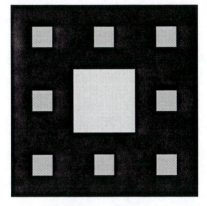

Third Generation

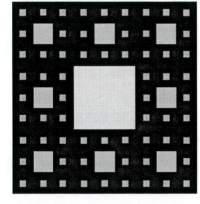

Fourth Generation

This page:
Fig. 3.7 Variation on the "Sierpinski Sponge".

Top left:
First Generation - the square initiator

Top right:
Second generation - the generator

Center left:
Third generation

Center right:
Fourth generation

Bottom:
A natural fractal found in ocean coral.

Slicing the Cube

Theoretically, there are an infinite number of ways in which the cube can be sliced. For practical purposes, we illustrate only a fraction of them in Fig. 3.8. The cube can be sliced as one would slice a loaf of bread, but these slices will not be very stable. The cube can also be sliced through the midpoints of opposite edges and elongated rectangular subunits can be made. If the cube is sliced along the diagonals of opposite faces, the resulting pieces are triangular wedges.

All of these subunits can then be assembled in many other configurations. They can also be sliced again and again to obtain many more shapes. Either way, each face also provides a surface for further transformation. Will these new pieces make interesting modular units for package design, sculpture, and architecture?

Changing the size of sliced units by a constant ratio and working with the idea of spiralling, has been the

Above:
Student work. Ann MacLean. A Golden wedge made from paper embellished with acrylic paint. The ratio of length to width is the golden ratio, 1 to 1.618 approx.

Right:
Fig 3.8 Three ways in which the cube can be sliced.

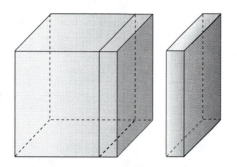
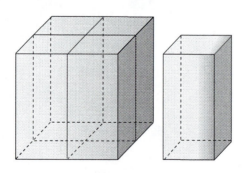
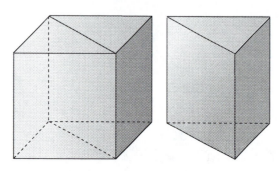

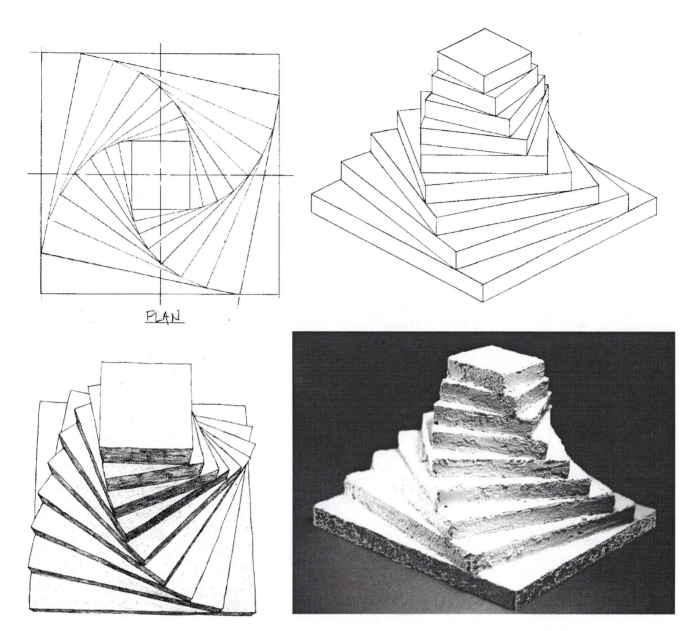

PLAN

springboard for a sculptural form as exhibited by the artwork of Robert Dumas. In the artwork depicted above, he has combined his drafting skills, his interest in geometry, his exploration of humble materials for modelling, and his desire to solve large scale outdoor sculptural problems. The progression from the two-dimensional inspiration, to the rendering of the three-dimensional form, to the actual model made of styrofoam, is shown at the top of this page. Perhaps this form could be con-

structed in granite or in terraces of grass and plantings. Given the operation of slicing, what kinds of models could you build?

The cube can also be sliced in a particular way to make a chamfered cube. Unlike the slicing operation that we have just described, however, the chamfered cube requires further manipulation. The construction on pages 144 and 145 gives one way that chamfering can be accomplished. How would the cube look if another side were chamfered also?

Above:
Student work. Robert Dumas. Sculptural progression.

Top left:
The two dimensional concept that sparked the sculptural idea.

Top right:
A line drawing of the stacking of the "slices".

Bottom left:
A shaded birdseye view drawing of the stacking.

Bottom right:
Styrofoam model coated with acrylic modelling paste.

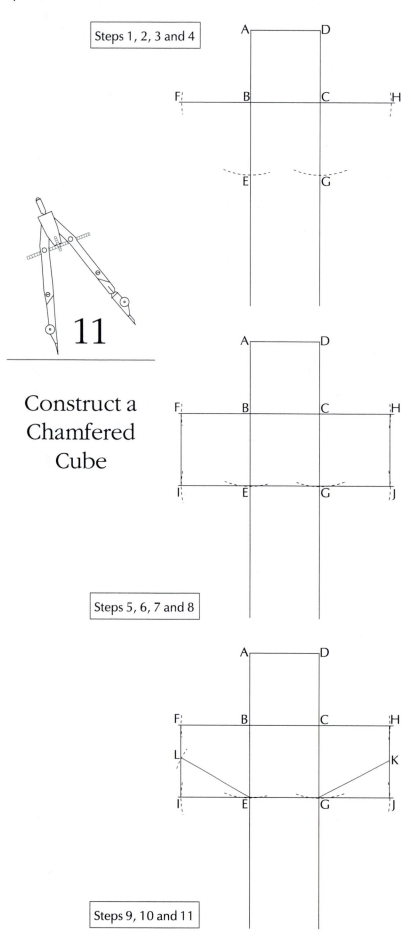

Steps 1, 2, 3 and 4

Steps 5, 6, 7 and 8

Steps 9, 10 and 11

11

Construct a Chamfered Cube

Given square ABCD

Initial Construction
1. Extend $\overrightarrow{AB}$ and $\overrightarrow{DC}$.

2. Extend $\overline{BC}$ in both directions.

3. Open the compass to measure AB. With the metal tip on B, cut an arc that intersects $\overrightarrow{AB}$ and another that intersects $\overrightarrow{CB}$ Label points of intersection E and F, respectively.

4. Without changing the compass setting, place the metal tip on C and cut an arc that intersects $\overrightarrow{DC}$ and another that intersects $\overrightarrow{BC}$ Label points of intersection G and H, respectively.

5. Draw a line through E and G, and extend it in both directions.
6. Using the same compass setting as in Steps 3 and 4, place the metal tip on E and cut an arc on $\overrightarrow{GE}$. Label the point of intersection I.

7. Once again, without changing the compass setting, place the metal tip on E and cut an arc on $\overrightarrow{EG}$. Label the point of intersection J.

8. Draw $\overline{FI}$ and $\overline{HJ}$.

9. Determine the triangular portion to be removed. To do this, draw a segment from G that intersects $\overline{HJ}$ at a point of your choosing. Label the point of intersection on $\overline{HJ}$, K.

10. Open the compass to measure GK, place the metal tip on E, and cut an arc that intersects $\overline{FI}$. Label the point of intersection L.

11. Draw $\overline{EL}$.

12. Using the same compass setting as in Step 10, place the metal tip on E and cut an arc on $\overrightarrow{BE}$. Label the point of intersection M.

13. Once again, without changing the compass setting, place the metal tip on G and cut an arc on $\overrightarrow{CG}$. Label the point of intersection N.

14. Draw $\overline{MN}$.

15. Open the compass to measure HK. With the metal tip on M, cut an arc that intersects $\overrightarrow{EM}$. Label the point of intersection O.

16. Without changing the compass setting, place the metal tip on N and cut an arc on $\overrightarrow{GN}$. Label the point of intersection P.

17. Draw $\overline{OP}$.

18. Erase all extraneous marks, including $\overline{IL}$, $\overline{IE}$, $\overline{GJ}$ and $\overline{JK}$.

19. Draw glue tabs as shown in the diagram.

Assembly
1. Cut out template along glue tab lines.

2. Score and mountain fold along all lines.

3. Fold up and glue as you would for a model of a cube.

Now you have constructed a chamfered cube.

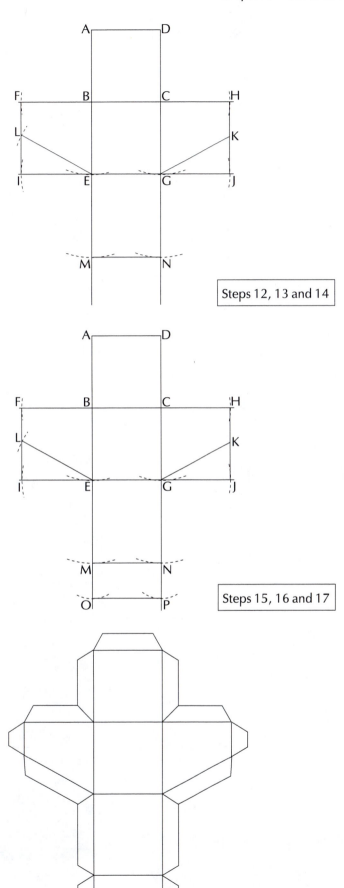

Steps 12, 13 and 14

Steps 15, 16 and 17

Steps 18 and 19

Skewing and Stretching the Cube

Two other ways to transform the cube are to skew it and stretch it, and sometimes both of these are done together. Before we describe these operations on three-dimensional objects, however, we must first consider the transformation of a single planar face. The square is just one of three regular, primal, or fundamental polygons. With the use of circumcircles and perpendicular bisectors, the three-sided equilateral triangle, the four-sided square, and the five-sided pentagon can be manipulated to give us three more regular polygons. The chart on this page illustrates the process by which the primal three are transformed into the six-sided hexagon, the eight-sided octagon, and the ten-sided decagon, respectively. Collectively, they become the six ancestor polygons that give rise to many of the polyhedra that we will consider in this book.

In this chapter, we will focus upon the lineage of the square and its two and three-dimensional progeny. The square is the ancestor of a a clan of quadrilaterals, or four-sided, planar figures. By tipping, stretching and compressing the square, its children and grandchildren come to life, as you can see in the chart on page 147.

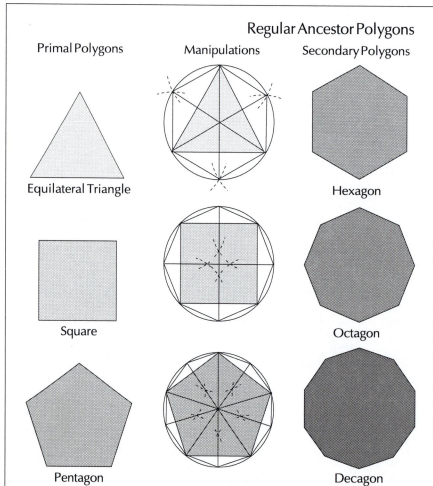

Regular Ancestor Polygons

Primal Polygons

Manipulations

Secondary Polygons

Equilateral Triangle

Hexagon

Square

Octagon

Pentagon

Decagon

1. Circumscribe a circumcircle around the polygon that is to be transformed.

2. Find the perpendicular bisectors of all sides. of the polygon. When drawing these in, extend them to intersect the circumcircle.

3. Connect all points where the bisectors intersect the circle. to the circumcircle with consecutive line segments.

The result is a new polygon with twice as many sides as the original one. If you substitute the new polygon for the original one and repeat the same process, other regular polygons can be made. The number of sides of the successive figures will always be twice as many as the generating one. Notice that the more sides the polygon has, the closer it comes to being a circle.

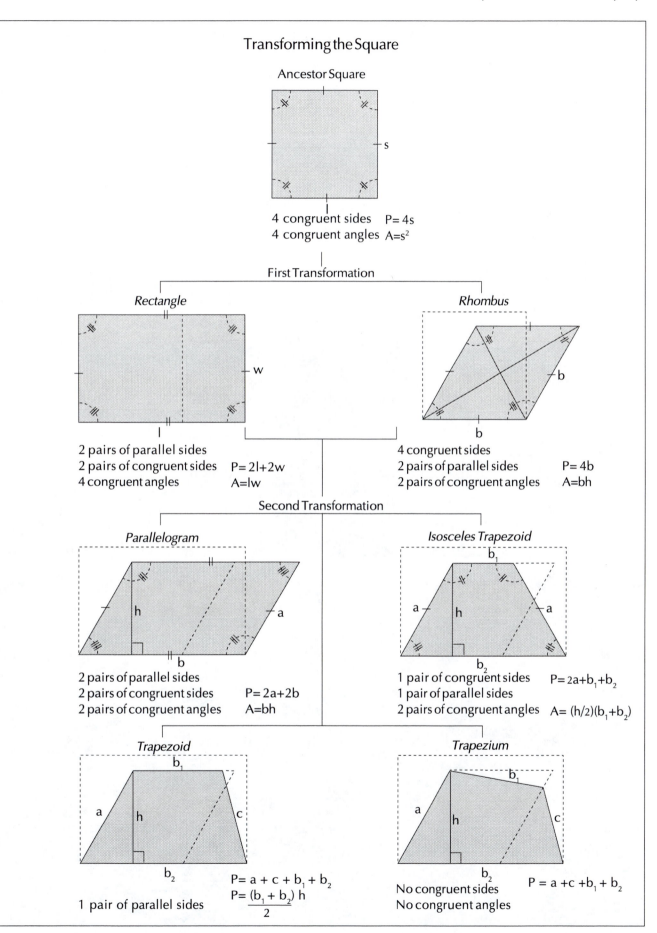

Transforming the Square

Ancestor Square

s

4 congruent sides   P= 4s
4 congruent angles   A=s²

First Transformation

Rectangle   *Rhombus*

w   b

l   b

2 pairs of parallel sides   4 congruent sides
2 pairs of congruent sides   P= 2l+2w   2 pairs of parallel sides   P= 4b
4 congruent angles   A=lw   2 pairs of congruent angles   A=bh

Second Transformation

Parallelogram   *Isosceles Trapezoid*

h   b₁
a   a   h   a
b   b₂

2 pairs of parallel sides   1 pair of congruent sides   P= 2a+b₁+b₂
2 pairs of congruent sides   P= 2a+2b   1 pair of parallel sides
2 pairs of congruent angles A=bh   2 pairs of congruent angles   A= (h/2)(b₁+b₂)

Trapezoid   *Trapezium*

b₁   b₁
a   h   c   a   h   c
b₂   b₂

                        P= a + c + b₁ + b₂   P = a +c +b₁ + b₂
                        P= (b₁ + b₂) h   No congruent sides
1 pair of parallel sides   2   No congruent angles

Tiling With Quadrilaterals

The basic design groupings that we illustrated for the triangle in Chapter 2 can be extended to include the quadrilaterals that we mention here. These types of polygonal organization are called tilings, and we can only give a taste of the material. For more information, we encourage you to research in the Grunbaum and Shephard book mentioned in the Further Reading section. We take the time to introduce this concept here, however, because tilings in two dimensions logically translate to tilings in three dimensions. The latter relates to the packing and stacking of polyhedra.

There are several important properties of 2-dimensional tilings to consider. First, these tilings are arrangements of convex polygons, (the tiles) that come together with no gaps between them. Second, they completely cover the plane in two independent directions. Third, the angles around any vertex of the tiling must sum to 360° in order fort the tiles to lie flat. Finally, any triangle or quadrilateral will tile the plane. Therefore, you can use equilateral, isosceles, or scalene triangle for tile units as well as non-regular quadrilaterals. These can be further manipulated by performing symmetry operations on the sides of the polygons to obtain a more organic unit or to develop a representational image.

Below:
Many architects use tilings to enhance the surfaces of buildings. You might want to do some research into Islamic architecture and tiling.

Right:
A detail of the tiling used as the surface of the conservatory at the Denver Botanical Gardens in Colorado.

Bottom:
View looking at the entire structure of the Conservatory at the Botanical Gardens in Denver, Colorado. Notice that the tilings are on a curved surface rather than a plane. Within each quadrilateral, there are four triangles which project out from the surface.

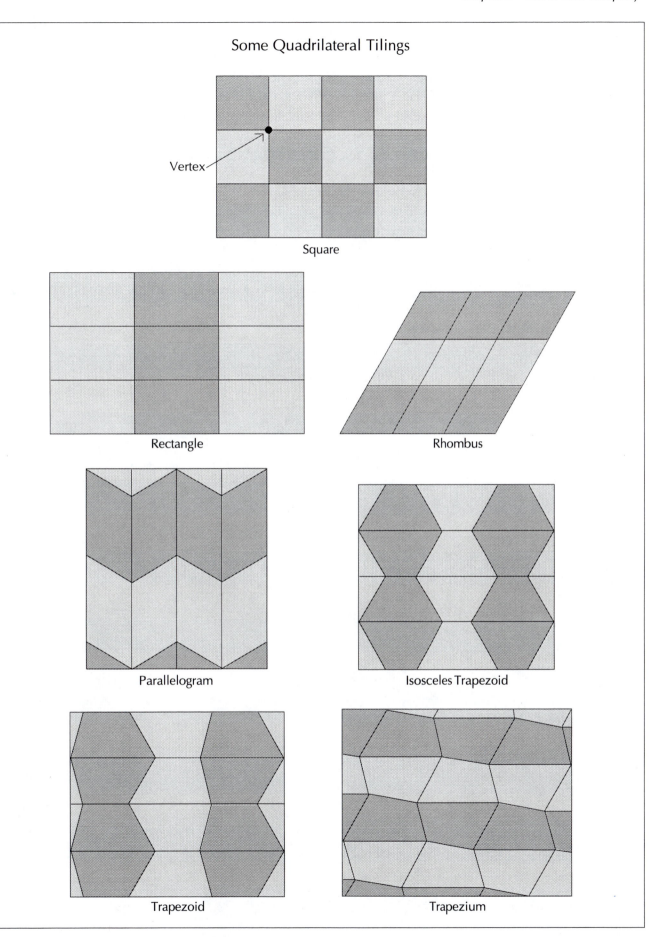

Some Quadrilateral Tilings

Vertex

Square

Rectangle

Rhombus

Parallelogram

Isosceles Trapezoid

Trapezoid

Trapezium

Two Dimensions Into Three

In the chart on page 145, we showed some of the members of the quadrilateral clan. These polygons can give rise to the polyhedra that you see in the chart on this page. In all of these solids, three polygons come together at each vertex, and six polygons are used to enclose the volume of space. In the examples of the parallelepipeds and the rhombohedron, six polygons are used. In the examples of the trapezohedra, there is a combination of trapezoids, trapezia and rectangles.

In the chart on page 148, we illustrated how the quadrilaterals can be used as tiles to make surface designs without gaps. Because the polyhedra that are constructed with these polygons have congruent faces, and since the generating polygons can be used to tile the plane, some of their corresponding polyhedra can also fill space with no gaps between them. (Can you discover which ones?) In so doing, we can liken filling space with polyhedra to *space-tiling*, and we obtain a three-dimensional structure.

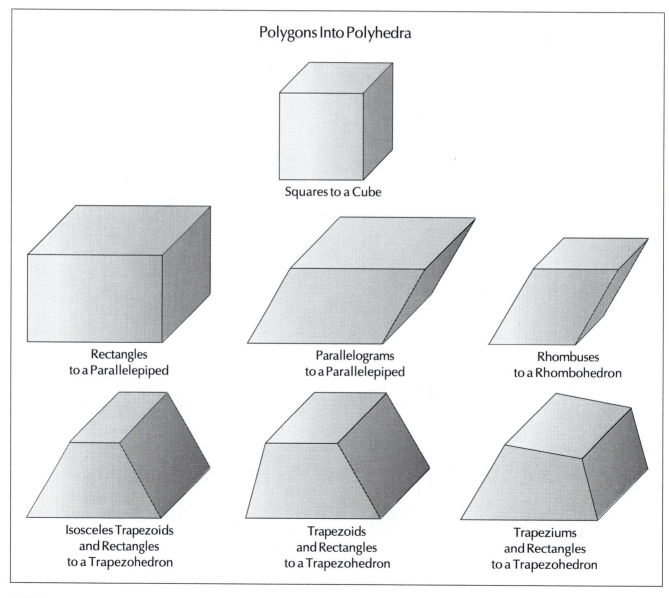

Polygons Into Polyhedra

Squares to a Cube

Rectangles
to a Parallelepiped

Parallelograms
to a Parallelepiped

Rhombuses
to a Rhombohedron

Isosceles Trapezoids
and Rectangles
to a Trapezohedron

Trapezoids
and Rectangles
to a Trapezohedron

Trapeziums
and Rectangles
to a Trapezohedron

If four squares are needed to fill the plane around a single vertex, how many cubes would be needed to fill three-dimensional space around the same vertex? What do cubes, rhombohedra and parallepipeds have in common? How does the symmetry of the cube relate to these other solids? Try making acetate models of these forms in order to see the symmetries.

The volume of an object is measured in cubic units (Fig. 3.9). How would you go about calculating the volume of a polyhedron that has square, rectangular, or rhombic faces? Would the formula be the same? Finding the volume of a polyhedron that has faces that are trapezoids or trapezia is another matter. The chart on this page illustrates one way to accomplish this task. By calculating the displacement of the liquid inside one container when another object is put into it, we can discover the volume of the submerged solid. For example, we can measure the volume of a trapezohedron if we place it inside a rectangular container that is partially filled with water.

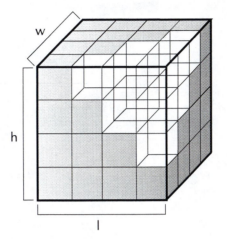

Left:
Fig. 3.9 The volume of an object is measured in cubic units. Notice that the internal stacking and packing of cubic units is a space tiling. Would the same thing be true of rhombohedral units?

Calculating Displacement

The volume of an irregularly shaped object can be determined by calculating the displacement of water in a container when the irregularly shaped object is submerged in it.

1. Add water to a clear rectangular container until it is approximately half full.

2. Calculate the volume of water by using the formula, V=lwh, where l and w are the length and width of the container and h is the height of the water.

3. Place the solid, whose volume is to be determined, into the container making certain that it is completely submerged. Then you had better redo step 2.

4. Recalculate the volume of water in the rectangular container using the same formula as in Step 2. This time, however, h is the measurement of the new water level.

5. Subtract the first calculation from the second calculation. The difference between the two is the volume, in cubic units, of the irregularly shaped solid.

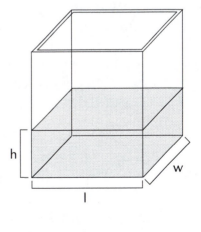

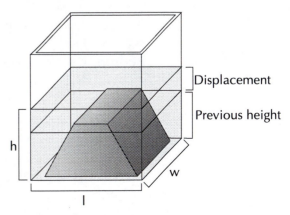

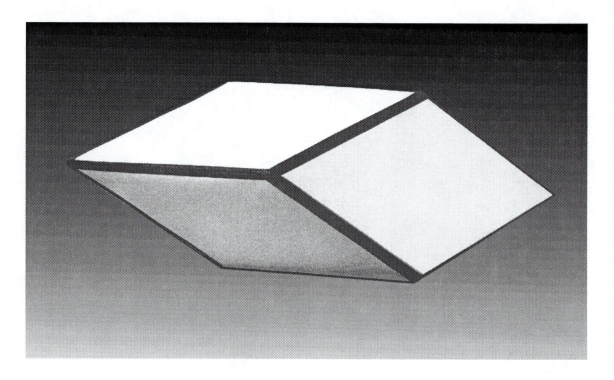

The Skewed Cube

When the square is skewed it is transformed into a rhombus, whose sides are all congruent, but whose two pairs of congruent angles never include a right angle . When the cube is skewed it is transformed into a rhombohedron, whose faces are all congruent, but whose four pairs of congruent angles are never 90°. Because the rhombohedron bears so many similarities to its parent cube, we have nicknamed it the "skewed cube". As you saw in the chart on page 150, any set of six congruent rhombuses will fit together to form a rhombohedron. We, however, have chosen to give them particular personalities, so we have used a select group of rhombuses that have Golden Ratio relationships to illustrate the building of a skewed cube.

The first figure with this connection is named the Golden Rhombus. Its diagonals are in the ratio 1:1.618

($\emptyset$). Its angles measure 116.6° and 63.4°, rounded to the nearest tenth of a degree (Fig. 3.10). The other two rhombuses are called the "fat" Penrose rhombus with its angles of 72° and 108° (Fig. 3.11A), and the "skinny" Penrose rhombus with its angles of 36° and 144° (Fig. 3.11B). These were discovered by, and named after, the Twentieth Century English mathematician, Roger Penrose.

Both of the Penrose rhombuses are formed by joining two triangles base-to-base. These triangles can be found in the regular pentagon and its interior pentagram, a regular, concave polygon. The ratios within the pentagon and its pentagram are Golden Ratios, that is, the ratios throughout these figures are 1:1.618 ($\emptyset$). Two different assembly procedures for the skewed cube are discussed and illustrated on pages 152 and 153.

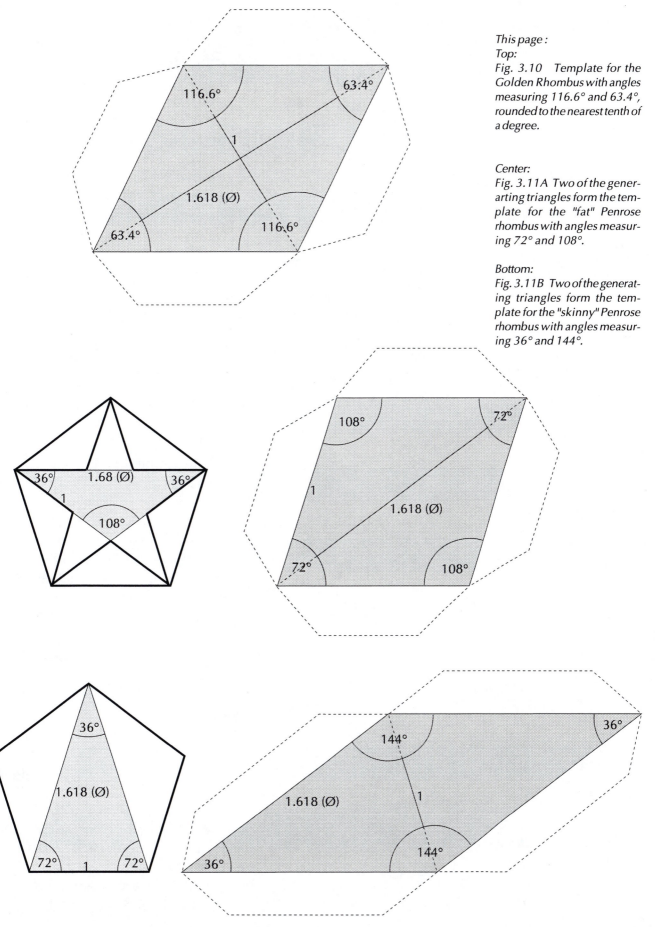

This page :
Top:
Fig. 3.10   Template for the Golden Rhombus with angles measuring 116.6° and 63.4°, rounded to the nearest tenth of a degree.

Center:
Fig. 3.11A Two of the generating triangles form the template for the "fat" Penrose rhombus with angles measuring 72° and 108°.

Bottom:
Fig. 3.11B Two of the generating triangles form the template for the "skinny" Penrose rhombus with angles measuring 36° and 144°.

This page:
Fig 3.12   Assembly of the skewed cube.

A. Label and number each rhombus.

B. Begin to glue rhombuses together into two groups of three.

C. The first group should include rhombuses 1, 2 and 3. The second group should include rhombuses 4, 5 and 6.

D. Glue the two groups of three rhombuses together and begin assembly.

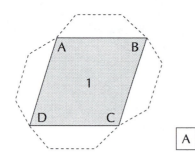

A

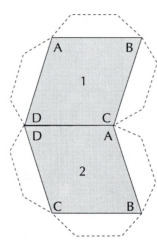

B

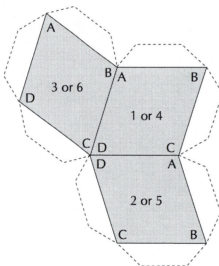

C

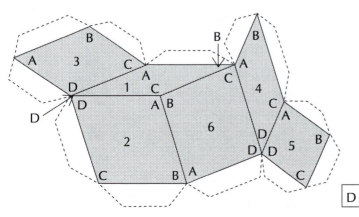

D

We suggest the following procedure for assembling a skewed cube with individual rhombuses. In Fig. 3.12, the "fat" Penrose rhombus has been used for illustration purposes, however, any other rhombus may be substituted for it.

1. Label each rhombus ABCD, making certain that the same orientation is used for each rhombus. Then give each individual rhombus a number from 1 to 6.

2. Glue rhombuses 1, 2 and 3 into a group in the following manner:

   a. Glue rhombuses 1 and 2 together at tabs DC and DA, respectively.

   b. Glue rhombuses 1 and 3 together at tabs DA and DC, respectively.

3. Glue rhombuses 4, 5 and 6 together in the same way as the first group, substituting rhombus 4 with 1, 5 with 2, and 6 with 3.

4. Complete the skewed cube by joining the two groups together in the following sequence:

   a. Glue together tabs AB of rhombuses 2 and 6.

   b. Glue together tabs BC of rhombuses 1 and 6.

   c. Glue together tabs AB of rhombuses 1 and 4.

   d. Glue together tabs BC of rhombuses 3 and 4.

   e. Glue together tabs AB of rhombus 5 and AD of rhombus 6.

   f. Glue together tabs DC of rhombuses 3 and 4.

   g. Glue together tabs BC of rhombuses 2 and 5.

   h. Glue together tabs CD of rhombus 2 and AD of rhombus 3.

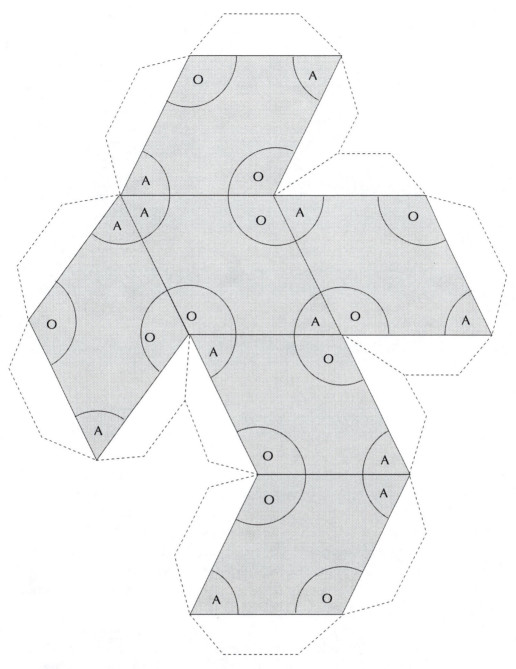

It is also possible to construct a skewed cube from a single template. Without first putting one together, and then taking it apart to form a flat net, it is unlikely that you would intuitively arrange the rhombic faces in a way that would give you the appropriate figure when folded and glued. In Fig. 3.13, we have used the Golden Rhombus to illustrate how to arrange the rhombuses into a single template.

Instead of the angle measures, however, we have substituted the letter, A, for the acute angles, and the letter, O, for the obtuse angles. In so doing, we have constructed a generic template that will serve for any group of six congruent rhombuses. When labeling your template pieces, remember to keep the rhombuses in the same orientation so that the combinations of acute and obtuse angles are maintained at the proper vertices.

Above:
Fig. 3.13   The single template for a skewed cube.

Stretching the Cube

Once again, let us begin with a single face of the cube. Rather than skew the square, however, this time we will stretch it in one direction only. In so doing, we have transformed it into a rectangle whose four congruent angles are 90°, but whose two pairs of congruent and parallel sides are not all the same length. The rectangle is the figurehead of a very large family of nonregular polygons that come in all sizes.

We would like to introduce you to the names and personality traits of members from two of its branches, the Dynamic Rectangles, and the Phi-Family Rectangles. All of the individuals from both groups have an inherent harmony that is derived from geometric relationships that specifically relate the smaller parts to the larger rectangle. If you recall, this is the quality that makes the Golden Ratio so special. The Dynamic Rectangles have a special property that is related to their reciprocal rectangles. A reciprocal rectangle is similar in shape to its parent, but is smaller in size. In the Dynamic Family, the reciprocal fits neatly, with no leftver pieces, the number of times indicated by the number under the radical sign. The Phi-Family Rectangles have connections to the Golden Ratio. The chart opposite indicates these.

In addition to inherent harmony (relationships between the subdivisions and the entire rectangle), there is also harmony among the members of the respective families. For example, if the $\sqrt{2}$ rectangle and the $\sqrt{3}$ rectangle from the Dynamic branch are used in conjunction with each other, the same kind of harmony that exists within each figure also exists between the figures. Likewise, in the Phi-Family, the $\sqrt{\varnothing}$ rectangle can be paired with the $\sqrt{5}$ rectangle to achieve a similar relationship.

In the Dynamic Family, the square becomes the generator of the $\sqrt{2}$ rectangle. This then becomes the generator for the $\sqrt{3}$ rectangle, and so on. Because the square is the parent of the first figure, and it begets the next, the square is essentially the progenitor of them all.

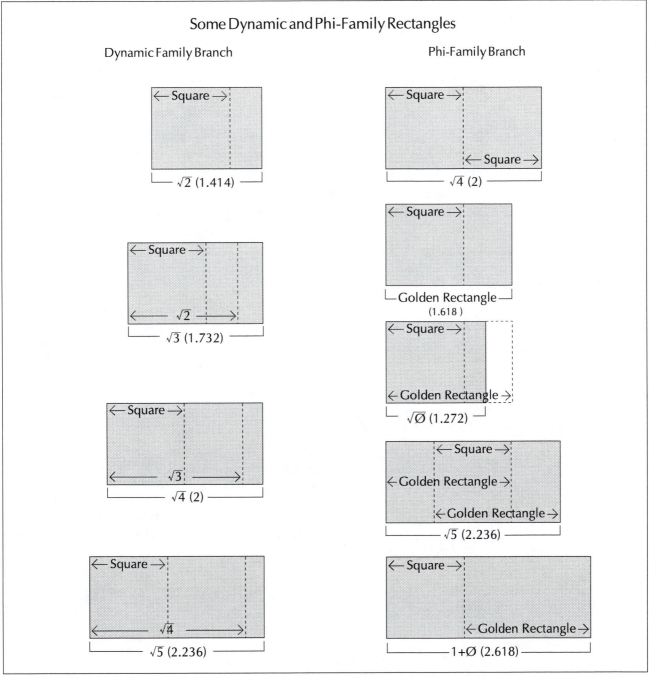

Some Dynamic and Phi-Family Rectangles

Dynamic Family Branch

Phi-Family Branch

The Phi-Family, however, is not as neat and tidy. In this case, the square first pairs with itself to form the √4 rectangle. It then moves on to become the generator for the Golden Rectangle. Then the latter becomes the figure to which the √Ø, the √5, and the Ø+1 rectangles are related. Individuals from these special branches have been illustrated in the chart on this page. Notice that family resemblance is so strong that two of the cousins are identical to each other.

Each family has its own inherent subdivisions which do not work from family to family. Experiment with simple divisions such as dividing the rectangles into halves, quarters, thirds. Notice the similarity, or lack of, between subdivisions and entire rectangle. Try finding the reciprocals of both. Try Golden Ratio subdivisions within the Phi-Family.

Making Blocks:
1, 2, 3, 4

As the square is the progenitor of the Dynamic and Phi-Family Rectangles, the cube is the forefather of two groups of polyhedra that we have called the Dynablocks and Goldbricks. One face of the cube becomes the constant unit for the width and height for all the blocks in both families. What differs from block-to-block, is their lengths. The chart on this page illustrates this concept as it takes us from a one-dimensional line, to a three-dimensional solid.

The length of the $\sqrt{4}$ blocks equals two whole units, since $\sqrt{4}$ = 2. The lengths of the remaining solids, however, have measurements that are irrational numbers,(decimals, that continue infinitely). An example is $\sqrt{5}$ = 2.2361..., which we choose to truncate to 2.236. While the concept of irrational numbers as infinite decimals may intrigue the mathematician for a lifetime, the artist needs a specific rational measurement for constructions. When we truncate an irrational number after three decimal places, the number can be used more easily in our constructions. An example of this is the Golden Ratio, 1:1.61803..., which we choose to approximate with the ratio 1:1.618.

As you can see in Fig. 3.14 on page 157, the names of the individual solids are derived from the rectangles that make up their faces. Also on page 157, is a master net from which you can build all of these blocks (Fig. 3.15). Notice that they all have unit squares for two of their faces. Make sure that you add glue tabs at the appropriate edges. Make yourself a full set of templates, a separate one for each block.

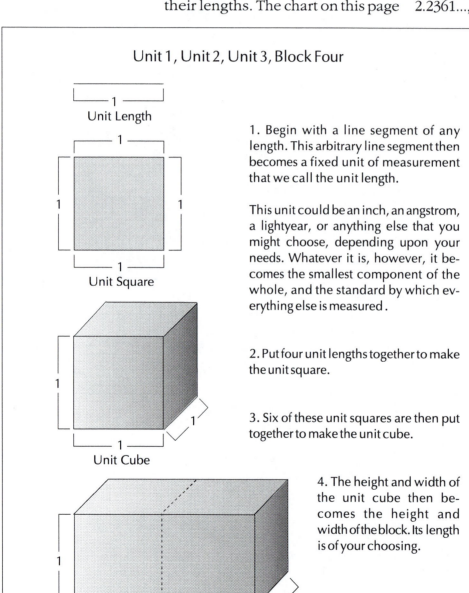

Unit 1, Unit 2, Unit 3, Block Four

Unit Length

Unit Square

Unit Cube

$\sqrt{4}$ Rectangle
$\sqrt{4}$ Block

1. Begin with a line segment of any length. This arbitrary line segment then becomes a fixed unit of measurement that we call the unit length.

This unit could be an inch, an angstrom, a lightyear, or anything else that you might choose, depending upon your needs. Whatever it is, however, it becomes the smallest component of the whole, and the standard by which everything else is measured.

2. Put four unit lengths together to make the unit square.

3. Six of these unit squares are then put together to make the unit cube.

4. The height and width of the unit cube then becomes the height and width of the block. Its length is of your choosing.

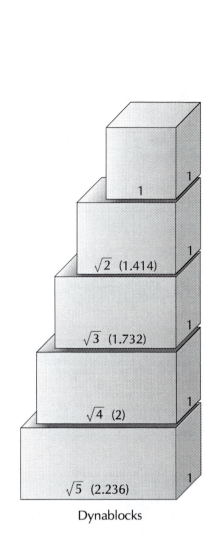

Dynablocks

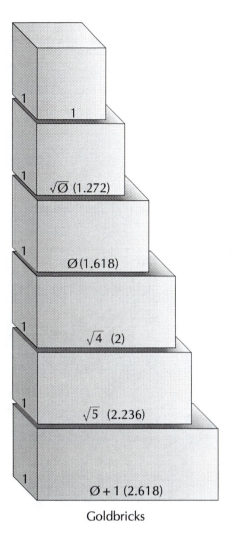

Goldbricks

Top:
Fig. 3.14 A stacking of the Dynablocks and Goldbricks for visual comparison. Notice that the $\sqrt{4}$, and the $\sqrt{5}$ blocks are found in both stacks.

Top left:
The Dynablocks are solids whose faces are rectangles from the family of Dynamic Rectangles.

Top right:
The Goldbricks are solids whose faces are members of the Phi-family Rectangles.

Bottom:
Fig. 3.15 Master net for the Dynablocks and Goldbricks.

A. Each block or brick has two square faces. Cut these out and add glue tabs to all four sides.

B. For the remaining faces, cut four of the same dimension rectangles, and then add glue tabs to all sides.

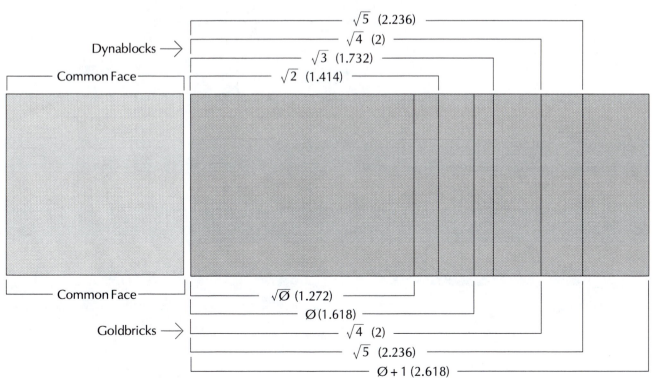

√∅ (1.272)

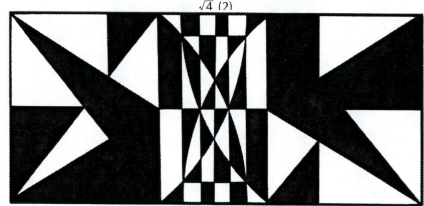

∅ (1.618)

Common Base

√4 (2)

This page:
Linda Maddox. Designs de-
veloped on polygons that re-
late to the two families of
parallelepipeds. Technical
pen and ink. If you want to
use these for your models,,
photocopy them and add
glue tabs and assemble.

√5 (2. 236)

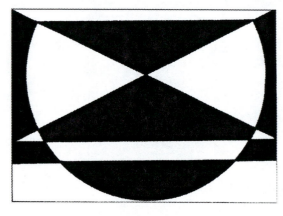

√2 (1.414)

√3 (1.732)

160

This page:
Student Works. Embellished Goldbricks made of paper.

Top:
David Robinson, colored pencil.

Bottom left:
Juliet Burley-Mason, colored pencil and photocopied elements.

Bottom right:
David Cockroft, colored pencil and embroidery thread.

161

I grew up in New York City. The natural world, to me, was made up of brick, concrete and asphalt. Trees, grass, rocks and dirt were contained in islands called "parks". In my 19th year, as I was driving from New York City to Alfred, New York, I realized that I had gotten it wrong. It was the cities that were islands and they were connected by tenuous strips of asphalt in need of constant maintenance lest they die and the cities be swallowed up by wild weeds. On that dark night on Route #17, I truly felt like one of P'an Ku's fleas. The feeling passed but returned later in the middle of the Rocky Mountains when my geology text came alive on "Going to the Sun Road" in Glacier National Park. That feeling visits me more often now and is a major source of inspiration for my work.

I begin by making projection drawings, (top, front and side view), of rectangular solids. Usually the top view is a Golden Section rectangle or a Root rectangle. Sometimes I use Fibonacci numbers to establish the dimensions of the rectangle; at other times, I establish one side of the rectangle and calculate the other side so that the result is a Golden rectangle or a Root rectangle. I establish the height of the solid in the same manner. I use the drawings as three dimensional templates. They provide the framework for sculptures that represent archetypes of geological phenomena; lakes, rivers, waterfalls, and the like. I first made these forms of pit-fired ceramics in 1977. In 1989 I began the series in lacquered wood.

These works are based on ancient architectural systems of proportion using variations of the golden section rectangle and root rectangles. They are archetypes of geologic phenomena. The basic forms are designed on the drawing board in orthographic projection. The blanks are then constructed from woods known for their carving properties and stability. The blanks are then carved and altered until the final form is realized. The raw wood is then dyed and six layers of clear lacquer are applied and hand rubbed between each coat. Additional coates of tinted lacquers are applied to develop richness and complexity in the color in much the same way that glazes are used in oil painting. At least three top coats are then applied and rubbed out to produce the final finish.

Charles DiCostanzo

This page:
Two of the works of artist Charles DiCostanzo.
Photos courtesy of the artist.
Top:
Mountain Waterfall. *1990.*
14"x14.25"x21" H. Lacquered poplar wood.

Bottom:
Stream Segment. *1992.*
23.375"x16.5"x3.875" H. Lacquered birch wood.

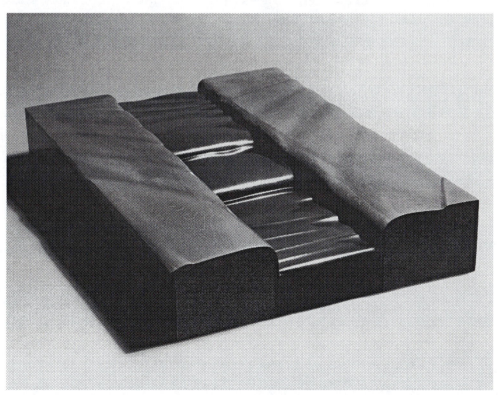

Architectural Connection: Chartres Cathedral, France

Above:
Artistic rendering of the Cathedral as it appears today with view looking down at the west facade.

The art and architecture of each age exemplifies the aspirations, the values, and the technologies of that time. In the Middle Ages, the architects and craftsmen of the Gothic period brought new light to the relationship between God and humankind. The elegance, harmony, and quality of the structure, the sculpture and the stained glass of the great Chartres Cathedral that represent the height of the Gothic style. Despite its outwardly complex look, this structure is essentially a pair of nonregular elongated pentagonal blocks.

The Middle Ages spannned 900 years between the fall of the Roman Empire, in the Fifth Century, and the onset of modern times, in the Fourteenth Century. The Middle Ages began with the disorder and decline of the Dark Ages (Fifth to the Tenth Century), and progressed to the Later Middle Ages, a period of social advancement from the Eleventh to the Fourteenth Centuries. The Gothic period, highlighted by its architecture, originated in France, and lasted 100 years from 1150 to 1250.

Legend has it that the Cathedral, located in the town of Chartres, some 90 km (55 miles) southwest of Paris, was erected above the site of an ancient Druid grotto that had been dedicated to a virgin giving birth. While the cult of the Virgin flourished in the latter part of the Middle Ages, at Chartres the Virgin Mary was revered as nowhere else. The relationship between Chartres and Our Lady the Virgin was fused for all time when the tunic reputed to have been worn by Mary at the birth of Christ was given to the church by Charlemagne's grandson, Charles the Bald, in 876. Some researchers believe that Charle-

magne, himself, was believed to be the only enlightened leader in an otherwise dark period of history.

The country cathedral of Chartres that we see today is not the original structure. There were five previous churches that rose up and fell down, prey to fire, before the Cathedral as we now know it came into existence. It was the sixth reconstruction of Chartres, which began after the fire of 1194, that brought it to its magnificent Gothic grandeur. It took many years and many skilled hands to complete the sacred place of worship that was dedicated in 1260.
Despite the fact that the name of the architect is unknown, it is believed that the design is that of one man learned in the traditions of his craft. Although a principal character, he was not the only person involved in such a major undertaking. Rather, the final rebuilding of Chartres Cathedral reflected the true spirit of the time. People of every social rank joined in to help with either labor or lavish donations. They believed that by doing so, they would secure a place in the new heaven that was the basis of the Christian movement.

The architect was the liason between raw material and completed splendor. He was the one to direct the groups of craftsmen whose skills and labor were needed to complete such an incredible amount of work. The master mason directed the stonework, the cutters shaped the stone, and the setters put the stone in place. Sawyers cut the timbers, and carpenters made all the wooden parts. The smiths created metal fittings, and the glaziers did the assembly work on the magnificent windows.

> The masters of Chartres, like the Platonists and Pythagoreans of all ages, were obsessed with mathematics; it was considered the link between God and world, the magical tool that would unlock the secrets of both.
>
> Otto von Simson
> The Gothic Cathedral

The structure of Chartres brought the divine to earth through the use of geometry, which was the basis of the closely allied arts of architecture and music which defined the Middle Ages. Fascinated by the concepts of proportion and mystical numbers, St. Augustine who outlined the architectural program of that age. The theories that influenced his thinking were connected to the writings of the Greek philosopher Plato, a student of Pythagoras, a person moved by mystical numbers and proportion.

Everything within the cathedral was based on geometric figures and the relationships among them. The contemplation of geometric order was thought to lead an individual from merely looking at the world of appearances to thinking about the order of the cosmos. The harmonies found within the geometric forms and relationships here on Earth hinted at the greater harmonies of the next world. The scale is not human but larger than life, but suggestive of the heavenly. Through geometry, the architect created a structure that, from the interior, seemed to dematerialize the enclosure in such a way that light coming in through the stained glass windows became palpable. The multiple vertical elements within the building suggested a restless and delicate shifting equilibrium.

In the plan of the Cathedral not only were the spiritual aspects of geometry called into play, but the practical as well. Most of the great pieces of architecture of the Gothic era were constructed according to a master floor plan. This master plan consisted of circles, divided into five, ten or twenty congruent arcs whose endpoints were connected by diagonals, all overlaid with a Golden Rectangle. The rectangle gave rise to the Golden Ratio automatically by those particular subdivisions. Some of these aspects are illustrated in Fig. 3.16 on page 167.

The builders of that time used some of the same techniques as the ancient Egyptians. Right angles were still constructed by using the 3-4-5 or Rope Knotter's Triangle. Linear measurements were often marked off by laying rods of particular lengths end-to-end. Therefore, all the harmony inherent in the master plan was preserved and repeated throughout the building by employing these techniques since the 3-4-5 Triangle has connection to the Golden Ratio.

At Chartres, the Golden Ratio and multiples of it appear in the measurements of the choir, transept and nave, and in the distances between the great supporting pillars. The connections to the Golden Ratio carry over from the floor plan to the elevation through the use of regular polygons, the pentagon especially.

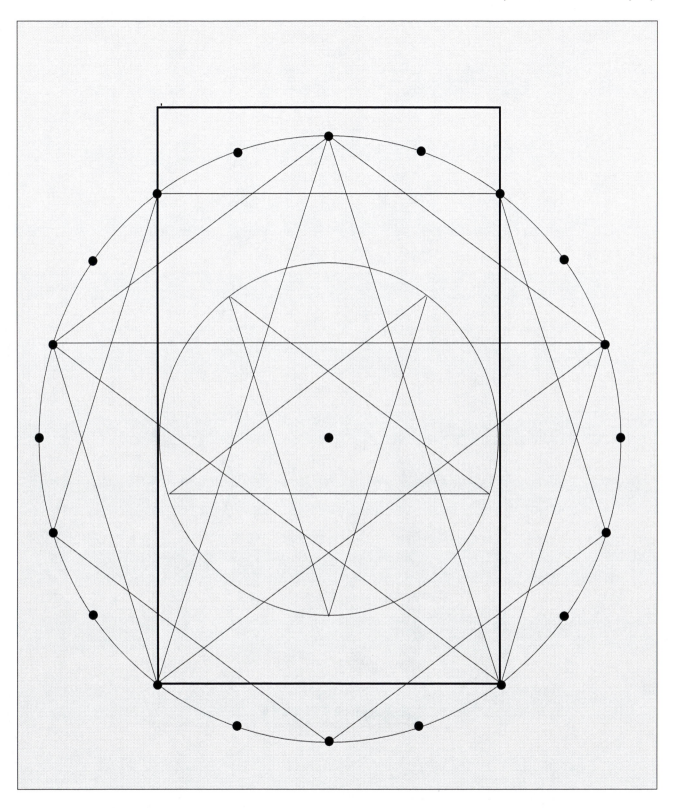

In fact, the geometry found in the design of the floor plan of this Cathedral is repeated everywhere within the structure of the church. Fig. 3.17 on page 168 illustrates the overall connection between the master plan and floor plan of Chartres while Fig. 3.18 on page 169 locates some of the areas of the Cathedral. Try this diagram on other churches.

Above:
Fig. 3.16 Some aspects of the master floor plan that were passed on from architect to architect.

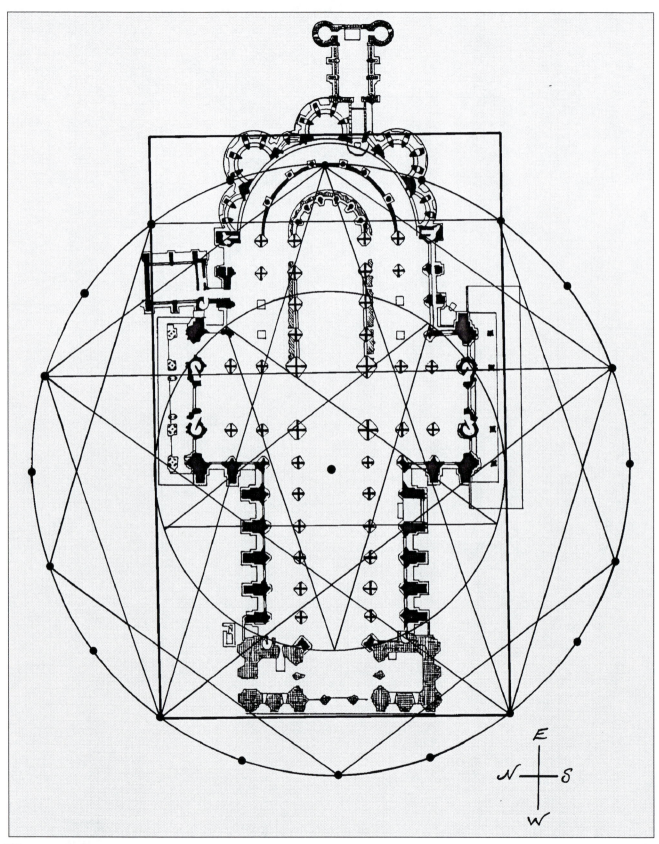

This page:
Fig. 3.17 The floor plan of Chartres Cathedral and its relationship to the master Gothic floor plan.

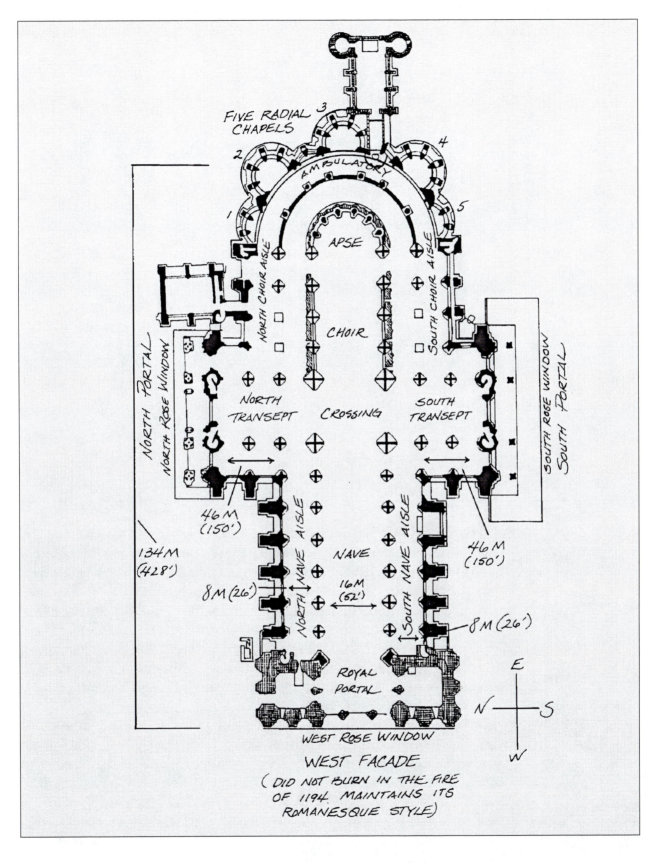

FIVE RADIAL CHAPELS

AMBULATORY

NORTH CHOIR AISLE

SOUTH CHOIR AISLE

APSE

CHOIR

NORTH PORTAL

NORTH ROSE WINDOW

SOUTH ROSE WINDOW

SOUTH PORTAL

NORTH TRANSEPT

CROSSING

SOUTH TRANSEPT

46 M (150')

46 M (150')

134 M (428')

NORTH NAVE AISLE

SOUTH NAVE AISLE

8 M (26')

NAVE

8 M (26')

16 M (52')

E

N — S

W

ROYAL PORTAL

WEST ROSE WINDOW

WEST FACADE

(DID NOT BURN IN THE FIRE OF 1194. MAINTAINS ITS ROMANESQUE STYLE)

This page:
Fig. 3.18 The location of specific elements of Chartres Cathedaral.

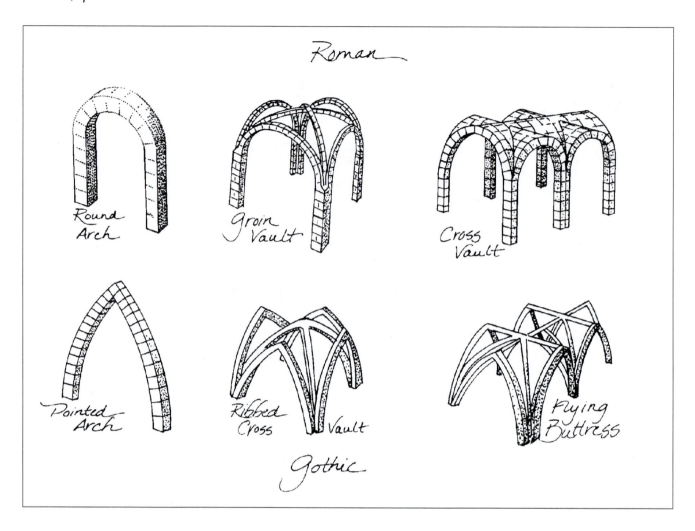

Roman

Round Arch

Groin Vault

Cross Vault

Pointed Arch

Ribbed Cross Vault

Flying Buttress

Gothic

Above:
Fig. 3.19 A comparison between Roman and Gothic arching systems.

Top:
The top row illustrates the Roman round arch; the groin vault which became the basic building module, which joins four round arches at right angles; and the cross vault.

Bottom:
The bottom row depicts comparable Gothic structures using pointed arches instead of round ones.

The desire to build higher and more spacious structures, coupled with much trial and error, led to the development of an arching system that was structured to carry most of the weight on its upright supporting elements. This provided the stability that allowed the walls to be heightened, and broken through, so that the lighter transparent material of the stained glass could be used in between stone sections. The Gothic system evolved from the round arch, the groin, and the cross vaults of Roman architecture. Fig. 3.19 gives a visual comparison between these two systems.

It was from Eastern sources, the Arab world, that Western architects learned about the pointed arch which ultimately came to symbolize the Gothic style. Architects were free to create sound, dynamic structures by joining several vaults of different spans. this could happen because their pointed arches could be made to meet at the same height despite the difference in width. The pointed arch became a basic design element as a module. This module was used in multiples, submultiples, and combinations.

As arches became higher, aisles were added on either side of the central nave, and as the number of stained glass windows increased, there was a need for greater support for the massive stone walls of the great cathedrals. The flying buttress, a masterpiece of structural engineering, was placed outside of the cathedral. It was the combination of the pointed arch, the ribbed vault, and the flying but-

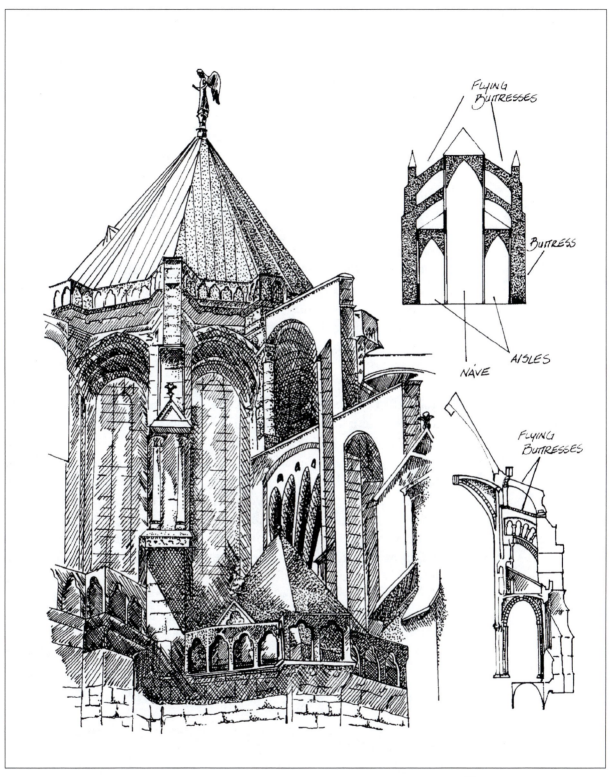

FLYING
BUTTRESSES

BUTTRESS

AISLES

NAVE

FLYING
BUTTRESSES

brought a balance between the oppos-
ing forces of thrust and counterthrust
of stone, mortal, metal, and stained
glass. (Fig. 3.20). All of these together
allowed the human participant inside
the structure to have the illusion of
little physical support, enabling him or
her to focus on the stained glass windows and the sculpture of the portals.
Inside the cathedral was all spirit and
evanescence. It was the celestial city
brought down to the earthly plane of
human comprehension. It brought
beauty and light into the dark corners.

Above:
*Fig. 3.20 Drawing of details
of the buttressing system
of Chartres Cathedral at the corner between the south transept and choir.*

Within this Gothic church there are visual elements that defy orthodox Christian explanation. Does the progression of light as it moves through the day and past the various rose windows suggest connections to the ancient study of alchemy? Is there a relationship to the rising and setting sun as it comes through particular windows? Does it, like Stonehenge in England, act as an astronomical site for observing the movement of the heavens?

Can we, who mostly understand fact, live with enigma? We, in the urban Twentieth Century, who are so used to electrical incandescence flooding us from all sides, have little ability to appreciate the significance that light held for peoples and times that had only firelight, candles, and natural illumination in a northern climate. Capturing and controlling the limited sunlight and channelling it through small colored pieces of glass outlined with lead was the miracle of Gothic cathedrals. These stained glass windows brought Divine mystery and delicacy into enclosures that were wrought primarily of stone, and which, from the outside, appeared massive and sculptural.

Stained glass windows were first made in the Ninth Century. However, it was in the Eleventh and Twelfth Centuries that the technique became an art. The process by which the windows were made was an elaborate one requiring many steps. It began with a sketch on a board that served as a template for the entire window, including the shapes of all the pieces needed to complete the design. Clear glass was cut into the desired shapes and laid onto the template. Coloring was then placed on top of the glass as it was made ready for the firing that would fuse it to the glass itself. Once cooled, these colorful pieces were assembled with the use of lead strips joined by soldering. Before the completed window could be raised into place and mounted, it was reinforced with iron crossbars.

Initially, both the colors used and the designs created were simple. As time progressed, however, and artisans became adept at filling more intricate patterns with a greater array of colors, these windows grew from simple figures to magnificent pictorial scenes. The stained glass windows that can be seen in Chartres Cathedral are some of the most spectacular in the world. There are 176 individual windows that present a variety of subjects, only some of which are exclusively biblical scenes. Many bear the trademarks of the guilds that paid for their construction, such as shoemakers and basketmakers. Others display the coats of arms of those who paid for their creation, men such as the Comte of Chartres and King Louis the Holy.

The most magnificent of these windows, however, are the rose windows. They are called rose windows because of the flowery images that are attained by the particular placement of stained glass within the stone walls. Their circular shapes appear to pierce the opaqueness of the dark and heavy walls with symmetrically placed petals of radiant, translucent color. The stone work that surrounds and holds these petal-like shapes in place is called tracery. When the rays of the sun played upon the outside of the building, the effect of the luminescence of the stained glass placed within the tracery of the stone was meant to create an awesome sight that would evoke the sense of being at

Opposite page:
Fig. 3.21
Top: An analysis of the structure of the north rose window.

Bottom:
Drawing of the North Rose and Lancet windows of Chartres Cathedral.

one with God and Heaven.

There are two such windows in Chartres. They are the famed North and south rose windows. The smaller of the two, the South Rose, thirty feet in diameter, is mounted at the end of the south transept. The North Rose, often referred to as the Rose de France, was donated by Blanche de Castile, the mother of Louis IX. Measuring forty feet across, it can be found at the end of the north transept. At the center of this flower is the image of The Virgin and Child. Its petals radiate outward, depicting angels, doves, kings and prophets. In each of the five lancet windows that are below the rose, the figure of a Holy person can be seen standing triumphantly over a sinful deed. One is St. Anne, and the other four are Old Testament figures. The north and south rose windows, according to Painton Cowen, function as guiding stars for the course of the metaphysical arc of the building which is the ship of Christianity.

If you look at Fig. 3.21, you will notice that the rose window has an underlying armature. It has a group of concentric circles that intersect with twelve radii. The vertices of the twelve squares lie on a circle, and the diagonals of these same squares lie on radii of the circles. Truly, the Cathedral of Notre Dame of Chartres is a magnificient example of the harmony and complexity that can be achieved through the application of geometric principles.

Try designing a model of a stained glass window using the structural analysis as an armature. Use colored acetates for the glass, black graphic tapes for the leading and illustration board for the stone walls. For subject matter consider the twelve months of the year or the zodiak.

Problems

1. Develop a model of a modifed cube, starting with a 5" square. Modify it in any way of your choosing.

2. Describe, in writing, the rotational symmetries of a $\sqrt{3}$ Dynablock.

3. Develop a new transformation for the cube. Give your operation a name and describe it mathematically.

4. Build a group of 3 rectangular solids out of paper using the following rectangles for the dimensions of faces:
a. 1:1.618
b. 1.618:2.236
c. 1:1.272

5. Construct a skewed cube and in writing describe its symmetries.

6. Find a floor plan for a Gothic cathedral other than Chartres. Compare and contrast it to Chartres through writing and visuals.

7. Develop a drawing of two cubes, one in parallel projection, and one in isometric projection, with angles other than those given in Fig. 3.1 on page 116. In writing, compare the look of the illusion. What kinds of things do you notice?

8. Using the symmetry chart on pages 128 and 129, compare, by diagramming, the symmetries of a cube and the symmetries of a $\sqrt{5}$ Goldbrick.

9. Build a template for a skewed cube from a rhombus with angles of your choice. Use the template to construct the skewed cube.

10. Develop a drawing which illustrates four different ways to slice a cube other than those given on page 136.

11. Imagine a 4" cube that is constructed with 1" unit cubes. How many unit cubes are needed? If only the exterior faces of the 4" cube are painted, how many unit cubes would have one side painted? How many would have two sides painted? How many would have three sides painted?

Projects

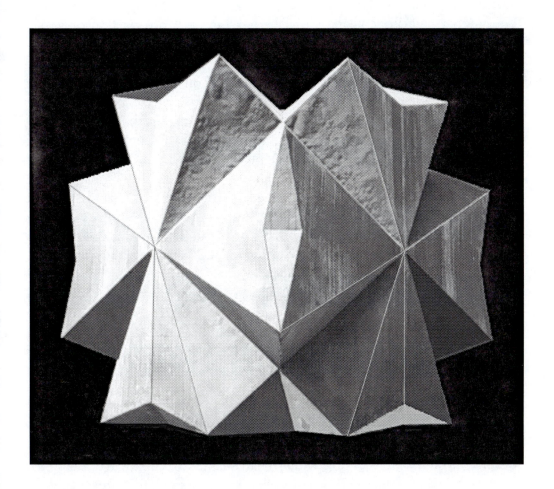

1. With the parallelepipeds as inspiration, design and execute a sturdy paper prototype for a set of children's alphabet blocks. Research the letter forms developed by Albrecht Durer and use them as the basis for designing the surfaces of your blocks.

2. Do an architectural rendering of a building you design using a modular approach with harmonic building blocks.

3. Research the totem poles of the Northwest Coast Indians. Create a three-dimensional model of a contemporary totem pole based on your research and any of the forms discussed in this chapter. Use watercolor paper and any water base medium you choose.

Above:
Granite sculpture in park in Toronto, Canada. Variation of cubic form.

4. Extend Project 3 by researching postal regulations and size limits, and design a totem pole as a flat piece, ready to be folded into a three-dimensional form, that could be sold by an educational mail-order business.

5. Design and execute a dollhouse from a single sheet of fomecore board or plywood. Use what you have learned from this chapter as the basis for the room modules. Do some research into the history of dollhouses, and make yours as realistic or as fantastic as you wish.

6. Build a wall relief sculpture out of different sized harmonic cells which may have one open side. Choose your material depending on your need for permanency and stability. Consider changes in size, color, and texture, or use only white and allow cast shadow to become the important visual element of your design.

7. Using fabric or fiber and sewing, crocheting, knitting, tatting, embroidering, basketry or weaving skills, create a bag that is derived from one of the harmonic structures discussed in this chapter. Make a paper pattern first so that you can work out the details of the shape and the surface design. Base your surface design on natural forms or structures.

8. Using wire, wood struts, or plastic rods, and beads for joints, create a skeletal structure that hints at natural growth but is built up from modular cubic or dynamic units.

9. Notch a pile of different sized and colored squares cut from sturdy board or plastic bottles, and join the units to create a three-dimensional sculpture that can be taken apart and reassembled in a variety of ways. Add design elements of your choice.

10. You can also play this game with friends, wherein the sculpture undergoes transformations as it passes from person to person, each adding his or her own choice of elements.

11. Design and execute a set of nesting gift boxes that have harmony in both the two-dimensional surface design and the three-dimensional form.

12. Using any of the solids discussed in this chapter and the technique of decoupage (a process of cutting out found images and adhering them to a surface), make a positive statement about the natural world.

13. Research and analyze the furniture design of the sect of American Shakers. Compare in drawings or photographs several different examples of chests, dressers, etc. What proportional system might they have used for their work? What conclusions can you draw from your analysis of their work?

14. Research, analyze, compare and contrast through visual documentation, a famous French cathedral other than Chartres, an English one and an Italian one. What conclusions can you draw?

Further Reading

Cowen, Painton. *Rose Windows*. London: Thames and Hudson, Ltd., 1990.

Feininger, Andreas. *The Anatomy of Nature*. New York: Dover, 1956.

Grunbaum, Branko and G. C. Shephard. *Tilings and Patterns*. New York: W. H. Freeman and Company, 1987.

Kappraff, Jay. *Connections*. New York: McGraw-Hill, Inc., 1991.

Lee, Lawrence, George Seddon, and Francis Stephens. *Stained Glass*. Secaucus, New Jersey: Chartwell Books, Inc., 1989.

Scully, Vincent. *Architecture*. New York: St. Martin's Press, 1991.

Williams, Christopher. *Origins of Form*. New York: Architectural Book Publishing Company, 1981.

Wong, Wucius. *Principles of Three-Dimensional Design*. New York: Van Nostrand Reinhold Company, 1977.

von Simson, Otto. *The Gothic Cathedral*. New York: Harper & Row, Publishers, 1962.

Westwood, Jennifer. *The Atlas of Mysterious Places*. New York: Weidenfeld & Nicolsin, 1987.

4 Spheres and Beyond

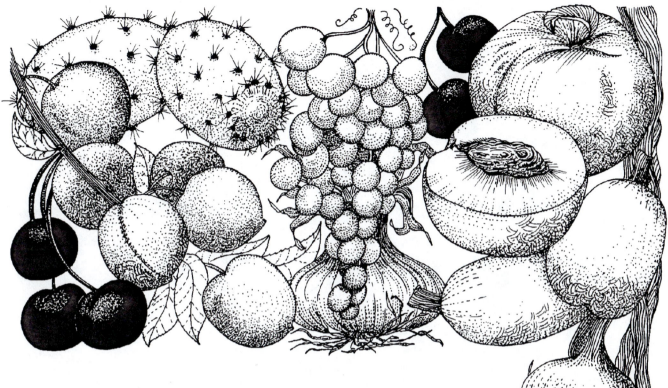

According to the theories of the physicist and mathematician, Albert Einstein, the universe is curved, with all its elements held together through the interplay of physical forces. Our Earth, other planets and the stars are basically spherical. This shape seems fitting since Nature always looks for economy in materials and work and the sphere is the form that affords the least possible surface area for a given volume regardless of its size or composition. Curved surfaces are stronger than flat ones and most materials are stronger when held in tension rather than in compression.

At a level closer to our inspection, we have the macroscopic world. In this human- sized realm we do not need microscopes nor telescopes to observe sphere-shaped forms. These include the fruits and vegetables that grace our tables and inspire our paintings of still lifes.

A sphere has the most symmetry of any shape. Its symmetry group is infinite. It can be divided into two identical halves by any cut that passes through its center. Because of this, it has an infinite number of planes of reflection. The sphere offers very little resistance to friction or pressure. If these are at all present, however, it tends to become more ovoid in shape as in the egg. Gravity, tension or pressure from being packed tightly, can effect the symmetry of the sphere.

Before looking at natural spheres such as the cell, let us make sure that we have a common vocabulary. The sphere and the circle have many of the same mathematical properties and, therefore, use the same terminology. There are some additions to the information on the circle that we provided in Chapter 1 and some new information in the relation of the circle to the sphere, all given on the charts on pages 180-185. We will need this information when we discuss polyhedra in the following chapter.

Above:
Spherical forms in the everyday realm.

Elements of the Circle

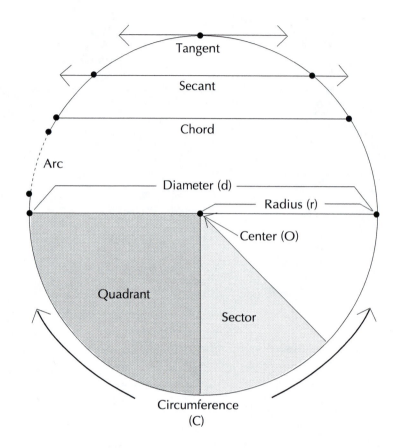

Circle

A circle is the simplest of all closed curves. It is described as the set of all points in a plane at a fixeddistance from a given point. This point is called the center of the circle and it names the circle. Usually it is designated as O.

Circumference (C)

The circumference is the distance around the circle.It is a real number rather than a geometric figure.

Arc

The continuous unbroken portion of the circle which lies between two points on a circle.

Chord

A line segment whose two endpoints lie on the circle.

Diameter (d)

A chord that passes through the center of the circle.The diameter is used for the number that gives the length of the line segment. Every diameter of a circle is contained in an axis of rotation about which the circle has infinite-turn symmetry.

Radius (r)

A line segment that connects the center of the circle to a point on the circle. It can also be the number that designates the length of such a line segment. It is half the length of the diameter.

Tangent

A line that intersects, or is tangent to, the circle at exactly one point. This line is in the same plane as, but lies outside of, the circle.

Secant

A straight line that passes through and intersects the circle at two points.

Sector

A region in the interior of the circle bounded by two radii and the arc intercepted by the radii.

Quadrant

A sector that contains one-quarter of the circle.

Elements of the Sphere

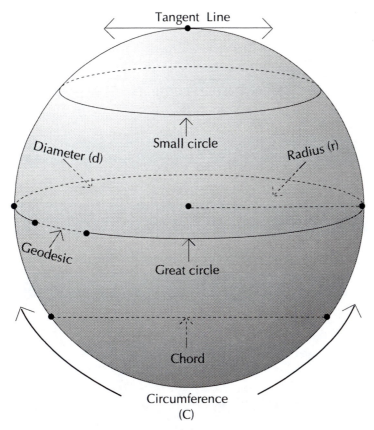

Sphere
A sphere is the simplest of geometric solids. It is described as the set of all points in space at a fixed distance from a given point. This point is referred to as the center of the sphere and it names the sphere. Usually it is designated as O.

Circumference (C)
The circumference is the real number which gives the distance around the sphere.

Chord
A line segment which joins two points on the sphere.

Diameter (d)
A chord that passes through the center of the sphere. Every diameter of a sphere is contained in an axis of rotation about which the sphere has infinite-turn symmetry.

Radius (r)
A line segment that connects the center of the sphere with *any* point on the surface. It can also be the number that designates the length of the line segment. It is half the length of the diameter.

Tangent Line
A line that intersects, or is tangent to, the sphere at exactly one point.

Small Circle
The intersection of the sphere with any plane that does not pass through the center of the sphere. The center of a small circle is not the center of the sphere.

Great Circle
The intersection of the sphere with a plane that passes through the center of the sphere. Every great circle divides a sphere into two halves. Every great circle determines a plane of reflection.

Geodesic Arc
The shortest path from one point to another on a surface on the sphere. A geodesic lies along the arc of a great circle. One and only one geodesic arc can be drawn through any two points of the sphere as long as the two points are not at opposite ends of a diameter.

Measuring the Circle

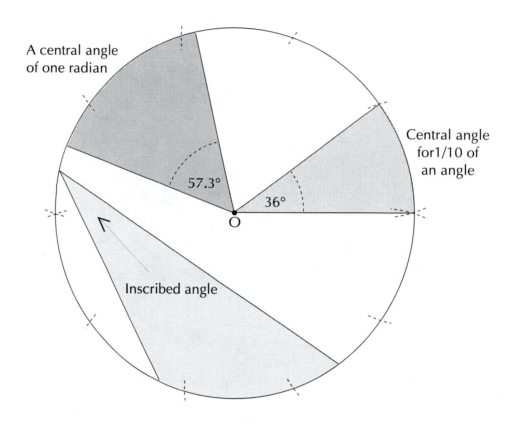

A central angle of one radian

Central angle for1/10 of an angle

57.3°

36°

O

Inscribed angle

$\pi=C/d\approx3.14$
The ratio of the circumference of a circle to its diameter.

Circumference (C) = $2\pi r$

Area (A) = πr^2

Inscribed Angle
An inscribed angle has its vertex on the circle and its sides formed by chords.

Central Angle
A central angle has its vertex at the center of the circle and its sides are formed by radii. The number of degrees in the central angle is the fraction of the complete circumference subtended by the angle, multiplied by 360° (which corresponds to one complete revolution). For example, the central angle corresponding to 1/4 of the circumference is 1/4 x 360° = 90°.

Arc Length and *Sector Area*
Arc length (S) = θ
θ= vertex angle of the sector only if it is measured in radians, not degrees.
Area of a sector (AS) = A =$ar^2/2$

Radian measure
A unit used to measure angles in some technical and scientific work. One radian is the angle at the center of a circle that corresponds to an arc exactly one radius in length.
By definition: 1 radian = 180°/3.14 = 57.296°.

To convert angle measurements from degrees to radians, multiply by 3.14/180 and round off.
For example: 43° = 43 x 3.14/180 or 0.75 radians, approximately.

To convert angles from radians to degrees, multiply by 180/3.14 and round off.
For example: 1.3 radians = 1.3 x 180/3.14 or 74.5°, approximately.

Measuring the Sphere

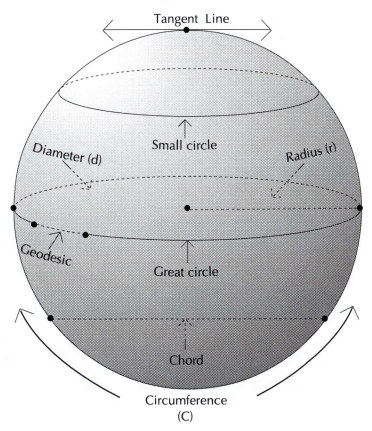

$\pi = C/d \approx 3.14$
The ratio of the circumference of a sphere to its diameter.

Surface Area (SA) $= 4\pi r^2$

Volume (V) $= 1/3r(4\pi r^2)$ or $4/3\pi r^3$

When doubling the diameter of a sphere, the surface increases by a factor of 4 and the volume increases by a factor of eight.

Area of a Circular Cross Section (small circles)
$A = \pi x^2$

Here we must use the Pythagorean Theorem to calculate the area of the small circles. Refer to the chart in Chapter 2 if necessary.
$$a^2 + b^2 = c^2$$

We will work through one example for you. Remember, in order to calculate these measurements we must insert real numbers.

r=15cm
h=9cm

and

a=x (radius of the small circle)
b=h
c=r (radius of the sphere)

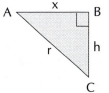

First, we must find the length of the radius of the small circle.

$x^2 + h^2 = r^2$
$x^2 + 9^2 = 15^2$
$x^2 + 81 = 225$
$x^2 - 81 = 225 - 81$
$x^2 = 144$
$x = 12$

Then, we can calculate the area of the small circle.

$A = \pi r^2$
$A = 3.14(12)^2$
$A = 3.14 \times 144$
$A = 452.16$ square cm

Organizing the Circle

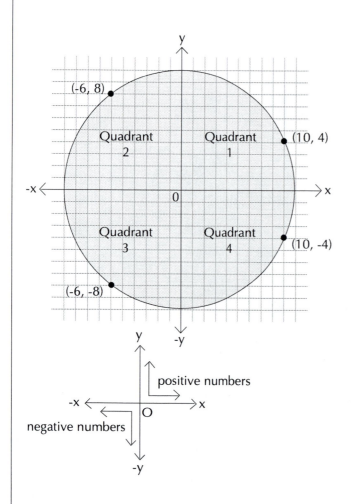

In order to locate a point, or position, in two-dimensional space, you need two co-ordinates. The first is used to measure the horizontal distance of the point from a fixed point (usually called the origin and denoted O).

The second co-ordinate is used to measure the vertical distance of the point from the origin O.

To facilitate this measurement, we place a horizontal co-ordinate axis, called the x-axis, and a vertical axis, called the y-axis on the plane.

Notice the use of positive and negative numbers to indicate position in the four quadrants.

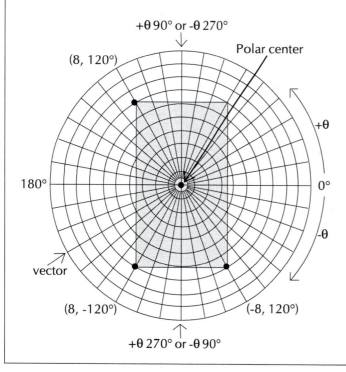

The Polar Grid

This is a grid of concentric circles that are organized around a center, which is referred to as a pole. Radii, which are called vectors, radiate out from the pole at specific angles. Locations on the polar grid are determined by the positions where the vectors are intersected by the circles. This system of organization also uses coordinates, but unlike the Cartesian system, polar mapping involves (r, θ), where r is the distance from the pole along a vector, and θ (theta) is the measure of the angle. For example, (8,120°)refers to the point which lies eight units from the pole along the 120° vector. Positive θ angles (+θ) are measured in a counterclockwise direction from the 0° vector and negative θ angles (-θ) in a clockwise direction. If r is a negative number (-r) the point will be located on the radius vector opposite the value of θ.

Organizing the Sphere

The grid and Cartesian coordinate system are also used to map points in three dimensions. Notice that by adding another dimension we now have a third axis, called the *z axis*. We now use ordered triples (x, y, z) to locate our points, and as you can see, we now have eight octants, rather than four quadrants.

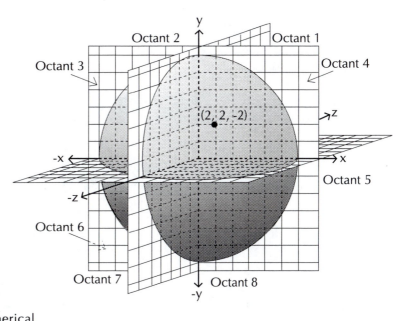

North Pole, South Pole, Longitudes anLatitudes

If we imagine that we are looking down on a sphere, the pole, the vectors, and the concentric circles of the polar grid become the basis for another way to locate points on the sphere. The three-dimensional counterpart is a system that can be used on any spherical surface where location and orientation are important. It is primarily used, however, to locate points on the surface of the Earth, which as you know, is roughly spherical. However, we are still only ocating two points. This time, they are on a curved surface. If you were piloting a plane, you would need to add the dimension of altitude.

Position on the Earth's surface is measured in terms of degrees of latitude and longitude, with its spatial orientation determined by the axis of rotation through its North and South Poles. Such measurement is independent of the size of the sphere. It is not truly a measure of distance, but rather, a measure of position in relation to the whole. It is dependent upon the fact that a circle contains 360°. Global positions are found by locating the points of intersection of the appropriate lines of longitude and latitude.

The great circles that pass through the poles become the half circles that are called meridians and form the lines of longitude. The prime meridian, which passes through Greenwich, England, has a longitudinal designation of 0°. All other measurements of longitude are in degrees east or west of this prime meridian, with numbers increasing in both directions from 0° to 180°. The lines of latitude are circles lying in parallel planes, all perpendicular to the axis of rotation. Of these, only the equator is a great circle, with its latitude designated as 0°, breaking the sphere into northern and southern hemispheres. Everywhere else, latitude is measured in degrees north or south of the equator, with numbers increasing in both directions until the poles are reached 90° away in either direction.

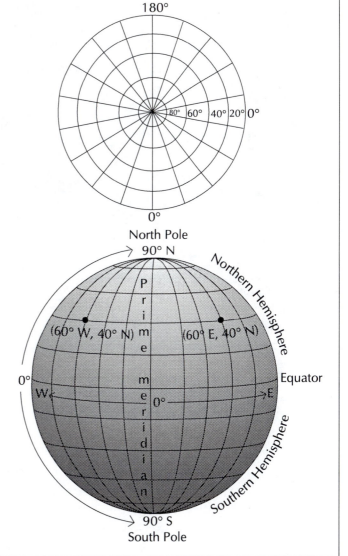

Spherical Tiling

These facing pages: Drawings after the Temari balls of English artist and author Mary Wood.

Spherical tiling has one of its roots in the sacred architecture of Islam in the Tenth Century, and bore fruit in the folk art of Japan. As a centuries-old craft, it consists of creating patterns from embroidery threads on the surface of a ball made from waste fibers. It is called temari, and it gives us a way into understanding the mathematics of a sphere.

Quiltmakers tile a flat plane, while the temari artist deals with a curved surface. Mathematically, this presents a different set of conditions. Probably, the artist who first undertook the decoration of a ball was not contemplating the use of geometry but, rather, was concerned with recycling silk and cotton threads, creating interesting pattern, using quality craftsmanship, and spending time in a meaningful way.

Essentially, what is required is a sphere that has a soft and pliable outer wrap. This ball is completely covered first by a layer of colored yarn and then with a matching shade of embroidery thread. In order for the ball to retain its solidity, the threads must follow the paths of great circles. The yarn and thread layers form the background onto which a pattern is

developed with additional colors.

By initially dividing and marking the sphere into manageable sections, the stage is set for the particular symmetries used in the ultimate design. In practical terms, a narrow strip of paper is wrapped around the widest part of the ball. It is removed, folded in half, and half again, and notched at the fold lines. It is then placed back on the sphere and pins are used to mark key points at the notches on the great circles containing the polar and the equatorial axes of the sphere.

Depending upon the complexi-

ties of the design, additional divisions are made between an equatorial point and a polar point. Once the subdivisions are made, the pattern is worked in decorative embroidery threads. For the most part, the temari designs are built on what appears to be simple divisions of the sphere by continuously bisecting it. First the sphere is halved, then quartered, then divided nto eighths, and then sixteenths. In many ways, working directly and experientially with the actual surface of a temari ball is much easier than the mathematical description of what is taking place.

If you would like to try one for yourself, we suggest that you read, and follow the directions in the book written by Mary Wood.

Right:
Fig. 4.1 A-C The planes of reflection of the cube become the basis for one kind of spherical tiling.

Top:
A. The cube sits symmetrically inside of a circumsphere. All vertices lie on the surface of the sphere.

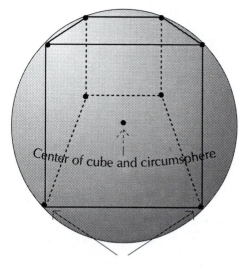

All vertices of the cube lie on the circumsphere

Center:
B. Two planes of reflection of the cube are seen intersecting the surface of the circumsphere creating great circles.

Bottom:
C. The tiling of a sphere, based on the nine planes of reflection of the cube.

The question that both the artist and the mathematician might ask involves the number and kind of congruent polygons needed to cover a sphere without overlaps or gaps. It is the same question that can be asked when tiling the two-dimensional surface. These are seemingly simple questions with more than simple answers.

Mathematicians know that a sphere can be covered completely with congruent spherical triangles which are not equilateral. These are obtained by first inscribing particular polyhedra within what is called, a circumsphere. The polyhedra that can be inscribed in a sphere have a center coincident with that of the surrounding sphere. All of the vertices of such polyhedra are equidistant from the common center of the polyhedron and the sphere, and lie upon the surface.

Fig. 4.1 A illustrates the circumsphere of the cube.

After inscribing the cube within the sphere, the nine planes of reflection of the cube are projected outward until they intersect the surface of the sphere. Refer back to the chart on page 135 if necessary. Fig. 4.1 B illustrates two planes of reflection that have been projected onto the sphere. The nine planes divide the surface of the sphere into a total of 48 spherical triangles, half of which are mirror images of the others. In Fig. 4.1 C, notice that the nine planes of reflection of the cube are coincident with the arcs of nine great circles of the sphere.

Different polyhedra inscribed within a sphere will yield different numbers and kinds of spherical triangles.. Mathematicians have determined, however, that the maximum

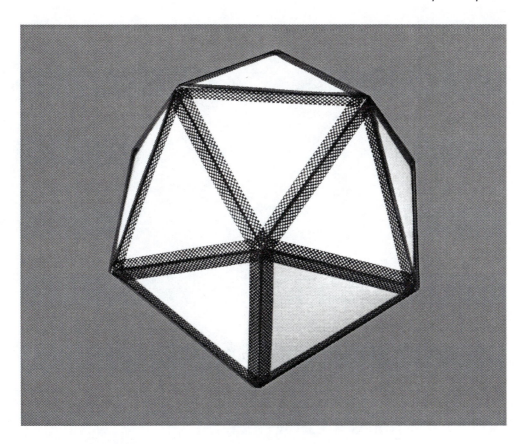

number of congruent spherical triangles that can tile the surface of
the sphere is 120. These triangles are obtained when a polyhedron, called the icosahedron, is inscribed within a
sphere.

The icosahedron is com-
posed of twenty equilateral triangles. According th
mathematicians, it is the
most symmetrical of all
possible convex polyhe-
dra with one type of con-
gruent regular face. This figure has fifteen planes of reflection, each of which passes
through opposite edges of the figure. Once again, as with the cube,
notice in Fig. 4.2, that each of these
planes determines a great circle on
the circumsphere. The mathematician H. S. M. Coxeter proved that
these great circles divide the sphere
into 120 congruent spherical trian-

Top:
Rochelle Newman. Model of
an icosahedron.Paper and
graphic tapes. Notice that 5
equilateral triangles come to-
gether at a vertex.

Bottom:
Fig. 4.2 A tiling of the sphere,
based on the planes of reflec-
tion found within the icosa-
hedron.

gles. Each has angles of 36°, 60°,
and 90°. Consider the difference between Euclidean triangles which
always have an interior angle sum of
180°, and spherical triangles, whose
sides are arcs of great circles, and
whose angles total more than 180°.

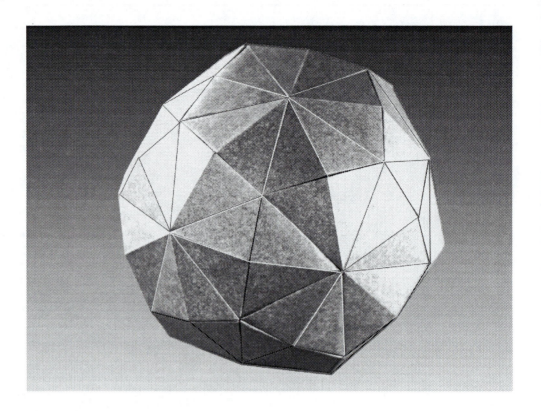

Spheres and Geodesics

The icosahedron can also be used as the armature for developing a polyhedron that we name the Neo-Geo-Sphere. This figure, however, is composed of 120 straight-edged triangles, rather than curvilinear ones. Its overall shape, nonetheless, approximates the sphere with its 120 geodesic triangles.

By definition, a geodesic line across *any* surface, is the shortest distance along the surface between the two points. Therefore, if the surface is curved, as is the case with the circumsphere, then the geodesic line is an arc. Polyhedra that are constructed with geodesic arcs can be called spherical polyhedra. The figures that we will concentrate on in this section, however, are adaptations of the spherical ones. Instead of using the arcs of great circles of the circumscribing sphere, we will adapt these geodesics into straight-

line chords, that we will call geodesic chords. The lengths of these are then translated into the edge lengths of the triangles that we will use to construct our figure.

In order to approximate the curved surface of the sphere we must do something to the icosahedron. One way in which to do this, is to triangulate it. Triangulation is the process by which an existing surface is subdivided into triangles. For this particular polyhedron, we use the edges and faces of the inscribed icosahedron as the template for triangulation, and then we use its layout as a pattern for construction.

The equilateral triangular face of the icosahedron can be subdivided into six congruent 30°, 60°, 90° right triangles, giving us a total of 120. These, however, will not work for the Neo-Geo-Sphere because they lie flat. Therefore, we must substitute triangles that when put together, will project into space. These deviate ever so slightly from the right triangle. Fig. 4..4 illustrates the difference between the 30°, 60°, 90° right triangle of the icosahedron, and the 34°26', 58°23', 87°11' triangles of the Neo-Geo-Sphere. A right and left-handed version of this new triangle must be paired in order to create the necessaary unit for constructing this polyhedron. In Fig. 4.5 we have given you the needed template. This size works well and gives you a model that is about 30 inches around.

There are two ways to approach the building of this figure. The first one involves putting glue tabs on the outside of the polyhedron. Lightweight paper is appropriate for this particular model. The second type has the glue tabs on the inside. This is the more difficult way, and it requires a much heavier paper and finer motor skills. Either way, the directions for building the Neo-Geo-Sphere follow.

Preparation
1. Duplicate the template 60 times.
2. For models with glue tabs on the outside, mountain fold the lines between triangles on each unit, and valley fold those at the glue tabs.
3. For models with the glue tabs on the inside of the polyhedron, mountain fold all the lines.

Assembly
1. Join five units together around a single vertex to form a *unit cluster.*
2. Repeat Step 1 eleven more times until you have a total of twelve unit clusters.
3. Join three of these unit clusters together at a single vertex.
4. Repeat this procedure until the figure is complete.

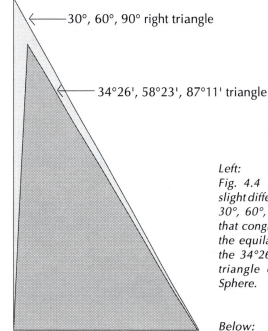

Left:
Fig. 4.4   There is only a slight difference between the 30°, 60°, 90° right triangle that congruently subdivides the equilateral triangle and the 34°26', 58°23', 87°11' triangle of the Neo-Geo-Sphere.

Below:
Fig. 4.5   A right and left-handed version of the 34°26', 58°23', 87°11' triangle group together to form the template for the Neo-Geo-Sphere.

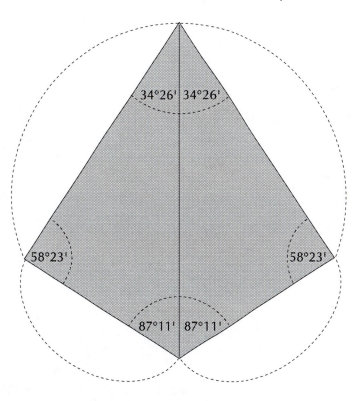

Geodesics and Domes

Above:
A simple skeletal geodesic dome used for children's play. Colored metal and bolts.
Notice that one vertex has five triangles coming together while the other vertex has six triangles coming together.

A contemporary development in architecture that relates to the sphere is the geodesic dome. This is essentially a very large geo-sphere that has a section removed so that it will sit upon a platform of some sort. Buckminster Fuller (1895-1983), "Bucky" to a great many, was responsible for the conception, development and subsequent use of the geodesic dome. He was one of those eccentric persons who did not follow the established way throughout the course of his very full eighty-seven years. He was lecturing, travelling, and inventing, almost up to the very end of his life.

At a crucial point in his career, Bucky decided to dedicate himself to the task of improving the quality of life on this "Spaceship Earth". To that end he set out to discover the principles that governed the natural world so that science and technology could be put to the service of humankind. He embraced an optimism that suggested all problems could be solved. So he set out to improve such commonplace objects as homes and automobiles.

In 1947, Fuller patented the design for the now famous geodesic dome. These spherical structures, made from interconnected, self-supporting members, staged one of their first appearances at the World's Fair, Expo 67, in Montreal, Canada. This particular three-quarter dome was constructed of steel pipe and transparent acrylic panels. It measured 200 feet from floor to the highest

point and 250 feet across.

A geodesic dome can enclose a large volume of space with no interior support. It is very light in weight in relation to its size, and in fact, has the highest strength rating per weight of any human-made structure. Since it can be constructed from prefabricated modular elements, it can be quickly assembled on site. In practical terms, a dome can be placed almost anywhere, as long as it is set upon a floor of wood or concrete or some other sort of platform. A wide range of materials can be used, thus adapting to a variety of locations and cultures. Domes have been erected in arctic climates as well as tropical ones, and have been built to house public events as well as private domestic living. At one point in his career, Bucky suggested a three mile dome be built over midtown Manhattan in New York City, a dream whose time has not yet come.

Above:
Drawing of a transformation that suggests a relationship between a tortoise and a geodesic dome. We told you it could be a platform of any kind...

Geodesics, Domes, and Polyhedra

Above:
Rochelle Newman. Model of a geodesic icosahedron. Paper and textured paint. Notice the combination of convexity and concavity.

For architectural and sculptural puposes, all geodesic arcs are translated into chords, and then into strut lengths. These are then used to construct three-dimensional forms, such as domes and polyhedra. Although we do not discuss the construction of domes in any great detail, we will say that any geodesic polyhedron can be cut off, or truncated, at particular locations, and set on a platform

to make a dome. The *Dome Handbook*, listed in our Further Reading section, gives the directions needed for constructing geodesic domes.

What we will discuss, here, however, is the construction of geodesic polyhedra. In order to do so, we couple the concept of the Neo-Geo-Sphere and the geodesic dome. Once again, we will use the icosahedron as the principle polyhedron inscribed within a circumsphere. When we made the geo-sphere, we triangulated the surface of the circumsphere into elemental unit triangles.

To make a geodesic polyhedron, we will triangulate the faces of the icosahedron, using the circumsphere as a guide. By breaking down the surfaces of any polyhedron into constituent triangles, we utilize the structural concept of the geodesic dome,

The triangle is the geometric plane figure which has maximum rigidity, accomplished with least effort.....omni-triangulated, omni-symmetric systems require the least energy effort to effect and regenerate their own structural stability.

Buckminster Fuller
Engineer

which is to couple the maximum volume-to-area ratio and weight bearing advantages of the sphere, with the structural strength and rigidity, as well as the simplicity, of the triangle. Rather than use the skeletal struts of a dome, which can then be covered with an appropriate material, we will construct our polyhedron with solid triangles whose edge lengths are equal to the required lengths of the struts.

Although there are many methods to triangulate the faces of a polyhedron, the one that we describe is called the "Alternate" method. It begins with the triangular subdivisions of a single face of the principle polyhedron. In the case of the icosahedron, this will be an equilateral triangle. The number of subdivisions will depend upon how nearly spherical the transformed polyhedron is to be. The more subdivisions, the closer the approximation of the sphere, and the more complex the completed figure.

Frequency is the term given to the initial number of congruent subdivisions along the edge of the polygonal face. Fig. 4.6 A-C illustrates three different frequencies. Subdividing an edge into two gives a 2-frequency unit, into three divisions, a 3-frequency unit, and into four, a 4-frequency unit, etc. The square of the frequency , 2^2, 3^2, 4^2, gives the total number of triangles needed to triangulate the face. Fig. 4.7 illustrates 1, 2, 3, 4, and 6-frequencies.

After deciding upon the frequency of the geodesic polyhedron, the edge lengths of the subdivision triangles must be determined. Since each one of these is essentially a chord of the circumsphere, they are called chord

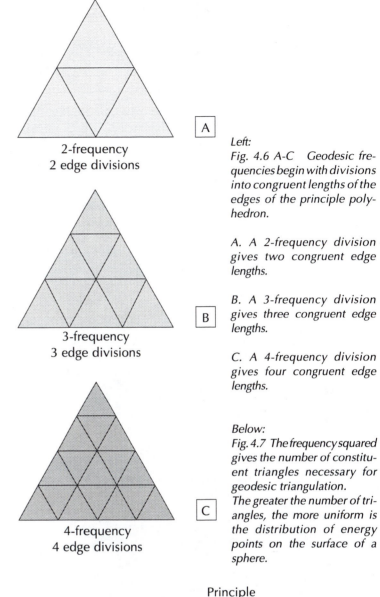

2-frequency
2 edge divisions

A

3-frequency
3 edge divisions

B

4-frequency
4 edge divisions

C

Left:
Fig. 4.6 A-C Geodesic frequencies begin with divisions into congruent lengths of the edges of the principle polyhedron.

A. A 2-frequency division gives two congruent edge lengths.

B. A 3-frequency division gives three congruent edge lengths.

C. A 4-frequency division gives four congruent edge lengths.

Below:
Fig. 4.7 The frequency squared gives the number of constituent triangles necessary for geodesic triangulation.
The greater the number of triangles, the more uniform is the distribution of energy points on the surface of a sphere.

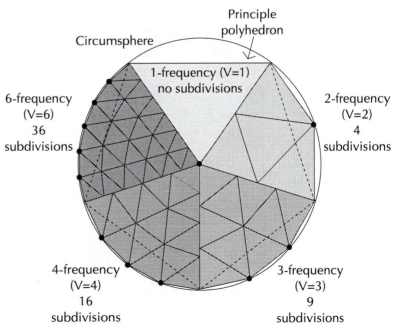

Principle polyhedron

Circumsphere

1-frequency (V=1)
no subdivisions

6-frequency
(V=6)
36
subdivisions

2-frequency
(V=2)
4
subdivisions

4-frequency
(V=4)
16
subdivisions

3-frequency
(V=3)
9
subdivisions

factors. The calculation of these is at best a tedious process, and it will not be discussed in this book. We do, however, refer you to the book by Anthony Pugh, which is listed in our Further Reading section, if you want to try the calculations yourself. His text also includes are tables of chord factors for your convenience. Whenever these are needed in this book, we will supply them.

There are three different chord factors for a 3-frequency icosahedron. They are:

a=.34862
b=.40355
c=.41241

These must then be translated into actual edge lengths, called struts. While these can be made from wood, or steel, or plastic, etc., our strut lengths will be the edge lengths of paper triangles.

In order to calculate the actual lengths, the overall size of the completed polyhedron must first be decided upon. Our geodesic icosahedron will have a circumsphere radius of 10 cm. Knowing this, we can now solve for each of the edge lengths with the equation:

Strut length=radius x chord factor
For example, to solve for a:

x=10 cm. x .34862
x=3.4862 cm.
x=3.5 cm. (rounded off)

To solve for b:

x=10 cm. x .40355
x=4.0355 cm.
x=4.0 cm. (rounded off)

To solve for c:

x=10 cm. x .41241
x=4.1241 cm.
x=4.1 cm. (rounded off)

We give the frequency and name of the polyhedron, its chord factors, edge lengths, numbers of triangles needed, and kinds of triangles in a blueprint that we will call a geodesic schematic. Fig. 4.8 gives the geodesic schematic for our model. This is an adaptation of the information that would be given for the construction of a 3-frequency geodesic dome.

Notice that the blueprint includes only the information for one face. Because the icosahedron is a symmetric figure with all faces con-

Below:
Fig. 4.8   The geodesic schematic for a 3-frequency geodesic icosahedron.

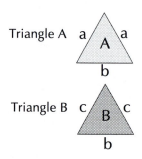

Geodesic Schematic
for a
3-frequency icosahedron

Chord Factors	Edge Lengths	Triangles Needed
a=.34862	a=3.5cm.	A=60
b=.40355	b=4.0cm.	B=120
c=.41241	c=4.1cm.	

Triangle A

Triangle B

gruent we need only look at one. We are now ready to construct a 3-frequency geodesic icosahedron.

Preparation
1. Duplicate triangle A 60 times.
2. Duplicate triangle B 120 times.
3. You should now have a total of 180 triangles.

Assembly
1. Join nine triangles together into a unit cluster according to the geodesic schematic.
2. Repeat this 19 more times, until you have a total of 20.
3. Join five of the unit clusters together at a single vertex. This makes a single cap. Build onto this group by finding a place where the next unit cluster will go. Try making each type triangle a different color.

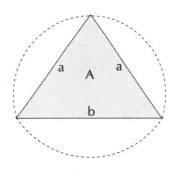

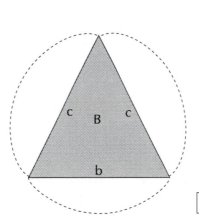

Above:
Lloyd Stranahan, engineer. A model of a 3-frequency geodesic icosahedron made of drinking straws and string.

Left:
Fig. 4.9 A and B Templates of the triangles needed to construct a 3-frqequency geodesic icosahedron.

Top:
Triangle A
You will need 60 of these (three per face.)

Bottom:
Triangle B
You will need 120 of these (six per face.)

Nature's Architecture: The Spheres of Biology

In Chapter 1, we compared those branches of science that study the history of the life of our earth to the facets of a diamond. In this chapter, we liken the study of life forms on earth to a seed pod with bodies of varying sizes and functions germinating inside of it. Biology is that part of science which is interested in the mystery of organisms, the living systems of plants and animals. Because this is such a vast and complex area, encased within the pod are two large seeds which represent the two main categories of biology. They are botany, the study of plants, and zoology, the study of animals.

Within the seeds of botany and zoology, there are two large bodies which represent the two different approaches of study. One is morphological, and as such, is concerned with the form, or structure, of organisms, and the other is physiological, concentrating on the functioning of the systems. It is not uncommon, however, for these bodies to meld, and research includes both the structural and functional aspects of the organisms.

Enclosed within morphology and physiology are smaller bodies which represent the particular fields of biology. For example, embedded in zoology, and inside the body of morphology, one finds the field of anatomy, which is concerned with the structure of an organism, as it is studied by dissection. Embedded in botany, and inside the body of physiology one finds the field of plant physiology.

In both of the seeds of biology, one might find the melding of the bodies of morphology and physiology. In this case, the fields include: biochemistry, which is concerned with atoms and molecules; cytology, which encompasses the study of cells as fundamental building units; histology, which concerns itself with the grouping of similar cells into tissues; and the field of genetics which concerns itself with the heredity of organisms.

Embedded within each of the fields, are the smallest bodies of the pod. These are the numerous entities which represent even more specific areas of investigation, such as bacteriology, the study of bacteria and icthyology, the study of fish. Finally, if one were to meld together the seeds of botany and zoology, the bodies of morphology and physiology, the fields, and the entities, one finds ecology, the heart of the pod, which is the study of groups of organisms and their environments.

Before we continue, let us remind you once again that science is that arena of investigation which embraces probability and not certainty. Scientists deal with observable phenomena in the material world. Data replaces absolute fact and theory replaces absolute truth. When new theories are formulated, some of the older ones become obsolete. The information that we present here is, to the best of our knowledge, current. Magazines and journals which come out more frequently than books are the best sources for the latest findings.

Above:
Artistic interpretation of the spheres of biology.

The Circle of Life

Above:
Gilah Yelin Hirsch. The Du-ality of At-one-ment. Oil on canvas, 21/2' round, 1979. Artistic interpretation of a DNA molecule.

When one steps into the circle of life, one steps into a sphere of intrigue. From its elusive definition, to its synthetically unattainable repro-duction, the matter of life has been cloaked in mystery since the begin-ning of time. While to date, we can-not create life in the laboratory, we can alter some aspects of it. The assumption is that these alterations are for the good; however, we must be aware that in some hands, this can be perilous. Recall Victor Fran-kenstein and his monster.

While we do not know the rea-sons for life, we do know that it has meaning, and that it matters. We know that it is the result of organiza-tion and chemical reaction, and as such, we can determine its existence. We can also measure the extent of its organization, and use the results to classify its constituent members into levels, from higher-to-lower, accord-ing to the complexity of the structure and function of its smallest, most basic units. No matter how simple or complex, however, we can be certain that all life, as all non-life, begins with the dance of the atoms.

When one speaks of life, one speaks of the cell, for the cell is the fundamental building unit of life, each one built up from particular

Elements and Molecules of Life

Major Elements		Weight %	Trace Elements		Weight %
Oxygen	(O)	65%	Potassium	(K)	—
Carbon	(C)	18%	Sulfur	(S)	—
Hydrogen	(H)	10%	Sodium	(Na)	—
Nitrogen	(N)	3%	Chlorine	(Cl)	—
Calcium	(Ca)	2%	Magnesium	(Mg)	—
Phosphorus	(P)	1%	Iron	(Fe)	—
	Total	99%	Copper	(Cu)	—
			Manganese	(Mn)	—
			Cobalt	(Co)	—
			Zinc	(Zn)	—
				Total	Less than 1%

Molecules

Lipids	(C, H, O, P)	1%
Carbohydrates	(C, H, O)	4%
Proteins	(C, H, O, N, S)	7%
Nucleic acids	(C, H, O, N, P)	1.5%
Water	(H_2O)	75-90%
Electrolytes *	(Na, Mg, P, S, Cl, K, Ca)	1.5%
Other inorganic compounds		Less than 1%

*Electrolytes are compounds that dissolve in water. As they do so, they release positive and negative ions that charge the water so that an electrical current can pass through it. Sour tasting acids release +H ions as they decompose. Bitter tasting bases release negative ions into the water. When acids and bases react chemically, they form salts.

The concentration of positive and negative ions is measured in pH units. The composition of these units is vital to the structure and function of a living system. Even slight shifts in pH levels can cause damage and sometimes death to the organism.

atoms clustered into molecules. The chart at the top of this page lists those elements and molecules that are most often found in the composition of all living things. It is important to remember that although these are present whenever there is life, particular combinations are specific to particular types of organisms. As a result, the percentages at which they are found, can and do, vary.

Although there are many different molecules found in all of the different life forms here on earth, none are found more frequently than the five basic molecules that we will discuss here. They are: lipids; carbohydrates; proteins; nucleic acids; and water. You may recall that we previously discussed the significance of water in Chapter 2. Interestingly enough, with the exception of water, all of these molecules are organic, and of those that are, all have carbon atoms in their structures. The charts on pages 205-207 show an artistic representation of a plant and an animal cell with details.

These facing pages: Munching out on the molecules. Some of those foods which are necessary for our good health.

The Lipids

At the simplest level of molecular organization, the lipid group contains the fats that most cells store as reserved energy. These molecules can also act as insulators and shock absorbers when deposited just under the skin and around internal organs. As a rule, saturated fats, such as those found in red meats are difficult to break down, and as such, should be consumed in moderation. On the other hand, unsaturated fats, such as those found in olive oil and other polyunsaturated vegetable oils are liquid at room temperature, and may actually aid in the decomposition of saturated fats.

At a more complex level of organization, we encounter the phospholipids which can be found in the structure of many cell membranes, and as the natural emulsifiers that prevent the separation of the substances in the aqueous solution within the cell. The phospholipids also play an important part in respiration and fat metabolism, the building up or breaking down of molecules. They also appear as enzyme activators, enzymes being the molecules that initiate most of the cellular chemical reactions necessary for life.

Also found at this level of complexity are the steroids. Cholesterol, one of the better known steroids, makes its presence in the heart, blood vessels and the liver. As you have seen, the lipid group is a diversified collection of molecules. There is, however, one characteristic that binds them together as a group. This is, that for the most part, they are all insoluble in water, but are soluble in fat solvents.

The Carbohydrates

Most of the energy that is required for cellular activity comes from that group of molecules known as carbohydrates. These are the sugars, such as glucose, fructose, and lactose. The solar energy absorbed by plants is converted and then is stored as carbohydrates. It is for this reason that plants are a major source of energy for *all* cells. Macromolecules of complex sugars are found in plants stored as starches and in their cell walls as cellulose. Through digestion, all complex sugars are broken down into simple sugars, the only form of carbohydrates that can be absorbed by the cells and then converted back into energy. Cellulose, however, cannot be digested so it becomes roughage and is excreted.

Some sugars are sweet to the taste and others are not. For example, lactose, a complex sugar found in the milk of all mammals is not sweet. The simple sugars, glucose and fructose, found in fruits and honey are sweet, glucose being less sweet than fructose. Glucose, sometimes referred to as dextrose or blood sugar, is also found in the bloodstream of animals. Sucrose, another complex sugar, found in sugar cane and sugar beets is sweet.

The Proteins

While all of the "molecules of life" are said to be essential to all living systems, the proteins are believed to be the most fundamental of these building units. Derived from the Greek word, *proteios*, meaning

"first rank", the name protein aptly describes the significance of this dual-roled group, as they play a part in both the structure and function of the cells in all living systems. In the structure of animals, they can be found in skin, bone and muscle, and in both plants and animals they are the catalysts, or activators, of the timely functioning of cells. These are the enzyme proteins that are responsible for the initiation of chemical reaction. Performing in this capacity, they determine metabolism and the formation of tissue, they give motion, and they protect organisms from harmful invasion by building up immunity systems.

The Nucleic Acids

While proteins can act as the catalysts that trigger essential chemical reactions inside living systems, it is the nucleic acids that determine the sequential structure, and therefore the ultimate functioning of the proteins. There are two different forms of nucleic acids, the first of which is called deoxyribonucleic acid, or DNA, and the second ribonucleic acid, or RNA. The chemical compositions of these macromolecules differ in the types of sugars that are found in them. One is called deoxyribose, and is specific to deoxyribonucleic acid, DNA, and the other is ribose, which is found in ribonucleic acid, RNA.

It is the awesome responsibilty of DNA and RNA molecules to collectively function as the perpetuators of life. They do so by the determination and facilitation of the synthesis, or construction, of proteins. The manner in which they do this expresses the most significant and extensive process of molecular pairing found in biology, whereby one molecule will bond only with a specific, complementary molecule.

DNA is often referred to as the basic molecule of life. When used in this context, the word basic does not suggest simplicity, but rather describes the primary importance of DNA as it functions as a master plan in all living things. In addition to having the capability to duplicate itself during cell reproduction, this double helix carries the encoded instructions for the sequencing of all proteins. The nitrogenous bases of the molecule function as a type of quality control, ensuring the follow-through of directions.

While DNA represents a master plan, RNA can be likened to the construction crew that builds the proteins. There are three different types of RNA, ribisomal (rRNA), messenger (mRNA) and transfer (tRNA), each one having a specific task. It is the duty of ribisomal-RNA to prepare the protein construction site by joining with existing proteins to act as building tools. Messenger-RNA carries a transcription of the encoded DNA instructions to the construction site and then functions as a template for the sequencing of amino acids. Finally, transfer-RNA transports the amino acids to the site so that they can be utilized in protein synthesis.

203

All living organisms are composed of the same basic materials enclosed in the cellular units. This material is called protoplasm, and it is a semi-fluid substance which contains molecules and particles of various sizes, in conjunction with water. The smallest particles mix homogeneously with the water to form a solution. The mid-sized particles float in the water to form a colloidal substance, and finally, the largest particles settle out to form a suspension.

We call protoplasm the material of life because it is the organization and interactions of its constituent parts that ultimately result in the characteristics of life. Biologists do not know how this occurs, but they none-the-less constantly strive to find the answers that will unlock the mystery of life. Until that time comes, however, if ever it does, life will come only from life, in a sequence that has not been broken.

The protoplasm of the cell is bound in an ultrathin, bilayered sheath called the plasma membrane. This covering selectively governs the intake, secretion and excretion of cell products. The plasma membrane alone separates the cells in an animal. Plant cells, however, have rigid, nonliving cellulose walls just outside of their membranes. The organization of the protoplasm inside the plasma membrane is specific to the type of cell and organism it is in.

In some cells, this life supporting mixture is separated between the nucleus and the cell proper. The protoplasm within the nucleus is called nucleoplasm, and it is enclosed in a nuclear membrane. It contains small bodies called nucleoli, and a chromatin material that forms into discrete chromosomes when the cell prepares to reproduce. The number of chromosomes formed is dependent upon the type of organism the cell is in.

The protoplasm within the cell proper is called cytoplasm. This is a somewhat translucent material that contains bodies of various sizes. The material closest to the cell membrane is thicker than that found in the center of the cell. When it is around the edge, it is said to be in a gel state, and it is called ectoplasm. When it is in the center, it is said to be in a sol state, and it is called endoplasm. The bodies found within the cytoplasm vary with different species of plants and animals.

The chart on page 205 illustrates what a generalized plant cell might look like and contain. The one on pages 206 and 207 shows the generalized form and content of an animal cell. It is important to remember that all cells will vary according to their specific functions and the type of organism.

Below:
A cluster of spherical cactus plants.

Artistic Interpretation of a Generalized Plant Cell

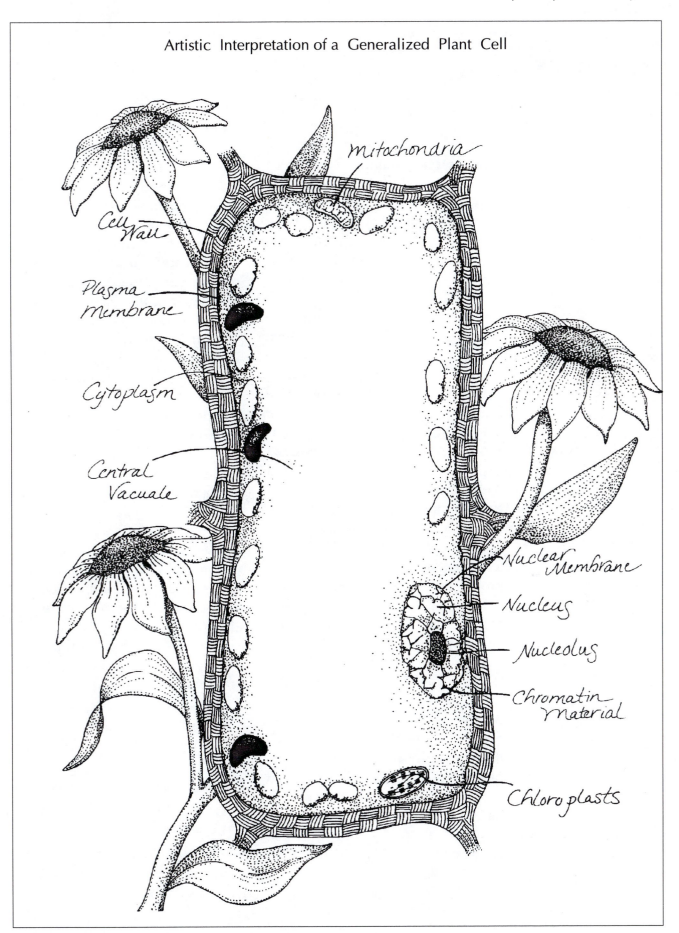

Animal Architecture

Our planet with its spatial dimensions of three, its gravity, its light to dark relationship, its seasons, in short, everything that makes for earth effects the evolution of all. Despite the diversity of animal species, there are only a few basic body armatures. Externally, species differ, but internally at the cellular level there is similarity. Size is the most important factor in the structure. The larger the organism, the more capabilities there are for specialization, but size also has a down side. Bigger is not necessariy better. As size increases, there is a greater problem of support for the animals. A size change requires a different locomotion system. All large creatures require muscles and these, in turn, require a skeletal structure for support. The unicellular protozoans succeed just as well as the elephant. Perhaps, even better, since nobody wants to hunt the protozoan into extinction. Habitats exist for all sizes and species evolve in relation to their habitats. Size either restricts or allows for complexity of the organs and tissues.

Cells are samll. At the cellular level, the larger the cell the more organelles can be allowed. An organelle is a specialized part of a cell that resembles and functions like an organ. An organ is a differentiated part of an organism, a living individual be it plant or animal, which is adapted for a specific function. A cell is the smallest structural unit of an organism that is capable of independent functioning.

Cell Size: Fifty white blood cells laid end to end would be no bigger than this period (.) This is an average size cell. In animals, the lower limit in size for a cell is a sac with a membrane large enough to hold a strand of nucleic acid and enough ribosomes to make the essential polypeptides. This size might be 3 micrometers in diameter.

The small size is an advantage to to cell because there is a large surface area compared to the contained volume. This is expressed as a ratio- surface: volume.

The area for exchange between the inside and outside of the cell is great. This allows for the cell to obtain nutrients and rid itself of water.

The small size allows for the interior of the cell to be close to the outer membrane. This allows for efficient internal communication between components within the cell and it allows for an efficient exchange of communication within its total environment.

Components of a cell:
1. plasma membrane
2. protoplasm which contains molecules and H_2O
3. nucleus which contains nucleoplasm which contains the genes
4. nucleoli are small bodies within the nucleus
5. chromosomes are inside the nucleus when the cell is ready to divide.

Artistic Interpretation of a Generalized Animal Cell

In order for an organism to qualify as living, it must be able to metabolize, grow, reproduce, respond to stimuli, and adapt to environmental circumstances. In order for the cell to qualify, it, too, must possess the same five characteristics, and it does. Each cell is capable of carrying out the above-mentioned prerequisites of life.

There is a direct relationship between the size of the cell and its function. When small, the surface area is many times greater than its volume. This is expressed as a ratio of surface area:volume. Thus, the area of exchange for obtaining nutrients and eliminating wastes is greater at the smaller size. This is most efficient. Also, the interior of the cell is in close proximity to its surface, making for efficient internal communication. No elaborate system is required to facilitate this communication. The typical cell is so small that a cluster of fifty of them would fit in the period at the end of this sentence.

The greatest number of living organisms, invisible to the naked eye, are composed of a single cell. Bacteria, protozoa, and yeast are in this count. These unicellular entities can all reproduce. Some of them live in total independence, as in the case of the protozoa, which group into colonies of cells that do not need to interact. Some of them, however, require host organisms to supply their nutritional needs. An example of these are the disease causing bacteria of pneumonia.

Procaryotric cells, such as those found in the unicellular bodies of bacteria, are most primitive with no real separation of constituent parts. Eukaryotic cells, which are found in the unicellular bodies of protozoa and yeast, and the multicellular organisms of most algae, and all of the higher plants and animals are another matter. Here, the protoplasm is separated into a distinct nucleus and cytoplasm.

While the sphere is a perfect form for unicellular plants and animals, it is not an especially suitable shape for larger, multicellular life forms that have directed locomotion. Rather, a complicated organism, such as a cat, a dog, or a human being, is the result of a cooperative venture among great numbers of spherical cells that combine to form other shapes. The more cells the organism has, the more sophisticated its living mechanism, the higher it ranks in the classifications of life.

As similar cells group, tissue is formed into structures such as muscles, bones, and blood. When tissues begin to organize, the results are the organs that perform specialized tasks, such as the brain, heart, and stomach. When organs interact, the results are organ systems, such as the human digestive system which involves the mouth, esophagus, stomach, intestines, liver, and pancreas. Finally, it is the organization and the interacting of the functions of the organ systems that give life to the multicellular organism.

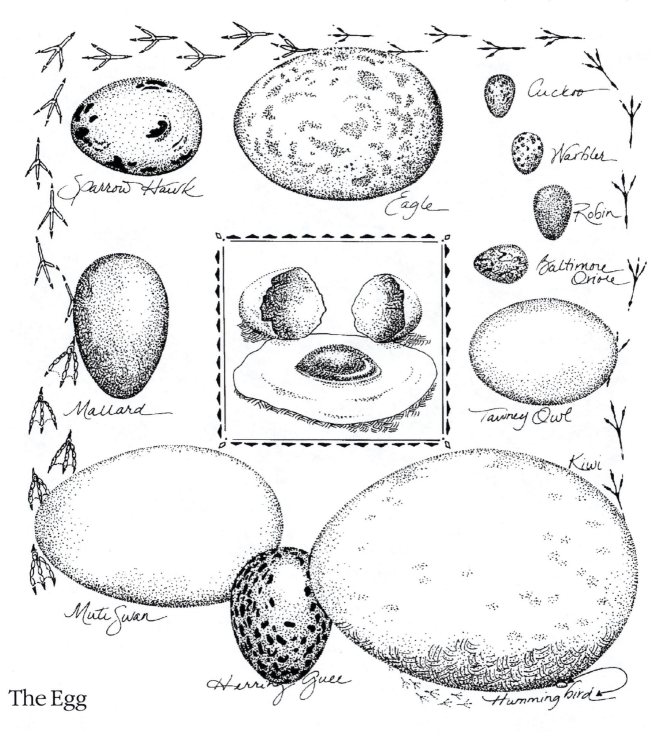

Sparrow Hawk

Eagle

Cuckoo

Warbler

Robin

Baltimore Oriole

Mallard

Tawney Owl

Kiwi

Mute Swan

Herring Gull

Humming bird

The Egg

Although many animals, such as, human beings, reptiles, and sharks produce eggs in a wide range of sizes and shapes, it is the egg of our fine feathered friends that we highlight, here. The yolk of a bird's egg is a single cell that is easily seen with the naked eye. Most of its mass is stored food, and if removed, the cell would shrink to typical size.

Each egg begins its development as a sphere, that wonderfully conservative shape that allows maximum volume for the minimum surface area. Muscular contractions of the bird modify this perfect form as it is squeezed through the oviduct. Although some remain completely spherical, others compress into the familiar ovoid form, among others.

Above:
Drawings of the egg of various creatures.

209

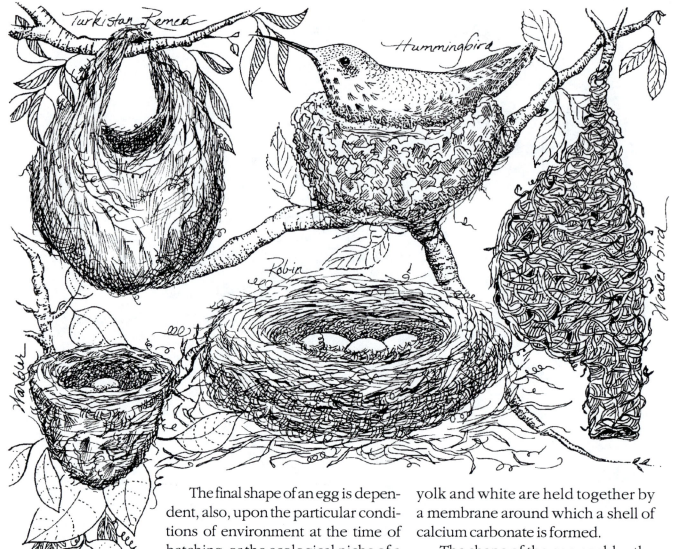

Turkistan Remez

Hummingbird

Robin

Weaver Bird

Marbler

Baltimore Oriole

Above:
Drawing of nesting birds.

The final shape of an egg is dependent, also, upon the particular conditions of environment at the time of hatching, or the ecological niche of a particular species. Eggs that rest safely in a nest can retain a form that rolls very easily, but the ovoid shape allows the parent to arrange them with their smaller ends toward the center of the nest so that they fit together better and the heat of the nesting bird is more evenly distributed. If the egg is to be incubated on a rocky ledge, it has to have a shape that prevents it from rolling off. A top-like form may result.

The egg is a natural package. It contains all the necessary food and water for the developing embryo. The yolk contains protein, fat, vitamins and some minerals. The albumen, or egg white, holds reserve water. The yolk and white are held together by a membrane around which a shell of calcium carbonate is formed.

The shape of the egg enables the shell to perform other functions beyond simple containment. The curved surface distributes pressure from the outside much the way an arch carries an architectural load. Therefore, in spite of its thinness, it can resist fracture due to compression, which means it has the strength to hold up to the weight of the incubating parent. This external strength also helps give it protection from predators. The same shape, however, that gives the egg strength from the outside makes it weak from the inside. Because of this, it can be easily shattered by the force of the beak when the time comes for the young one to peck its way out.

The egg is both an actuality of life and a symbol of it. Egg decorating has a long history in the cultures of many European and Asian countries. The Ancient Romans decorated eggs and, in fact, the oldest known example dates from the 4th century A.D., and was found in a sarcophagus.

Today the people of Poland and the Ukraine carry on the tradition of intricate egg decoration. Given on Easter morning, the egg is a symbol of all of nature's fertility. Ukrainian folk lore has it that the decorated eggs, particularly the red ones, are a protection from evil and a guarantee of the very existence of the world. A simple, single colored one is given to be eaten, while the time-consuming decorated examples are meant to be displayed. The images on these eggs allude to time honored natural forms, such as, plants, roosters, flowers, birds, and geometric configurations that suggest natural elements.

Early pagan practices have been incorporated into later Christian ones, and today in many cultures, at Easter, eggs of chickens, ducks, and geese are decorated with dyes and added elements. They are given as a way to bring attention to, and to celebrate the season of beginnings and renewed hope. On the following pages we shall look at some methods that can be used to transform natural eggs into art objects, suitable for sharing at any time of the year.

Above:
Unadorned chicken eggs and decorated ones.
The Czechoslovakian eggs are patterned by applying small pieces of straw to the dyed surface. Try a variation using self-adhesive contact paper or graphic tapes instead of the straw.

211

Initial Egg Preparation

There are several different ways to prepare eggs for decoration, and the intended use should be taken into consideration. Regardless, the surface should be clean and grease free. If the egg is to be eaten, simply hardboil it as usual.

If the egg is to be kept for display, there are three different approaches you can take. One is to hardboil it for a half an hour. This will prevent the egg from spoiling, and the egg will have a sturdiness that will help prevent breakage as you work. The surface of a boiled egg will take dye more easily.

Another approach is to blow out the inside of the egg. This is done by piercing both ends with a needle, "scrambling" the egg by inserting the needle into the yolk and rotating it several times, and then blowing into one end so that the contents come out the other. This process requires patience and can make your jaws very sore, but the advantage is that you can attach a hanger to the egg. The pinholes are easily concealed with wax or whatever material you apply to the egg.

The Ukrainians simply wash the eggs and decorate them as is. Over time, exposure to the air will cause the contents to dry out, and the egg will last for a very long time. If you use this method, be sure to store or display the egg in such a way as to allow the air to circulate about it.

Decorating Suggestions for Dyed Eggs

To color eggs, use commercial egg dyes or the more brilliant packaged fabric dyes, or try some found-around-the-house natural ones. To use natural dyes, try tea, coffee, beet juice, spinach, or onion skins. Boil the material until the desired color is achieved. Strain the liquid through cheese cloth to obtain a clear solution. Add some vinegar to the dye bath to increase the luminosity of the colors.

Place the egg in the dye bath until the desired color is achieved. Darker colors require a much longer time in the bath. Some can take an hour or more.

Dry the egg thoroughly. Rub a drop of salad oil onto the entire surface to preserve the color and add a lustre to it. Although relatively easy to make, these dyed eggs can be brilliantly beautiful.

The Patterned Colored Egg

This process requires time and forethought. In many ways it is similar to the design process used in creating the temari balls. This time, though, the pattern is produced by dividing an ovoid form into sections and developing pattern components within those areas. One could simply use a random approach to pattern, but systematic preparation is needed for a more structured pattern.

Partitioning the egg into design "fields" is both a mathematical and an artistic problem. What types of symmetric divisions does the egg lend itself to? All planes of symmetry pass through the egg lengthwise, so congruent areas can be obtained by drawing the equivalent of great circles (great ovoids?) through both ends of the egg. Fig. 5.12 illustrates some ways to subdivide the surface to prepare it for design elements. A piece of string wrapped around the egg can act as a guide for drawing lines.

Lightly pencil the major divisions of your pattern onto the egg surface.

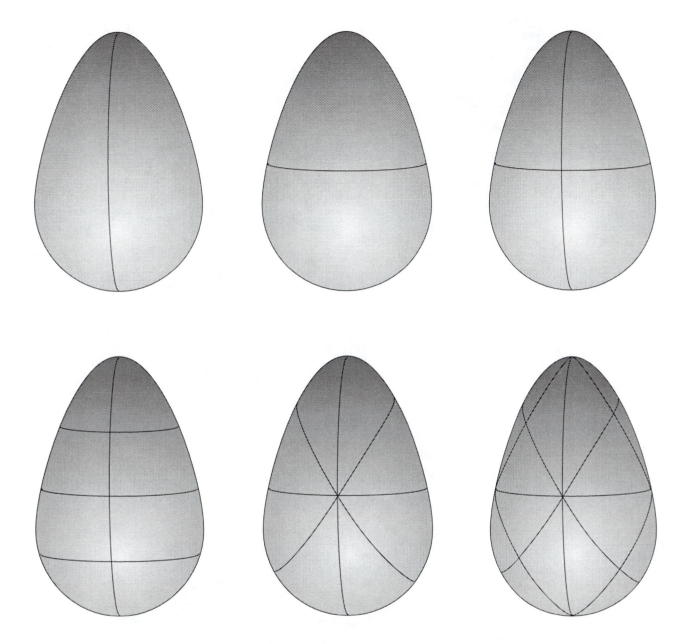

Do not erase the pencil lines or they will cause smudging. Wash off if necessary and start again. Draw the design on with wax crayons or wax pencils. Dip the egg into the dye solution until the desired color is obtained. This is one of the simplest ways to obtain what is called a wax resist design. Where there are crayon or pencil marks, the dye will not adhere. If you want to get involved with more complex processes, see the books listed in the Further Reading section.

Displaying the Egg

When your eggs are thoroughly dry, they can displayed in a variety of ways. Group several of them in a basket or wooden bowl. Hang them individually by inserting christmas tree ornament hangers at one end. Set them up on a stand. Or make a wooden tree with branches from which to hang the eggs. Whichever method you choose, keep them out of direct sunlight to prevent the colors from fading.

Above:
Fig. 4.10 Some ways to subdivide the egg into design areas. Photocopy the above and try some surface decorations of your own.

This page:
Students works. Decorated eggs using acrylic paint or ceramic paint, glitter, and permanent markers.
These were not easy to do. Patience is the key.

This page:
The shapes of the ceramic artworks are reminiscent of the egg. Potter Leslie Thompson of California combines a natural material, clay, with forms suggestive of those found in nature and enhancesthe surface with geometric patterns that solve the mathematical problem of tiling a curved surface.

The Vegreville Egg

Above:
An overall view of the Vegreville egg in a public park in Vegreville, Canada.

If one is not a bird, how does one go about constructing a form that would have the shape of an egg, but not its contents? In 1974, such a problem was presented to artist/geometer/computer designer, Ron Resch. His interest was to combine theoretical geometry with a real world situation. This sculptural undertaking was rather unusual, since the task of producing eggs is usually left to the biological processes of the female of the species.

Undaunted by this limitation and innocent to the mighty task he had undertaken, Resch thought that constructing an egg would be fairly easy, based on the belief that there had been a major body of research done on the morphology of eggs. Wrong! While it takes about twenty-four hours for a hen to form an egg, it took him two years and 12,000 man-hours to solve this problem. The egg he eventually built was a thirty-one foot, two thousand pound ovoid.

Let us back up a minute. Why was he given this task in the first place? In Alberta, Canada in the very small town of Vegreville, fifty-five miles east of Edmonton, the townspeople wished to celebrate the centennial year of the Royal Canadian Mounted Police by erecting an appropriate monument. An equestrian statue could have been the first thing that came to mind. But no. The ultimate choice was to have a sculpture in the form of a painted pysanki, the traditional decorated Easter egg of the Ukrainian people. The decision was related to the fact that the regional population is of that heritage.

The final solution that Ron Resch

Above:
Two views of the Vegreville egg. Notice the tiling units and how the straight edges are abutted to create the curvature of the form.

arrived at, after much deliberation, false starts and experimentation, was to enclose a volume of space with tiles designed with the traditional pysanki patterns in mind. A plane surface is a relatively easy tiling problem, but an egg is a continuously changing surface. What kinds of tiles can cover this form and leave no gaps? Resch's interest was both practical and economical. He wanted to use the fewest number of different tile shapes that could articulate the egg form.

He reached for the basic tile unit of the equilateral triangle. There are 2,208 congruent equilateral triangles and 524 star shapes developed from equilateral but nonregular hexagons on the egg. These vary in width depending upon their position on the surface. The angle at which each tile is joined to another varies from less than one degree at the widest point in the middle of the egg to only seven degrees at the pointed end. Thus, the appearance of the egg is smooth despite the fact that it is composed of the flat polygonal tiles.

Ultimately, in six weeks, he and his assistants painted and constructed the first internally braced architectural shell in which the surface closes in on itself. It is built out of two and a half tons of anodized aluminum in bronze, gold, and silver. The egg measures 25.7 feet long and 18.3 feet wide. Instead of resting securely in a nest, it is mounted on a base that allows it to swing freely when buffeted by the severe winds typical of the region. It stands alone on the flat plane of a city park. Perhaps it waits for Ron Resch to create the chicken that laid it.

Problems

1. Find the surface area and volume of a sphere that has a radius of twenty meters.

2. Draw a diagram similar to the one in the chart on page 185 that would indicate the location of a point on a sphere that is 35° South and 120° East.

3. Construct a Neo-Geo-Sphere out of bristol board.

4. Construct a model of a 2-frequency geodesic dome from an icosahedron such that the radius of the circumsphere is twelve centimeters. Chord factors are:

a=.546533
b=.618034

5. Research the use, versatility, and applicability of the geodesic dome. Write up your findings.

6. Research the architecture of various nomadic cultures that use a hemi-sphere as the basis for their building structures. Do a written and visual comparison of their dwellings. Be concerned with how the practical impacts the aesthetic.

7. Research the dome architecture of the church of Hagia Sophia as well as the onion domes found in the architecture of Russia. Compare and contrast them through the building of three-dimensional models of aspects of the architecture.

8. Subdivide the surface of a natural or a plastic egg into four congruent areas. Add further subdivisions of your own choosing to define areas that you would find interesting as an armature for a decorated egg.

9. Develop a system for locating points on an ovoid surface?

10. Research the work of the followers of Buckminster Fuller. How have his ideas been changed?

11. Find the radius of a sphere that has a volume of 729 cubic inches.

12. Find the radius of a hemisphere that has a volume of 16 cm^3.

13. Research the habitats, nests, eggs, feeding habits, etc. of three different bird species. Document your findings through drawings, collage, and writings.

Projects

1. Construct a Neo-Geo-Sphere and transform it into a hanging ornament. Or develop a large hanging sculpture for an interior space.

2. Construct an ovoid form for use as a sculptural work using unusual materials. Develop openings within the form to let light become part of the work.

3. Do a painting on a sphere based on the concept of temari pattern.

4. Use the concept of temari patterns and beads and glue to completely cover a sphere in a mosaic fashion.

5. Research the sizes, patterns, and shapes of eggs of a variety of species of birds. Use this information as a basis for a two or three-dimensional artwork.

6. Build a geodesic dollhouse. Give it a floor plan and landscape the exterior.

7. Use sugar cubes and/or styrofoam to create a model of an igloo after you have researched its form.

8. Use the idea of a geodesic polyhedron to construct a prototype for a carnival ride. Build it out of recycled materials.

Above:
Metal Ornament. Sphere with open meshwork.

9. Using a hemisphere and the concept of spherical tilings, design a fantasy hat that celebrates a specific event.

10. Use broken pieces of eggshells to create an elegant decorative pin or brooch designed in the shape of a rooster, hen, or an egg.

11. Construct a hanging container in the form of an egg using only found natural materials.

12. Create a Global Village Using Geodesic forms.

Using the following "Baker's Clay" recipe, construct a group of geodesic or hemispheric forms that become the basis for an architectural complex. Place these forms in a setting of your own design and construction. Be as realistic or as fantastic as you choose. You might like to do some research into tribal architecture before you begin this project.

4 cups flour
1 cup table salt
1 1/2 cups water (approx.)
2 Tbs. oil (approx.)

Mix together thorougly and knead until smooth and pliable. Keep in a plastic bag in order to prevent the materials from drying out.

You will also need:

beaten egg (optional)
small amount of milk, regular or evaporated (optional)
round baking bowls for armatures of hemispheres (optional)
tacky white glue
acrylic paints
tin foil to line baking sheets
a rolling pin
templates for your pattern pieces
small knife for cutting out the pattern pieces
items that you might want to embed into the dough before baking or glue on after baking.

Roll and cut out the necessary pieces for your models. Place on foil lined baking sheets. Bake at 300-350° for at least one hour so that dough dries out thoroughly. If you like a brown color, brush with milk or beaten egg, or evaporated milk. This will also make your pieces shiny. Assemble in the particular environment that you have created.

Further Reading

Ball, W. W. R. *Mathematical Recreations and Essays*, revised by H. S. M. Coxeter. New York: McMillian, 1967.

Hoffman, Paul. *Archimedes' Revenge: The Joys and Perils of Mathematics*. New York: W. W. Norton and Company, Inc., 1988.

Herder and Herder. *Decorating Eggs*. London: Search Press, 1968.

Laycock, Mary. *Bucky for Beginners*. Hayward, California: Activity Resources Company, Inc., 1984.

Luciow, Johanna, Ann Kmit and Loretta Luciow. *Eggs Beautiful*. Minneapolis, Minnesota: Ukrainian Gift Shop, 1980.

Marks, Robert W. *The Dymaxion World of Buckminster Fuller*. Carbondale, Illinois: Southern Illinois University Press, 1960.

Prenis, John (edited by). *The Dome Builder's Handbook*. Philadelphia: Running Press, 1973.

Pugh, Anthony. *Polyhedra a visual approach*. Palo Alto, California: Dale Seymour Publications, 1990.

Wenninger, Magnus J. *Spherical Models*. Cambridge: Cambridge University Press, 1979.

Wood, Mary. *The Craft of Temari*. Turnbridge Wells, England: Search Press Limited, 1991.

5 *Perfect Partnerships*

The concept of complementarity is essential to the world outlook of many cultures — nothing is seen in isolation but always as a duality. Space and form. Gravity and fusion. Sun and moon. Day and night. Winter and summer. Earth and sky. Black and white. Yin and Yang. These are all complementary pairs requiring both partners to be fully understood, as each is seen in relationship to the other. Contemporary science, too, is looking at natural phenomena with this concept in mind. Scientists such as Niels Bohr and Fritjof Capra have turned to Eastern philosophy as a way to model aspects of the physical world.

In Chapter 2 we introduced the equilateral triangle and its offspring, the tetrahedron. In Chapter 3, you met the square, the progenitor of the cube. You also became acquainted with four other regular polygons, the pentagon, the octagon, the hexagon and the dodecagon. Now you will see how all six of these polygons are used to construct a variety of polyhedra. On page 225, we have provided templates for all of these figures.

Give me day
    and I long for night.
Set me steadfast
    before my flight.

Give me youth
    and I long for age.
Give me foolishness
    to offset sage.

Give me heat when
    my heart is moved,
and give me cool when
    my head needs proof.

Give me you when
    I've had enough of me,
and through the two
    comes the Unity.
        Rochelle Newman

Above:
Rochelle Newman. Models. Polyhedra with triangular and square faces. The pattern, developed from an harmonic subdivision of the polygons, reaffirms the number of sides. The unit was designed by hand first, then photocopied onto bristol paper and then joined together, working one vertex at a time.

We will look at the genealogy of polyhedra, from ancestor polygons to polyhedra progeny. Interestingly enough, through particular operations, one form can evolve into another. We will focus upon the complementarity of these manipulations, and the effect that they have upon the polyhedra and their families.

The Regular Polygon

The number of sides   n

The vertex angle $m=\dfrac{(n-2)180}{n}$

The central angle $CA=2\pi/n$

The circumcircle radius $cr=1/2s\ \csc\ \pi/n$

The intercircle radius $itr=1/2s\ \cot\ \pi/n$

The perimeter $P=s\cdot n$

The area $A=1/2itr\ s\cdot n$

Key
n = the number of sides
m = the measure of an interior angle
s = the measure of a side of the polygon

The Polygon and the Polyhedron

Facing page:
A set of polygons that you can use for generating polyhedra.

Try experimenting with combinations of polygons to see what kinds of three-dimensional forms you can construct.

Remember that symmetry does play a very big part in polyhedra.

A polyhedron is composed of a particular type and number of polygons that come together in a particular way to form its vertices, faces and edges. The polygons that we will use as faces are all regular, and as such, have both congruent edge lengths and congruent interior angles. If you recall, they all can be generated with circumscribed circles and perpendicular bisectors. Generated in this way, however, you will have to scale them proportionately if you intend to use them to build models. While each individual polygon will have its eges congruent If If two polygons are inscribed an edge of the polygon with the greater number of edges will be shortenthan an edge of the polygon with fewer sides. The vital statistics of any polygon, and the formulas needed to find, them are given in the chart on this page.

By using diagonals, polygons can be broken down into component isosceles or equilateral triangles. These can then be further subdivided into elemental right triangles. On the facing page there is a set of the six polygon templates for your use. Due to the limited amount of area, however, they are small and should be enlarged proportionately when using them to build models. We also suggest using a heavy weight paper for firm support and a fast drying glue, such as a white tacky type. Work one vertex group at a time, letting it dry throughly before adding the next one to it. As you continue to combine groups, the polyhedron will come together quite miraculously due to the constraints of three-dimensional space.

Polygons for Polyhedra

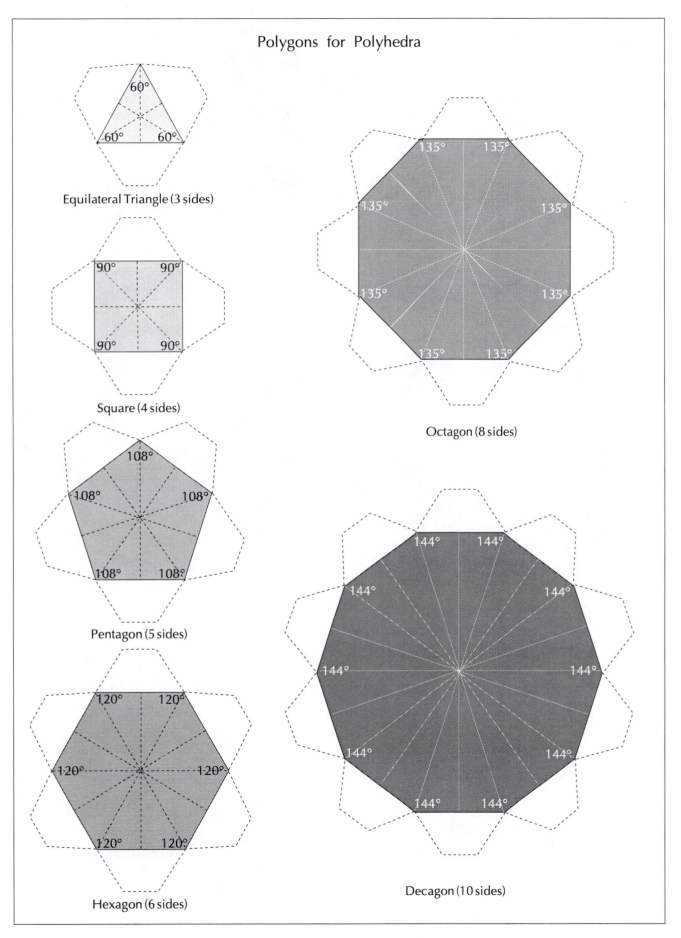

Equilateral Triangle (3 sides)

Square (4 sides)

Pentagon (5 sides)

Hexagon (6 sides)

Octagon (8 sides)

Decagon (10 sides)

This page:
Linda Maddox. Polygonal de-
sign variations. Note that the
edge lengths are not congru-
ent. If you want to use these
as templates, they must be
sized appropriately and glue
tabs must be added.

$$F + V = E + 2$$

Euler's Formula

Mathematicians come in many shapes, sizes, textures, and colors. They come from diverse backgrounds, cultures, and geographic locations. The 18th Century mathematician, Leonhard Euler, came from Basel, Switzerland. Euler, a remarkable individual, worked in every branch of mathematics during his seventy-six year lifetime, and in each of them, his contributions were major.

Despite the fact that he lost one eye at an early age, and the use of the second at age sixty, Euler wrote on algebra, the calculus, and mechanics, among other subjects. His high quality research produced about 800 pages of writing per year, for the greater part of his lifetime, and all without the advantages of a word processor. It would seem that his mathematical quest did not take up all of his time, however, since he also married and helped to produce thirteen children. Was he into Fibonacci numbers? Who knows?

The particular piece of Euler's work that interests us here, appropriately called Euler's Formula, illuminates the connection between the numbers of faces, vertices, and edges of every convex polyhedron. The equation F + V = E + 2, where F= number of faces, V= number of vertices and E = number of edges, gives a product in which the sum of the faces and vertices will always be two more than the edges. Let us look at the tetrahedron and the cube to verify this formula. For the tetrahedron, 4 faces + 4 vertices =8, and 6 edges + 2 =8. For the cube, 6 faces + 8 vertices =14 and 12 edges +2=14. It isevident that by using this formula, the number of faces, vertices, and edges can be found in any particular polyhedron if two of these three variables are known.

Above:
Drawing of Leonhard Euler, 18th Century mathematician.

For the mathematical proof of this theorem, look in any text that gives information on algebraic topololgy or graph theory.

Right:
Fig. 5.1 A-D The radii of circumcircles and intercircles are used to form right triangles which are used in the computation of areas, among other things.

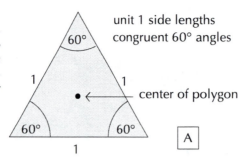

unit 1 side lengths
congruent 60° angles

center of polygon

A

Circumcircles, Intercircles and Triangle Forming Radii

Every regular polygon has a circumcircle and an intercircle. We have used an equilateral triangle with unit 1 edge length and congruent 60° angles as our example (Fig. 5.1 A). The radius of the circumcircle is the angle bisector of the inscribed polygon (Fig. 5.1 B). Notice that the sides of the equilateral triangle are chords of the circumcircle. The radius of the intercircle is the perpendicular bisector of the escribed polygon (5.1 C). Notice that the sides of the equilateral triangle are tangent to the intercircle. Together, the two radii and one-half of a side of the polygon form a right triangle, to which the Pythagorean Theorem can be applied.. Notice that the centers of the circumcircle, the polygon, and the intercircle are coincident with each other. Since the radius of the circumcircle bisects the 60° angle, we get two 30° angles. Because the radius of the intercircle cuts the edge length in half, the right triangle has a side length .5. It is a 30°, 60°, 90° right triangle withside of .5 (Fig. 5.1 D).

This information allows us to use the Pythagorean Theorem to calculate the area of the inscribed polygon, in addition to many other things. We, however, have saved you the aggravation of this lengthy process by calculating the areas of the six regular polygons for you. They are included in the chart on page 229. These are needed if you want to calculate the lateral surface areas and total surface areas of the various polyhedra that we are about to explore.

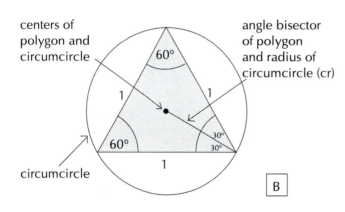

centers of
polygon and
circumcircle

angle bisector
of polygon
and radius of
circumcircle (cr)

circumcircle

B

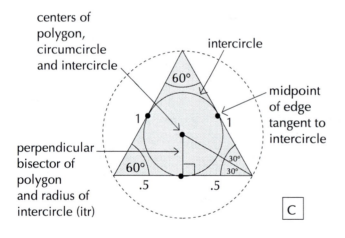

centers of
polygon,
circumcircle
and intercircle

intercircle

midpoint
of edge
tangent to
intercircle

perpendicular
bisector of
polygon
and radius of
intercircle (itr)

C

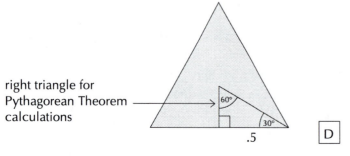

right triangle for
Pythagorean Theorem
calculations

D

Areas of Regular Polygons

$$A = 1/2\ itr\ s\ n$$

Each polygon has its own unit 1 edge length

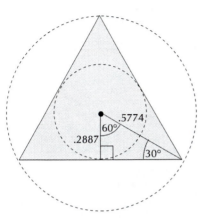

Area of an equilateral triangle:
.4330 square units

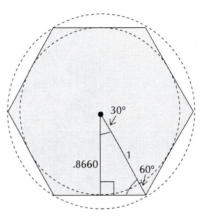

Area of an hexagon:
2.5981 square units

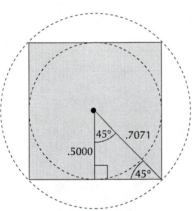

Area of a square:
1.0000 square units

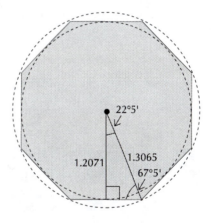

Area of an octagon:
4.8284 square units

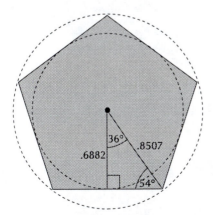

Area of a pentagon:
1.7205 square units

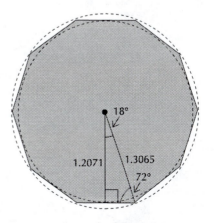

Area of a decagon:
7.6942 square units

This page:
Student works which use a natural theme on the faces of triangles and squares that make up this particular polyhedron. Paper and mixed media.

Top:
Kirk Hansbury

Bottom:
Karen Landry

Polyhedra Clans and Families

Since the subject of polyhedra is vast, for purposes of organization, we would like to introduce our own classification system. It is one that might make for a more user friendly approach to the study of these three-dimensional, multifaceted objects. If you follow the chart on pages 232 and 233, which presents our analysis of the clans and families of polyhedra, and the chart on pages 234 and 235, which illustrates our determination of their lineage, you will have a better understanding of the concept of our system. Notice that each is given a birth name which is sometimes followed by a name of our own notation. Since these forms share the common origin of ancestor polygons, and since they are all three-dimensional figures that completely enclose space without gaps, we have gathered them into a single kingdom of polyhedra. We then divide the realm into the clans of regular, semiregular, vertically regular, and non-regular polyhedra. These groups are then further subdivided into branches of convex and non-concave polyhedra. From there the families are given surnames and each member has an individual identity. Because each family has multiple members, and because some of these memberships are infinite, we will focus only upon a select group of them. All of those that we will look at have a finite number of individuals. These include the Platonic Solids, the Kepler-Poinsot Family, the Archimedean Solids, and the Convex Deltahedra. Although this is a finite collection, each of these could be transformed in a great many ways to produce an endless variety of form variations.

Above:
Student work. Model.
Joe Conselyea. Unadorned polyhedron. Balsa wood and silver automobile tape along the edges. This tape is extremely strong.

Look at what happens at each vertex. Notice the repetition of the particular polygons of squares, triangles and pentagons.

Kingdom of Polyhedra

Regular Clan

Convex
Branch

Concave
Branch

Platonic Solid
Family

Stellated
Family

Tetrahedron

Hexahedron
(Cube)

Octahedron

Dodecahedron
(Regular
Dodecahedron)

Icosahedron
(Regular
Icosahedron)

Kepler
Group

Poinsot
Group

Small Stellated
Dodecahedron

Great
Icosahedron

Great Stellated
Dodecahedron

Great
Dodecahedron

Semiregular Clan

Convex
Branch

Facially Regular
Prism Family

Archimedean
Solid Family

Truncated
Tetrahedron
(Archi 3-6-6)*

Rhombicuboctahedron
(Archi 3-4-4-4)

Truncated Cube
(Archi 3-8-8)

Rhombicosidodecahedron
(Archi 3-4-5-4)

Truncated
Dodecahedron
(Archi 3-10-10)

Icosidodecahedron
(Archi 3-5-3-5)
(Quasiregular)

Truncated
Octahedron
(Archi 4-6-6)

Snub Cuboctahedron
(also called Snub Cube)
(Archi 3-3-3-3-4)

Truncated
Cuboctahedron
(also called
Greater
Rhombicuboctahedron)
(Archi 4-6-8)

Snub Icosidodecahedron
(also called Snub
Dodecahedron)
(Archi 3-3-3-3-5)

Truncated
Icosidodecahedron
(also called Greater
Rhombicosidodecahedron)
(Archi 4-6-10)

Truncated
Icosahedron
(Archi 5-6-6)

Cuboctahedron
(Archi 3-4-3-4)
(Quasiregular)

*This notation indicates the alternate referral name
of the polyhedron, and in some cases, its vertex net

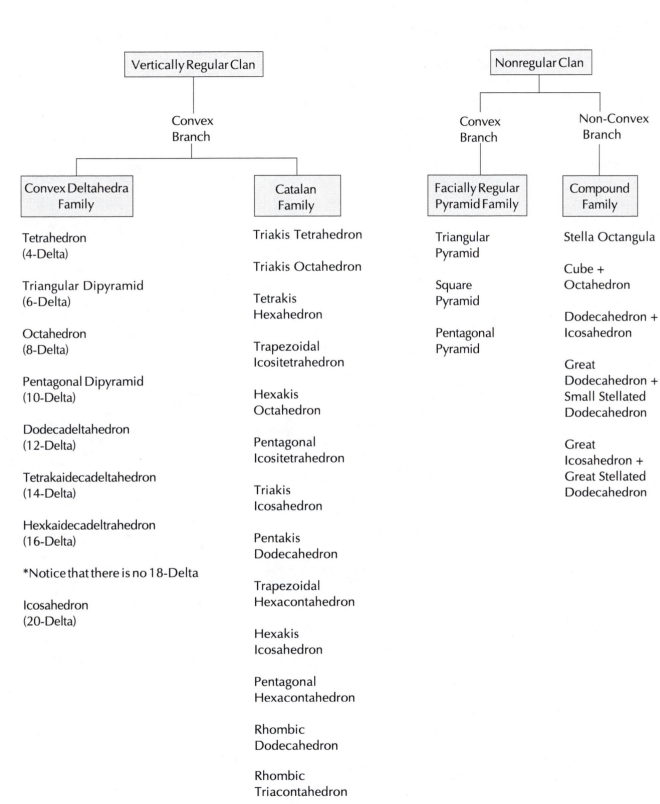

Clan and Family Analysis

Vertically Regular Clan

Convex Branch

Convex Deltahedra Family

Tetrahedron
(4-Delta)

Triangular Dipyramid
(6-Delta)

Octahedron
(8-Delta)

Pentagonal Dipyramid
(10-Delta)

Dodecadeltahedron
(12-Delta)

Tetrakaidecadeltahedron
(14-Delta)

Hexkaidecadeltrahedron
(16-Delta)

*Notice that there is no 18-Delta

Icosahedron
(20-Delta)

Catalan Family

Triakis Tetrahedron

Triakis Octahedron

Tetrakis Hexahedron

Trapezoidal Icositetrahedron

Hexakis Octahedron

Pentagonal Icositetrahedron

Triakis Icosahedron

Pentakis Dodecahedron

Trapezoidal Hexacontahedron

Hexakis Icosahedron

Pentagonal Hexacontahedron

Rhombic Dodecahedron

Rhombic Triacontahedron

Nonregular Clan

Convex Branch

Non-Convex Branch

Facially Regular Pyramid Family

Triangular Pyramid

Square Pyramid

Pentagonal Pyramid

Compound Family

Stella Octangula

Cube + Octahedron

Dodecahedron + Icosahedron

Great Dodecahedron + Small Stellated Dodecahedron

Great Icosahedron + Great Stellated Dodecahedron

Polyhedra Genealogy

This chart indicates which polygons generate particular polyhedra. We consider the equilateral triangle, the square, and the pentagon to be the primal polygons.
The first generation requires only a single polygon.
The second generation requires two types of polygons.
The third generation requires two or three types of polygons.

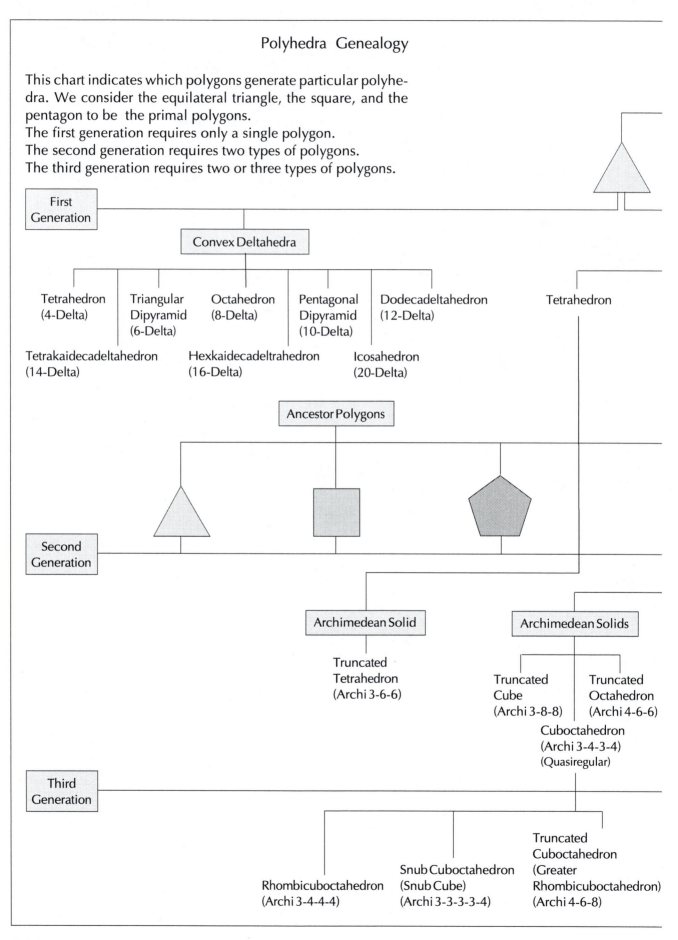

First Generation

Convex Deltahedra

Tetrahedron
(4-Delta)

Triangular
Dipyramid
(6-Delta)

Octahedron
(8-Delta)

Pentagonal
Dipyramid
(10-Delta)

Dodecadeltahedron
(12-Delta)

Tetrahedron

Tetrakaidecadeltahedron
(14-Delta)

Hexkaidecadeltrahedron
(16-Delta)

Icosahedron
(20-Delta)

Ancestor Polygons

Second Generation

Archimedean Solid

Archimedean Solids

Truncated
Tetrahedron
(Archi 3-6-6)

Truncated
Cube
(Archi 3-8-8)

Truncated
Octahedron
(Archi 4-6-6)

Cuboctahedron
(Archi 3-4-3-4)
(Quasiregular)

Third Generation

Rhombicuboctahedron
(Archi 3-4-4-4)

Snub Cuboctahedron
(Snub Cube)
(Archi 3-3-3-3-4)

Truncated
Cuboctahedron
(Greater
Rhombicuboctahedron)
(Archi 4-6-8)

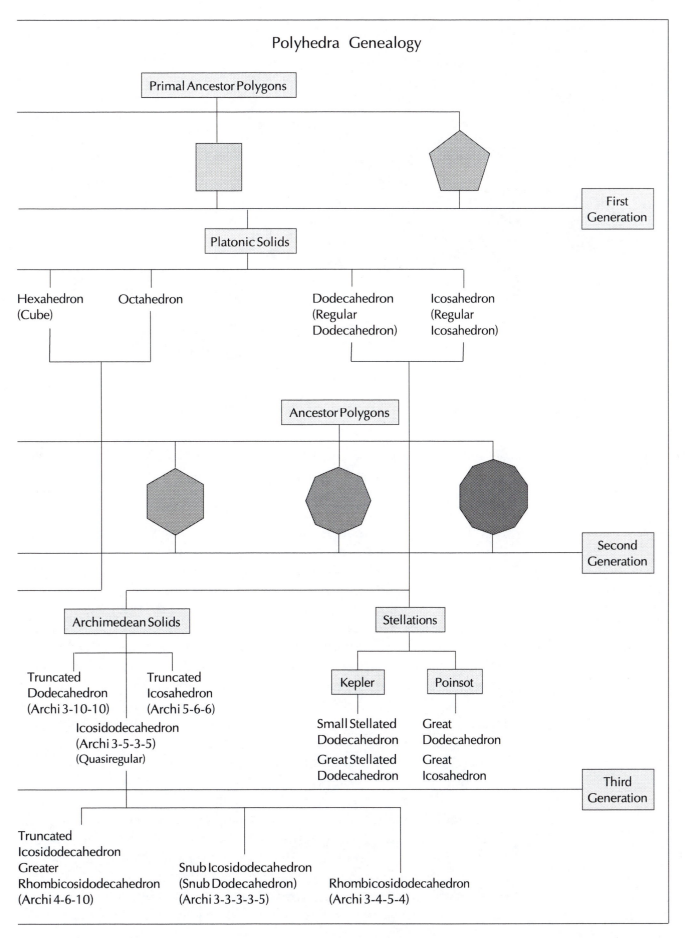

Polyhedra Genealogy

Primal Ancestor Polygons

First Generation

Platonic Solids

Hexahedron (Cube) Octahedron Dodecahedron (Regular Dodecahedron) Icosahedron (Regular Icosahedron)

Ancestor Polygons

Second Generation

Archimedean Solids Stellations

Truncated Dodecahedron (Archi 3-10-10) Truncated Icosahedron (Archi 5-6-6) Kepler Poinsot

Icosidodecahedron (Archi 3-5-3-5) (Quasiregular) Small Stellated Dodecahedron Great Dodecahedron

Great Stellated Dodecahedron Great Icosahedron

Third Generation

Truncated Icosidodecahedron Greater Rhombicosidodecahedron (Archi 4-6-10) Snub Icosidodecahedron (Snub Dodecahedron) (Archi 3-3-3-3-5) Rhombicosidodecahedron (Archi 3-4-5-4)

The Convex Deltahedra

Above:
Rochelle Newman. Models. A family portrait of the Convex Deltahedra. There are eight members in this family. Bristol paper and graphic tape to define the edges. These all have a constant edge length so that you can see their relative size.

Try building a group of Concave Deltahedra. Could you turn the ones depicted in the above photograph from convex to concave?

In the kingdom of polyhedra, there is one unique closely knit family whose faces are astoundingly similar, while their body types and personalities vary from one to the other. These are the Convex Deltahedra, the "landed gentry" of the vertically regular clan. This family, descending from the primal ancestor, the equilateral triangle, kept themselves in seclusion until the 20th Century when they made a decision to go public. Until that time, they were quite content to associate exclusively with their cousins, the Concave Deltahedra.

The family surname, Deltahedra, is a direct reflection of the delta, Δ, the fourth letter of the Greek alphabet, which forms their family shield and describes their faces. Because of their Greek heritage, however, their birth names are quite lengthy as they also include the number of faces each individual has, such as, the Tetrakaidecadeltahedron, with its fourteen

faces. When the Deltahedra entered school, their teachers were somewhat apprehensive as to how students would react to them. They were determined that they not be cast off and forgotten because of the lengths and sounds of their names.

When the town in which they reside adopted computers with only 16-bit addressing capability, the Deltahedra felt it was time to shorten their names, rather than settle for whatever the computer might do to such abbreviations when records were entered into the system. They were quite clever when choosing their new referral names, and none of their descriptive quality was lost. The Greek name for the number of faces that each has is now translated into Arabic numerals, and Deltahedra is shortened to Delta. The Hexkaidecadeltahedron is now pleased to be called the 16-Delta and the teachers, students, and data entry clerks are

Polyhedra Personality Profile

Deltahedra
Family Name

Delta
Referral Name

8
Family Count

	Ancestors — Parent Polygons						Gene Pool — Symmetries: Axes/Planes							Bone Structure			
	Equi. Triangles	Squares	Pentagons	Hexagons	Octagons	Decagon	2-turn	3-turn	4-turn	5-turn	6-turn	Total # Axes	Total # Planes	Total # Edges	Total # Vertices	Vertex Nets	Interfacial Angles
4-Delta (Referral Name) — *Tetrahedron* (Birth Name)	4						3	4				7	5	6	4	3-3-3	70° 32'
6-Delta (Referral Name) — *Triangular Dipyramid* (Birth Name)	6						1	2				3	4	9	5	3-3-3 / 3-3-3-3	98° 13'
8-Delta (Referral Name) — *Octahedron (Square Dipyramid)* (Birth Name)	8						6	4	3			13	9	6	12	3-3-3-3	109° 28'
10-Delta (Referral Name) — *Pentagonal Dipyramid* (Birth Name)	10						5			1		6	6	7	15	3-3-3-3 / 3-3-3-3-3	119° 6'
12-Delta (Referral Name) — *Dodecadeltahedron* (Birth Name)	12						1					1		8	18	3-3-3-3 / 3-3-3-3-3	X*
14-Delta (Referral Name) — *Tetrakaidecadeltahedron* (Birth Name)	14						3	1				4		9	21	3-3-3-3 / 3-3-3-3-3	X
16-Delta (Referral Name) — *Hexkaidecadeltahedron* (Birth Name)	16						4		1			5		10	24	3-3-3-3 / 3-3-3-3-3	X
20-Delta (Referral Name) — *Icosahedron* (Birth Name)	20						15	10		6		31	10	12	30	3-3-3-3-3	138° 11'

all pleased as well. The database at the Town Hall includes much of the information found in the chart on this page.

For your own modest building, the chart on pages 238 and 239 give the nets for constructing all the Deltahedra. Included on these pages, is the matriarch tetrahedron that you met in Chapter 2. You will also see the three reflective members of the family, the dipyramids, and the three eccentric ones. They are the 12-Delta (Dodecadeltahedron), the 14-Delta (Tetrakaidecadeltahedron) and the 16-Delta (Hexkaidecadeltahedron). You will note that they broke the mold after these three and no 18-Delta came into being. There was, however, one more sibling after them, our "Golden Boy", the 20-Delta (Icosahedron). This is the polyhedron that you met in Chapter 4. He has a marvelously adaptive personality, as you will see, when you meet the Royal Family in the next section of this chapter.

This page:
*These angles are unavailable to us at this time. If the reader can figure out the necessary ones, please send the information on to us.

The Eight Convex Deltahedra

Nets*

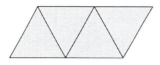

*If you want to use these as templates, enlarge them and add the necessary glue tabs.

4-Delta
(Tetrahedron)

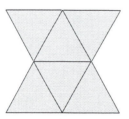

6-Delta
(Triangular Dipyramid)

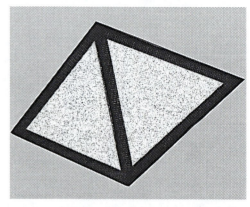

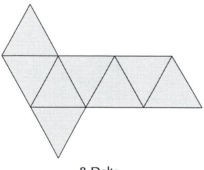

8-Delta
(Octahedron) (Square Dipyramid)

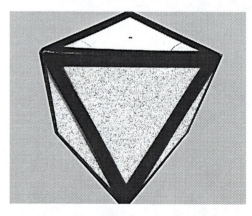

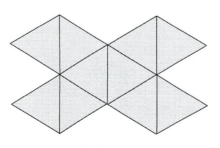

10-Delta
(Pentagonal Dipyramid)

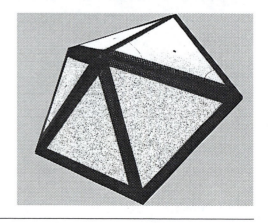

Nets

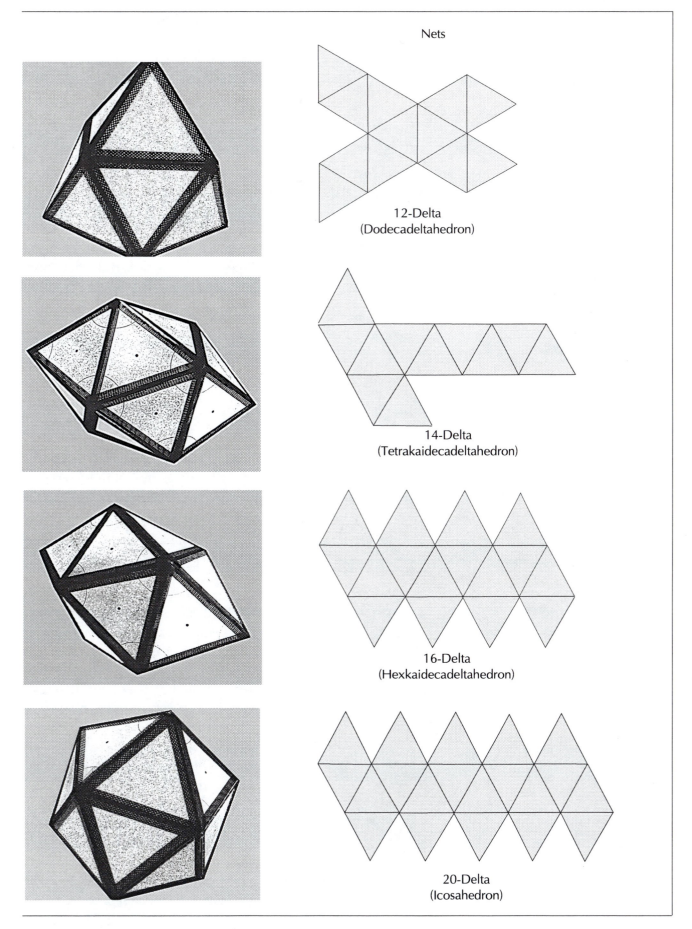

12-Delta
(Dodecadeltahedron)

14-Delta
(Tetrakaidecadeltahedron)

16-Delta
(Hexkaidecadeltahedron)

20-Delta
(Icosahedron)

Above:
Fig. 5.2   The 4-Delta, or tetrahedron is also known as a triangular pyramid.

Right:
Fig. 5.3 The facially regular square pyramid has a square base and four equilateral triangular sides.

Below:
Fig. 5.4 The 10-Delta, or pentagonal dipyramid is two pentagonal pyramids joined base-to-base and edge-to-edge.

Try building hexagonal, octagonal, or decagonal pyramids. Turn them into dipyramids.

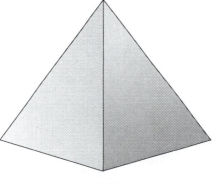

4-Delta
(Tetrahedron)
(Triangular Pyramid)

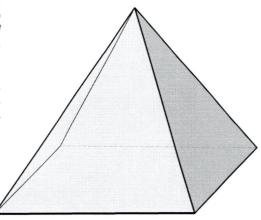

Square Pyramid

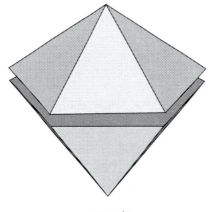

10-Delta
(Pentagonal Dipyramid)

We can now consider some of the characteristics that make each member an individual. The tetrahedron is sometimes referred to as a triangular pyramid. This is because when she sits on any surface, her fourth face acts as a stable base, while the remaining three triangles form her sides (Fig. 5.2). Although there are an infinite number of pyramids whose sides are isoscees triangles,, the facially regular ones, those made with regular polygonal bases and equilateral triangular sides, form a finite family of three. These are named by their bases and they include the triangular pyramid, the square pyramid (Fig. 5.3), and the pentagonal pyramid.

Whenever the triangular pyramid, the pentagonal pyramid, or the square pyramid lean their bases against the surface of a mirror to reflect upon the events of the day, whole new personalities emerge as they transform into Deltahedra. They become the 6-Delta, or triangular dipyramid, the 10-Delta, or pentagonal dipyramid (Fig. 5.4), and the 8-Delta, or octahedron, respectively. Essentially, a dipyramid is two identical pyramids joined base-to-base and edge-to-edge.

The symmetries of the pyramid are inherited directly from those of the base. The pyramid has the same rotational symmetry as the base and, no other. The axis of rotation passes through the vertex of the pyramid and the center of the base. Each axis of reflection in the base is contained in a plane of reflection that also passes through the vertex of the pyramid. Dipyramids have exactly the same symmetries as the related pyramids, with the addition of a plane of reflection through what was the base of the original pyramid and two 2-turn rotation axes through opposite pairs of edges, opposite pairs of vertices or an opposite edge and vertex of the base.

This page:
Student works which use one of the deltahedra as the armature for an ocean theme. Watercolor paper, colored pencils, and acrylic paint.

Can you identify which deltahedra were used?

Top left:
Karen Petteruto

Top right:
Terry Shedd

Bottom:
Jeff Spero

The Platonic Solids:
The Royal Family

Above:
Rochelle Newman Models. A family portrait of the five Platonic solids, the Royal Family, of first generation polyhedra. Bristol paper with graphic tape to define the edges. All of the solids have a constant edge length so that you can see the sizes relative to each other.

Having just met the landed gentry of the first generation of polyhedra, we would now like to introduce you to the only other first generation family of forms. These are the Platonic Solids, the Royal Family of the kingdom of polyhedra. They are the members of the convex branch of the *regular clan.* Like the Convex Deltahedra, they, too, have a single kind of polygonal face per polyhedron. Rather than all of them being equilateral triangles, however, the Platonic Solids come from three different primal ancestors. They are the equilateral triangle, the square, and

the pentagon. What makes them regal and select is that they are the *only* five regular convex polyhedra, and as such, they form a very closed finite family.

The Platonic Solids are named after the classical Greek philosopher, Plato (427-348 B.C.), who found them most beautiful. They were used to develop a geometrical description of the physical world. In Pythagorean cosmology these five were symbolically associated with five natural elements: the tetrahedron with fire, the cube with earth, the octahedron with air, the icosahedron with water, and the dodecahedron with the Universe. Their descriptions can be found in Book XII of the geometry books, *The Elements,* of the mathematician Euclid. Interestingly enough, in Scotland, archaeologists have discovered a set of these solids that were hewn out of stone. The origin of these has been attributed to the builders of the Neolithic period of prehistory, one thousand years prior to their discovery by Plato.

The given names of this family refer only to the number of faces, such as, tetrahedron, which has four faces, or octahedron, which has eight faces. Because there are so many derivatives of the dodecahedron and the icosahedron, we shall refer to them as the regular dodecahedron and the regular icosahedron. Again, as with the Convex Deltahedra, the matriarch of this family is a tetrahedron. In addition to this, the Platonic Solid Family also has a patriarch, the cube. The octahedron has a very reflective personality, and the regular dodecahedron and the regular icosahedron are the Golden Pair because of their Golden Ratio connections.

The chart at the bottom of this page offers a personality profile of each member of the family. They each have been given a birth name. If they are known by any other names, they are also listed. Their ancestor polygons have been noted along with their gene pools of symmetry and the particular bone structure that defines their individual body types. This family is intimately linked to both the Archimedean and Catalan solids through symmetry and duality.

Polyhedra Personality Profile	Ancestors Parent Polygons						Gene Pool Symmetries: Axes/Planes							Bone Structure			
Platonic Solids — Family Name / Same — Referral Name / 5 — Family Count	Equi. Triangles	Squares	Pentagons	Hexagons	Octagons	Decagon	2-turn	3-turn	4-turn	5-turn	6-turn	Total # Axes	Total # Planes	Total # Edges	Total # Vertices	Vertex Nets	Interfacial Angles
Same — Referral Name / *Tetrahedron* — Birth Name	4						3	4				7	5	6	4	3-3-3	70° 32'
Cube — Referral Name / *Hexahedron* — Birth Name		6					6	4	3			13	9	12	8	4-4-4	90°
Same — Referral Name / *Octahedron* — Birth Name	8						6	4	3			13	9	12	6	3-3-3-3	109° 28'
Regular Dodecahedron — Referral Name / *Dodecahedron* — Birth Name			12				15	10		6		31	10	30	20	5-5-5	116° 34'
Regular Icosahedron — Referral Name / *Icosahedron* — Birth Name	20						15	10		6		31	10	30	12	3-3-3-3-3	138° 11'

Duality

Below:
Fig. 5.5 The cube and octahedron are dual partners. Notice that the midpoints of the edges of both polyhedra intersect. Also, the centers of the faces of the cube correspond to the vertices of the octahedron.

Try diagramming the relationship between the tetrahedron and tetrahedron or the dodecahedron and the icosahedron.

There is a special relationship, called duality, between some polyhedra. This is a condition in which two different polyhedra have intimate connections. These are similarities in the numbers of edges, and the number and kind of symmetries, and exchanges in the faces and vertices, and the vertex nets. Although there are other families which have duals, only the Platonics keep the duality within the family.

There are three pairs in which partners share symmetries and edges while exchanging vertices and faces, and vertex nets. Because the tetrahedron pairs with another tetrahedron, however, the number of faces and vertices stay the same. The chart at the bottom of this page shows these connections. Fig. 5.5 illustrates the dual relationship between the cube and the octahedron. Notice that the centers of the faces of both polyhedra become the locations, which when extended, mark the positions of the vertices of the dual partner. Also, the midpoints of edges of the pair intersect each other.

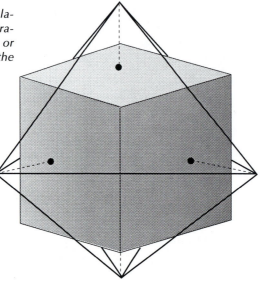

Duality Similarities			Duality Exchanges	
Dual Polyhedra	Edges	Symmetries	Faces and Vertices	Vertex Nets
Tetrahedron to Tetrahedron	6 6	(3) 2-turn, (4) 3-turn	4 ⤢ 4 4 ⤢ 4	3-3-3 3-3-3
Cube to Octahedron	12 12	(6) 2-turn, (4) 3-turn, (3) 4-turn	6 ⤢ 8 8 ⤢ 6	4-4-4 3-3-3-3
Regular Dodecahedron to Regular Icosahedron	30 30	(15) 2-turn, (10) 3-turn, (6) 5-turn	12 ⤢ 20 20 ⤢ 12	5-5-5 3-3-3-3-3

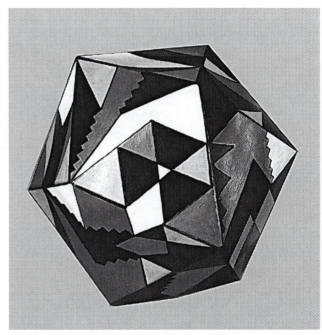

The Golden Pair

As you saw in the case of duality, the regular dodecahedron and the regular icosahedron share this particular relationship. This Golden Pair also exhibits a symmetry relationship that is different from the other Platonics Solids. These are the only two members of this family to have pentagonal, or 5-turn symmetry. While in the regular dodecahedron this symmetry is seen in the pentagonal facial structure, it is at the vertices of the regular icosahedron that this 5-turn symmetry shows. The pentagon is filled with Golden ratios. These ratios are used for developing the patterns on faces of one of the polyhedra shown.

In many cases, 5-turn symmetry is associated with organic forms, while 2, 3, 4, and 6-turn symmetries are displayed by the crystalline structures. There is, however, no sharp dividing line between the organic and inorganic realms. Viruses exist at the boundary of the crystal kingdom. Up until recently, these were the most complex substances that crystallize. Scientists have now discovered a group called the quasi-crysals which have a relationship to Penrose tiles.

Above:
Rochelle Newman. Models. Artful manipulations of the regular dodecahedron and the regular icosahedron. Acrylic paint and watercolor paper.
Fibonacci subdivisions were used on the faces of the solid at the upper left while Golden ratio subdivisions were used on the solid at the lower right. Both are painted in hues of the three primary colors.

The following poem is a modification of a rhyme from Mother Goose

There was an old woman who lived in a shoe,
Who had so many kids she knew not what to do.
She cried "When J last counted they numbered to twelve!
J dread no more space for the laces to swell!"

"No fear," called a baker, "J'll come to your aid
With the best gingerbread that J ever have made!
We'll build such a house as you never have seen.
(But J can"t promise you it'll be easy to clean.)"

Said the woman, "Let's begin this project together,
Jn order to keep my brood safe from the weather.
My first girl's a mixer, she'll help with the DOUGH.
Why a DECK can be added if we're not moving too slow!"

"Quite right, we must hurry," the baker concurred,
"For your children at times are unruly J've heard.
A room for each child is what J think you'll need.
To keep them from fighting, we'd better take (A) HEED.

The exterior structure will give us twelve walls.
'Tis a problem to choose a design that won't fall..."
"Not so," quipped a youngster, they knew him as RON,
" We'll simply create a DOUGH DECK A HEED RON!"

"Of course!" the group chorused, "Now let us all toil."
And to sturdily build it they used frosting royal.
All the children excitedly joined in the task
To bestow it with beauty in which they could bask.

The baker succeeded in doing her duty.
With help she created a Vision of Beauty.
Her Math built the structure, and Art decorated,
 So with Nature they comfortably 'co-habitated'.

Ann MacLean

246

This page:
Student work. Artful variations of the regular dodecahedron and the regular icosahedron.

Top:
Ann MacLean. A gingerbread "dough-deck-a-heedron". Gingerbread, royal frosting, and other assorted delights.

Bottom:
Greg Scanlon. Recycled toy parts, fomecore and metallic paint. Can you find the icosahedron nucleus within the body of this well disguised spacebird?

The Stellated Family: The Duchy of Transformation

The Golden pair yields the Stellated family. Stellation is a process which involves the systematic and simultaneous extension and intersection of all of the planar faces of a polyhedron. Such an undertaking encloses new volumes of space in what can be considered a type of cap that has been placed on the faces of the original polyhedron. Although all convex polyhedra can have caps joined to their faces to transform them into new figures, not all polyhedra can be stellated. Stellation, by definition is a limiting condition. There are restrictions which confine the number and types of transformations allowed. The interfacial angles of the nucleus polyhedron must be obtuse, or greater than 90°. Also, the rotational symmetries of the original solid must be preserved. For example, in Fig. 5.6, the planar faces of a cube are extended. As you can see, other than the edges of the cube, there are no intersections and thus no new modules of space are enclosed. If, however, the same operation is performed on the dodecahedron, the planes do intersect. If you look at Fig 5.7, you will be able to see the pentagram that is formed by these extensions. The face parallel to the viewer has not been stellated so as to accentuate the pentagonal face of the original regular dodecahedron.

It was our famous Johannes Kepler (1571-1630), who, in 1619, discovered the small stellated dodecahedron and the great stellated dodecahedron. In 1809, two centuries later, Louis Poinsot (1777-1859), discovered their cousins, the great dodecahedron and the great icosahedron. In fact, the small stellated dodecahedron and the great dodecahedron are dual partners, as are the great stellated dodecahedron and the great icosahedron. All four of these polyhedra are second generation forms from the non-convex branch of the regular clan. Together they form what we call the Duchy of Transformation. All four have a relationship to the pentagram. The Kepler pair has

Right:
Fig. 5.6 If the planes of the faces of a cube are extended, they will only intersect at the edges of the cube. Therefore, the cube cannot be stellated.

Below:
Fig. 5.7 When the planes of the faces of the regular dodecahedron are extended, they enclose new modules of space. Therefore, the regular dodecahedron can be stellated. Each face will have five extensions. When we multiply this by the twelve faces of the figure, the first stellation of the regular dodecahedron requires sixty extensions, or manipulations.

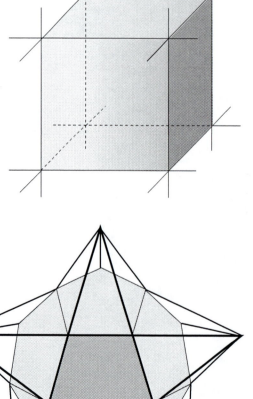

faces that are pentagrams, and the Poinsot pair has vertex figures that are pentagrams. It should be noted that the small stellated dodecahedron and the great dodecahedron do not satisfy Euler's Formula in its usual form, and therefore, were thought not to exist.

Although we only give visuals for four members of the Stellated Family, there are actually many more. In fact, our Golden Pair yields a finite group of three stellations of the regular dodecahedron, all of which are included here, and a whopping 59 of the regular icosahedron. While we give the stellation that results in the great icosahedron, the book, *Polyhedron Models*, by Magnus Wenninger, listed in our Further Reading section gives many more.

In Fig 5.8, we give a schematic that illustrates where the components for the template pieces for the small stellated, great, and great stellated dodecahedra are placed. In Fig. 5.9, on pages 250 and 251, we give a schematic for all 59 stellations of the regular icosahedron. It should be noted that this is our approach to determine the various shapes necessary for these stellations. In both cases, we began with a single face and worked outward in a process of extending lines and enclosing new areas. The shaded areas indicate where the components for the template pieces are located. Notice all of the Golden connections that are seen in the divisions of the sides of the equilateral triangles of the icosahedron. As with the case of the geodesic schematic, these diagrams, too, are conceptual aids, and, therefore, do not represent what physically happens. Actual template pieces are given on pages 252 and 254.

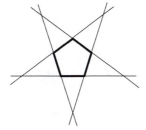

Left:
Fig, 5.8   A schematic for the three stellations of the regular dodecahedron.

Step 1
A. Begin with a regular pentagon.
B. Extend the sides in both directions until they intersect to form a pentagram.

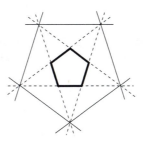

Step 2
Connect the vertices of the pentagram to form a pentagon. Notice that this one is in a different orientation and larger than the original one.

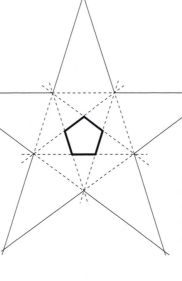

Step 3
Extend the lines of the new pentagon until they intersect to form another pentagram. Notice with this extension and intersection, the pentagram is similar to the original pentagon.

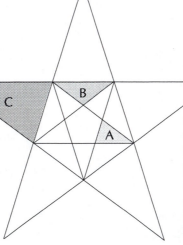

Step 4
Completed schematic for the three stellations of the regular dodecahedron. Shaded areas indicate the necessary components for:
A. The small stellated dodecahedron
B. The great dodecahedron
C. The great stellated dodecahedron

249

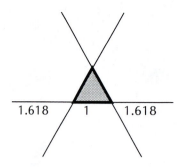

1.618   1   1.618

Step 1
A. Begin with an equilateral triangle with sides of unit length.
B. Extend the sides 1.618 in both directions.

Step 2
Connect the endpoints of the extended sides to form three new triangles.

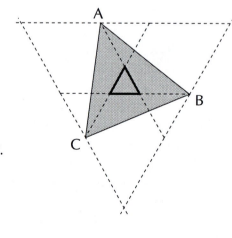

A

B

C

Step 3
Extend the endpoints of the newly drawn connecting lines until they intersect. A large equilateral triangle is formed.

These facing pages:
Fig. 5.9 The schematic for the 59 stellations of the regular icosahedron.
The shaded areas in Step 8 indicate those pieces that are used as the components for the template of the great icosahedron. See page 254 for the necessary template.

Step 4
Enclose triangle ABC.

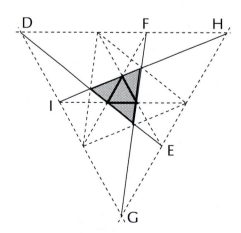

D   F   H

I

E

G

Step 5
Connect D to E, F to G, and H to I to enclose an equilateral triangle.

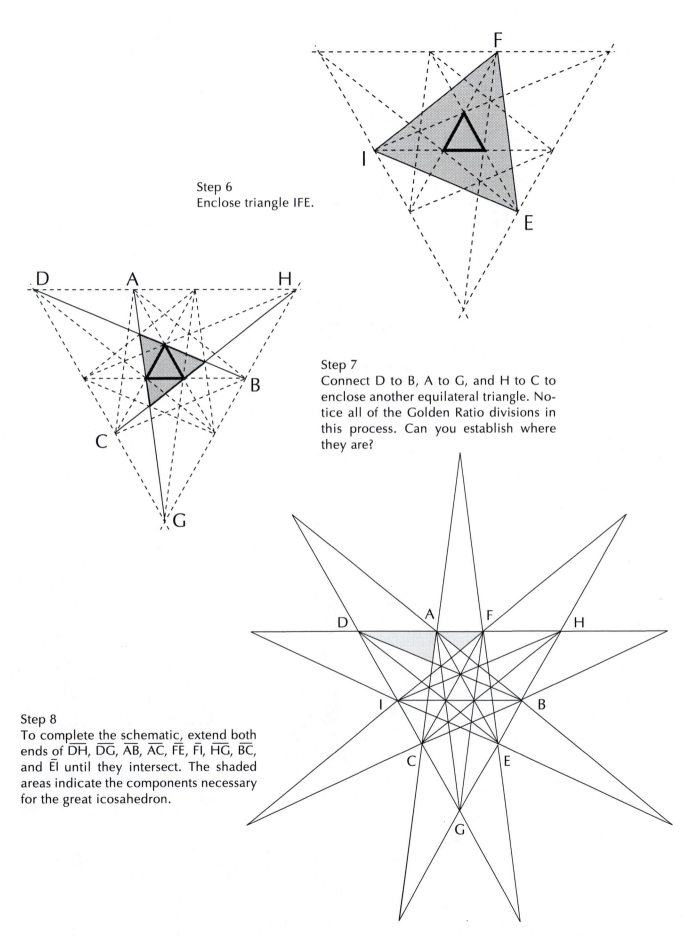

Step 6
Enclose triangle IFE.

Step 7
Connect D to B, A to G, and H to C to enclose another equilateral triangle. Notice all of the Golden Ratio divisions in this process. Can you establish where they are?

Step 8
To complete the schematic, extend both ends of $\overline{DH}$, $\overline{DG}$, $\overline{AB}$, $\overline{AC}$, $\overline{FE}$, $\overline{FI}$, $\overline{HG}$, $\overline{BC}$, and $\overline{EI}$ until they intersect. The shaded areas indicate the components necessary for the great icosahedron.

251

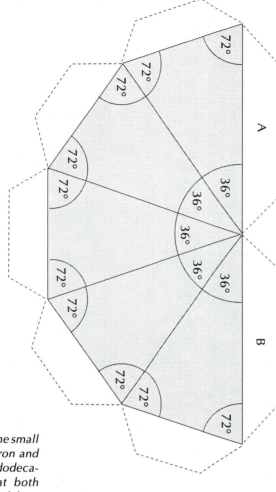

This page:
Template pieces for the small stellated dodecahedron and the great stellated dodecahedron. Notice that both polyhedra are derived from the same isosceles Golden Triangle.

Top:
Fig. 5.10 Template for the small stellated dodecahedron.

Bottom:
Fig. 5.11 Template for the great stellated dodecahedron.

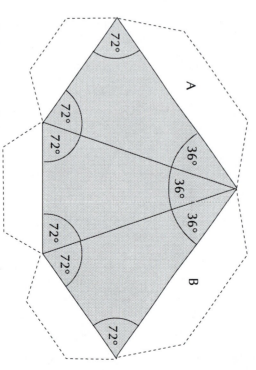

The Kepler Pair

Both of these polyhedra use the same isosceles Golden Triangle. Each one, however, requires a different number of them for its unit clusters. The following gives the preparation and assembly procedure for making these two forms.

The Small Stellated Dodecahedron
Preparation
1. Duplicate the template in Fig. 5.10 twelve times.
2. Score and mountain fold all lines.
3. Glue tabs A and B together to form a *unit cap*.
4. Repeat this eleven more times until you have twelve unit caps.
Assembly
1. Join three unit caps together at a vertex of the base of each, forming a concave vertex.
2. Add a single cap at a time making certain that three caps come together at each new concave vertex.
3. Continue on in this manner until the form is complete.

The Great Stellated Dodecahedron
Preparation
1. Duplicate the template in Fig. 5.11 twenty times.
2. Score and mountain fold all lines.
3. Glue tabs A and B together to form a *unit cap*.
4. Repeat this 19 more times until you have twenty unit caps.
Assembly
1. Join five unit caps together at a vertex of the base of each, forming a concave vertex.
2. Add a single cap at a time making certain that five caps come together at each new concavevertex.
3. Continue on in this manner until the form is complete.

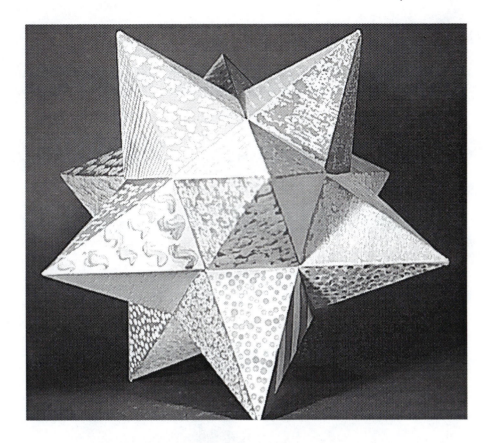

This page:
Artful models of the small stellated dodecahedron and the great stellated dodecahedron.

Top:
Student work. Priscilla Dullea. Small stellated dodecahedron. Acrylic paint on paper.

Bottom:
Rochelle Newman. Great stellated dodecahedron. Photocopied elements on paper. The structure is based on Golden Ratio subdivisions.

This page:
Template pieces for the great dodecahedron and the great icosahedron.

Top:
Fig. 5.12 Template for the great dodecahedron. Notice that this is derived from the 36°, 36°,108° triangle found in the pentagram.

Bottom:
Fig. 5.13 Template for the great icosahedron. Notice that the 82° 14', 75° 32', 22° 14' triangles are in right and left-handed orientations.

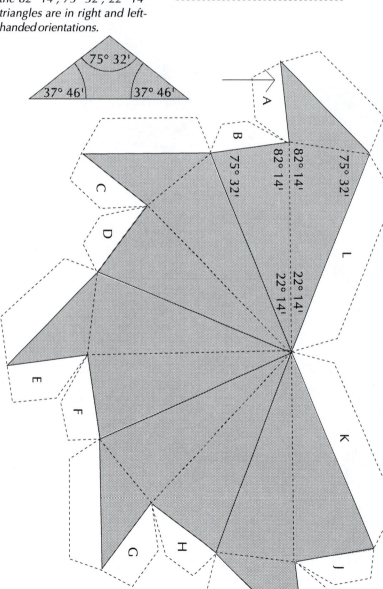

The Poinsot Pair

This pair requires three different triangles. The great dodecahedron uses a single 36°, 36°, 108° triangle which is derived from the connection between the pentagram and pentagon. The great icosahedron requires two, one isosceles triangle with angles of 37° 46', 37° 46', 75° 32' that is used in right and left-handed orientations, and one scalene triangle with angles of 82° 14', 75° 32', 22° 14'.

The Great Dodecahedron
Preparation

1. Duplicate the template in Fig. 5.12 twenty times.

2. Score and mountain fold all solid lines.

3. Score and valley fold all dashed lines.

4. Glue tabs A and B together to form a *unit cup,* as opposed to a *unit cap.*

5. Repeat this 19 more times until you have twenty unit cups.

Assembly

1. Join five unit cups together at a single vertex where they come together as a cap (a 36°vertex).

2. Add a single cup at a time making certain that five cups come together at each new vertex.

3. Continue on in this manner until the form is complete.

The Great Icosahedron
Preparation

1. Duplicate the template in Fig. 5.13 twenty times.

2. Score and mountain fold all solid lines.

3. Score and valley fold all dashed lines.

4. Glue pairs of tabs together in the following sequence: A to B, C to D, E to F, G to H, I to J, and K to L to form a *unit cap.*

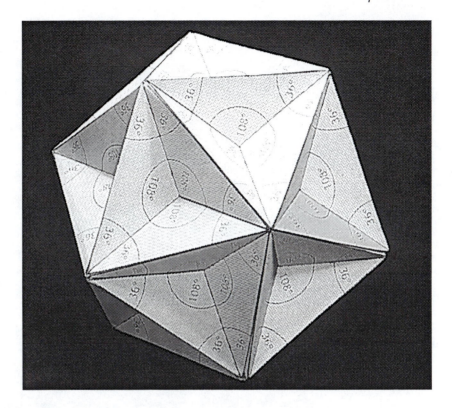

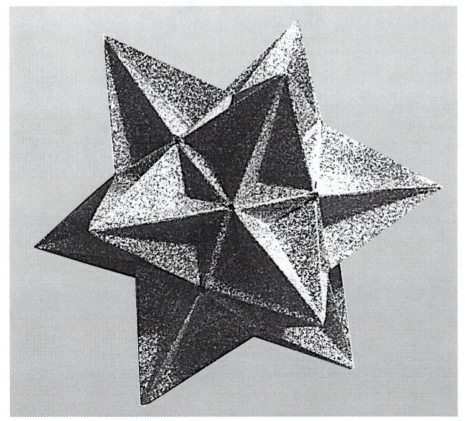

This page:
Artful models of the great dodecahedron and the great icosahedron.

Top:
Rochelle Newman. Great dodecahedron. Angles at vertices are marked. It could now be given a coat of textured paint.

Bottom:
Donna Fowler. Great icosahedron. Textured paint on paper.

5. Repeat this 19 more times until you have twenty unit caps.
Assembly
1. Join three unit caps together at a single base vertex.

2. Add a single cap at a time making certain that three caps come together at each new vertex.
3. Continue in this manner until the form is complete.

The Capping Process

Once the fundamentals are known of how polyhedra are born of polygons around a vertex, one can start to improvise on basic themes. Before I knew about the restrictions of stellation, I innocently went about the business of putting pyramidal caps onto polyhedra. I was interested in making more artful models using contemporary materials and technology. I first decided that I wanted to construct caps composed of only equilateral triangles. On each face of these I wanted a pattern structure that would carry the harmony of the Golden Ratio and one that would suggest the notion of "triangleness". A template was made using hand construction techniques. Then this template was photocopied the number of times necessary for the particular polyhedron. I was curious to see what would happen if I used different kinds of papers which would take the inks very differently. In the model pictured above, there was a graininess about the ink that I liked. Rather than building a nucleus dodecahedron, I made the cap templates without the fourth face and just joined them in groups starting with a single vertex and moving on until the figure totally enclosed space. I could have just as easily used caps of isosceles triangles or ones that had been chamfered, skewed or truncated. I could have begun with a polyhedron that had two or three different polygonal faces requiring different caps. The possibilities are limitless as well as most pleasureable.

Rochelle Newman

This page:
Flower forms suggestive of natural stellations.

What do you think are the advantages for having a flower form with spikes? In fact, what are the advantages of having flowers at all? You might like to research the evolution of the morphology of a particular species of flower. You could then document your findings in a visual manner.

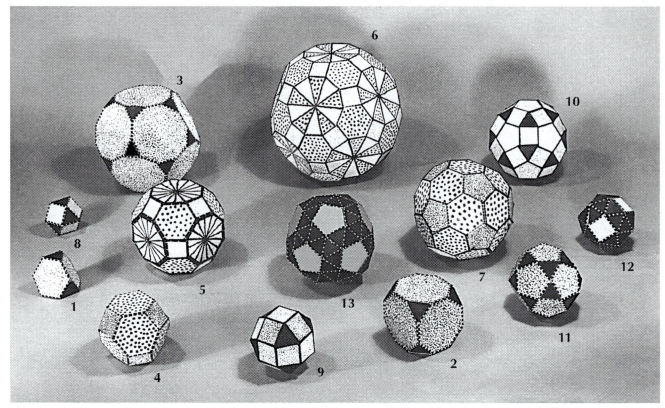

Above:

Rochelle Newman. Models. Artful variations of the Archimedean solids. Marker and graphic tapes on paper. Each member is identified by a number. All models have a constant edge length so that you can see their relative size.

1. *Truncated Tetrahedron (Archi 3-6-6)*
2. *Truncated Cube (Archi 3-8-8)*
3. *Truncated Dodecahedron (Archi 3-10-10)*
4. *Truncated Octahedron (Archi 4-6-6)*
5. *Truncated Cuboctahedron (Archi 4-6-8)*
6. *Truncated Icosidodecahedron (Archi 4-6-10)*
7. *Truncated Icosahedron (Archi 5-6-6)*
8. *Cuboctahedron (Archi 3-4-3-4)*
9. *Rhombicuboctahedron (Archi 3-4-4-4)*
10. *Rhombicosidodecahedron (Archi 3-4-3-5)*
11. *Icosidodecahedron (Archi 3-5-3-5)*
12. *Snub Cuboctahedron (Archi 3-3-3-3-4)*
13. *Snub Icosidodecahedron (Archi 3-3-3-3-5)*

The Archimedean Family: The Duchy of Archimedes

A complementary relationship exists between the Platonic Family and another distinguished group, the Archimedean Family, named after Archimedes, a contemporary of Plato. In the 17th Century, Johannes Kepler was the first to give drawings of the Archimedean polyhedron. This family is descended from the convex branch of the semiregular clan. Its members comprise most of the second and all of the third generation of forms. In fact, you can say that this family is a chip off the old block. By this, we mean that every Archimedean polyhedron can be obtained by truncating, or cutting off, various parts of the Platonic solids. We will discuss the process of truncation a little further on.

Because the birth names of these polyhedra are so lengthy, this family

like the Deltahedra, have chosen to take an abbreviation-Archi. This, in combination with their vertex nets, names them and gives them their distinctive personalities (See chart) Each vertex of an Archi is like every other vertex so that naming such a polyhedron by its vertex net is unambiguous.

The Archimedean solids are a visually diverse family of many shapes. Some have very angular bone structures, while others tend to be on the roly-poly side. Their faces range from equilateral triangles to regular decagons (ten-sided figures). All of these forms can be constructed using the polygonal templates furnished on page 225, if you follow their vertex nets. The chart on page 259 gives the personality profile of this diverse group.

Polyhedra Personality Profile

Archimedean Solids
Family Name

Archi
Referral Name

13
Family Count

Referral Name / Birth Name	Equi. Triangles	Squares	Pentagons	Hexagons	Octagons	Decagon	2-turn	3-turn	4-turn	5-turn	6-turn	Total # Axes	Total # Planes	Total # Edges	Total # Vertices	Vertex Nets	Interfacial Angles
Archi 3-6-6 — Truncated Tetrahedron	4			4			3	4				7	5	18	12	3-6-6	109° 28' T/H 70° 32' H/H
Archi 3-8-8 — Truncated Cube	8				6		6	4	3			13	9	36	24	3-8-8	125° 16' T/O 90° O/O
Archi 3-10-10 — Truncated Dodecahedron	20					12	15	10		6		31	10	90	60	3-10-10	142° 37' T/D 116° 34' D/D
Archi 4-6-6 — Truncated Octahedron		6		8			6	4	3			13	9	36	24	4-6-6	125° 16' S/H 109° 28' H/H
Archi 4-6-8 — Truncated Cuboctahedron		12		8	6		6	4	3			13	9	72	48	4-6-8	144° 44' S/H 135° S/O 125°16' H/O
Archi 4-6-10 — Truncated Icosidodecahedron		30		20		12	15	10		6		31	10	180	120	4-6-10	159° 6' S/H 148° 17' S/D 142° 37' H/D
Archi 5-6-6 — Truncated Icosahedron			12	20			15	10		6		31	10	90	60	5-6-6	142° 37' P/H 138° 11' H/H
Archi 3-4-3-4 — Cuboctahedron	8	6					6	4	3			13	9	24	12	3-4-3-4	125° 16' T/S
Archi 3-4-4-4 — Rhombicuboctahedron	8	18					6	4	3			13	9	48	24	3-4-4-4	144° 44' T/S 135° S/S
Archi 3-4-5-4 — Rhombicosidodecahedron	20	30	12				15	10		6		31	10	120	60	3-4-5-4	159° 6' T/S 148° 17' S/P
Archi 3-5-3-5 — Icosidodecahedron	20		12				15	10		6		31	10	60	30	3-5-3-5	142° 37' T/P
Archi 3-3-3-3-4 — Snub Cuboctahedron	32	6					6	4	3			13	9	60	24	3-3-3-3-4	153° 14' T/T 142° 59' T/S
Archi 3-3-3-3-5 — Snub Icosidodecahedron	80		12				15	10		6		31	10	150	60	3-3-3-3-5	164° 11' T/T 152° 56' T/P

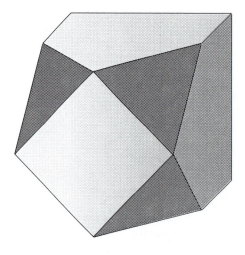

This page:
The truncation of a cube.

Top:
Fig. 5.14 When one face of a cube is truncated at the midpoints of edges the resulting face is also a square. Notice that at the four vertices, there are places to set in equilateral triangles.

Center:
Fig. 5.15 Four vertices of this cube have been truncated. Notice the three triangles and an octagon are parallel to you.

Bottom:
Rochelle Newman. Artful Model of a truncated cube. Notice that a triangle and two octagons come together at a vertex (Archi 3-8-8).

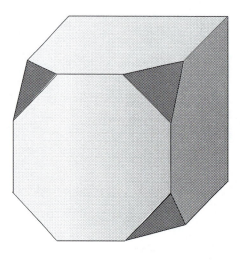

Truncated Partners

Truncation, like duality, is a manipulation based on a mathematical concept. To truncate means to cut off, and truncation is the act of cutting off the vertices of a polyhedron at specific places in a symmetrical fashion. We will limit our discussion to truncations that alter each vertex in the same way. When a polyhedron is truncated, two things can happen to the resulting form. If the cuts are made at the midpoints of the sides of the faces, the resulting faces are regular and similar to the orginal face. Thus the new polygon is similar in shape, but smaller in size. Fig. 5.14 illustrates a cube with one face truncated at the midpoints of the edges.

When, however, the truncation cuts are made at specific points between the midpoints of the edges and the vertices, the number of sides of the original polygonal face will double. Fig. 5.15 illustrates a cube that has one face truncated halfway between the midpoints of the edges and the vertices. When cut in this way: the triangular faces of the regular polyhedra will become hexagons; squares will become octagons; and pentagons will become decagons. Care must be taken with the placement of the cuts if the new polygonal faces are to be regular as well.

Once truncation is complete, there will be areas that need to be filled with new polygons. Their shapes are dependent upon the number of polygons that come together at each vertex of the original polyhedron. In the tetrahedron, cube, and dodecahedron, three faces come together at

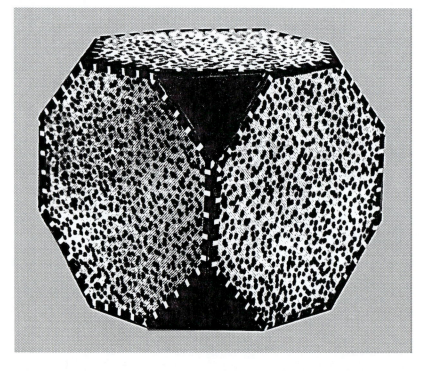

each vertex. Therefore, when these polyhedra are truncated at the midpoints of edges, a new equilateral triangular face appears. A square face appears when the octahedron is truncated since four equilateral triangular faces come together at each vertex of the octahedron. In the icosahedron, five equilateral triangles come togetherat each vertex, so we get a regular pentagonal face after this type of truncation.

Dual pairs of Platonic Solids give rise to second generation Archi offspring through the process of truncation. Although these children do not resemble their parents physically, they do have some of the same characteristics. A major similarity appears in their gene pools, whereby progenitor and progeny both have the same kind and number of rotational symmetries. The chart at the top of this page lists the Platonic parents and Archimedean children. If the cuboctahedron and the icosidodecahedron are further truncated, they give rise to the third generation of Archimedean polyhedra. These relationships are also found in this chart. The chart at the bottom of this page, which continues on pages 262-265, shows the connection between all parents, children, and grandchildren.

Platonic and Archimedean Generations

Parents Platonic Dual Partners	Children Archimedean Second Generation
Tetrahedron Tetrahedron	Truncated Tetrahedron (Archi 3-6-6)
Cube Octahedron	Truncated Cube (Archi 3-8-8) Cuboctahedron (quasiregular) (Archi 3-4-3-4) Truncated Octahedron (Archi 4-6-6)
Dodecahedron Icosahedron	Truncated Dodecahedron (Archi 3-10-10) Icosidodecahedron (quasiregular) (Archi 3-5-3-5) Truncated Icosahedron (Archi 5-6-6)
Quasiregular Parents Archimedean Second Generation	Children Archimedean Third Generation Platonic Grandchildren
Cuboctahedron (Archi 3-4-3-4)	Truncated Cuboctahedron (Archi 4-6-8) Rhombicuboctahedron (Archi 3-4-4-4) Snub Cuboctahedron (Archi 3-3-3-3-4)
Icosidodecahedron (Archi 3-5-3-5)	Truncated Icosidodecahedron (Archi 4-6-10) Rhombicosidodecahedron (Archi 3-4-5-4) Snub Icosidodecahedron (Archi 3-3-3-3-5)

Progeny By Truncation of the Platonic Solids
Second Generation

Parent - Tetrahedron

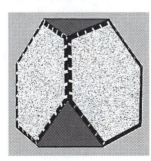

Parent - Tetrahedron

Child
Truncated Tetrahedron
(Archi 3-6-6)
F = 8
V = 12
E = 18

Dual
Triakis Tetrahedron

F = 12
V = 8
E = 18

Polygonal Analysis
1. The principle equilateral triangles of the parents are transformed into hexagons.
2. The original vertices are filled with equilateral triangles.

Parent Cube

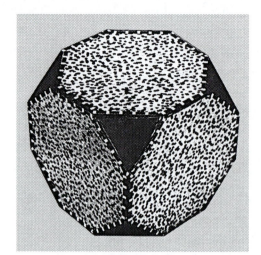

Child
Truncated Cube
(Archi 3-8-8)
F = 14
V = 24
E = 36

Dual
Triakis Octahedron

F = 24
V = 14
E = 36

Polygonal Analysis
1. The original square faces of the cube are transformed into octagons.
2. The original vertices are filled with equilateral triangles.

Child
Cuboctahedron
(Archi 3-4-3-4)
F = 14
V = 12
E = 24

Dual
Rhombic Dodecahedron

F = 12
V = 14
E = 24

Quasiregular
This figure stands halfway between the dual parents, and as such, partakes of both their names and faces. Because of this, each square face of the cuboctahedron is surrounded by equilateral triangles.

Polygonal Analysis
1. The octagonal faces of the truncated cube are transformed back into squares.
2. The hexagonal faces of the truncated octahedron are transformed back into equilateral triangles.
3. The new vertices are now 3-4-3-4.

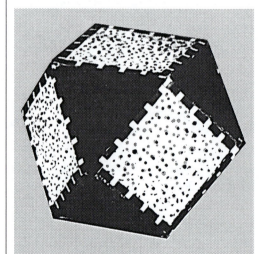

Child
Truncated Octahedron
(Archi 4-6-6)
F = 14
V = 24
E = 36

Dual
Tetrakis Hexahedron

F = 24
V = 14
E = 36

Polygonal Analysis
1. The original equilateral triangular faces of the octahedron are transformed into hexagons.
2. The original vertices are filled with squares.

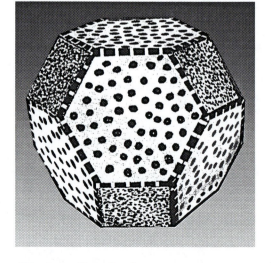

Parent Octahedron

Parent - Dodecahedron

Parent Dodecahedron

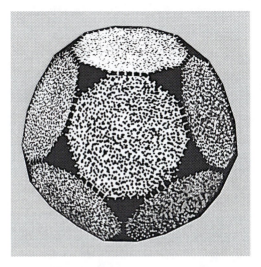

Child
Truncated Dodecahedron
(Archi 3-10-10)
F = 32
V = 60
E = 90

Dual
Triakis Icosahedron

F = 60
V = 32
E = 90

Polygonal Analysis
1. The original pentagonal faces of the dodecahedron are transformed into decagons.
2. The original vertices are filled with equilateral triangles.

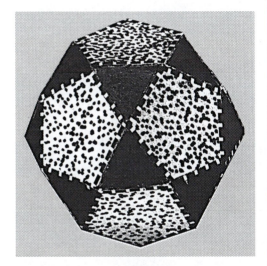

Child
Icosidodecahedron
(Archi 3-5-3-5)
F = 32
V = 30
E = 60

Dual
Rhombic Triacontahedron

F = 30
V = 32
E = 60

Quasiregular
This figure stands halfway between the dual parents, and as such, partakes of both their names and faces. Because of this, each pentagonal face of the dodecahedron is surrounded by an equilateral triangle.

Polygonal Analysis
1. The decagonal faces of the truncated dodecahedron are transformed back into pentagons.
2. The hexagonal faces of the truncated icosahedron are transformed back into equilateral triangles.
3. The new vertices are now 3-5-3-5.

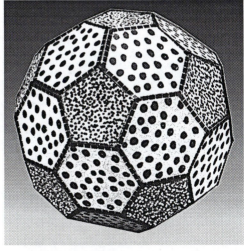

Child
Truncated Icosahedron*
(Archi 5-6-6)
F = 32
V = 60
E = 90

Dual
Pentakis Dodecahedron

F = 60
V = 32
E = 90

Polygonal Analysis
1. The original equilateral triangular faces of the icosahedron are transformed into hexagons.
2. The original vertices are filled with pentagons.

*This is the C_{60} of the Fullerene family.
The $_{60}$ refers to the number of vertices.

Parent - Icosahedron

Parent Icosahedron

Third Generation

Parent - Cuboctahedron

Parent - Cuboctahedron

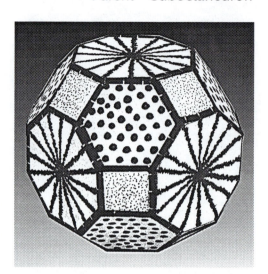

Child
Truncated Cuboctahedron
(Archi 4-6-8)
F = 26
V = 48
E = 72

Dual
Hexaxis Octahedron

F = 48
V = 26
E = 72

Polygonal Analysis
1. The original square faces of the cuboctahedron are transformed into octagons.
2. The original equilateral triangular faces are transformed into hexagons.
3. The original vertices are filled with squares.

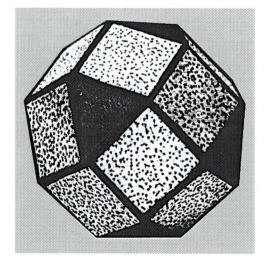

Child
Rhombicuboctahedron
(Archi 3-4-4-4)
F = 26
V = 24
E = 48

Dual
Trapezoidal Icositetrahedron

F = 24
V = 26
E = 48

Polygonal Analysis
1. The hexagonal faces of the truncated cuboctahedron are transformed back into equilateral triangles.
2. The octagonal faces are transformed back into squares.
3. The new vertices are now 3-4-4-4.

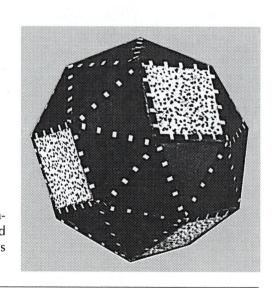

Child
Snub Cuboctahedron
(Archi 3-3-3-3-4)
F = 38
V = 24
E = 60

Dual
Pentagonal Icositetrahedron

F = 24
V = 38
E = 60

Polygonal Analysis
The snub cuboctahedron is derived directly from the the parent cuboctahedron by a modified truncation in which there is a cutting, a twisting, and an inserting of equilateral triangles. There are no planes of reflection in this child which allows it to occur in right and left-handed forms.

Parent - Icosidodecahedron

Parent - Icosidodecahedron

Child
Truncated Icosidodecahedron
(Archi 4-6-10)
F = 62
V = 120
E = 180

Dual
Hexaxis Icosahedron

F = 120
V = 62
E = 180

Polygonal Analysis
1. The original pentagonal faces of the icosidodecahedron are transformed into decagons.
2. The original equilateral triangular faces are transformed into hexagons.
3. The original vertices are filled with squares.

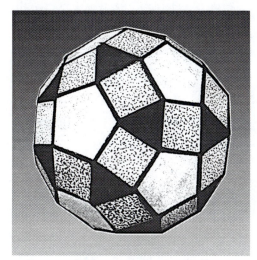

Child
Rhombicosidodecahedron
(Archi 3-4-5-4)
F = 62
V = 60
E = 120

Dual
Trapezoidal Hexacontahedron

F = 60
V = 62
E = 120

Polygonal Analysis
1. The hexagonal faces of the truncated icosidodecahedron are transformed back into equilateral triangles.
2. The decagonal faces are transformed back into pentagons.
3. The new vertices are now 3-4-5-4.

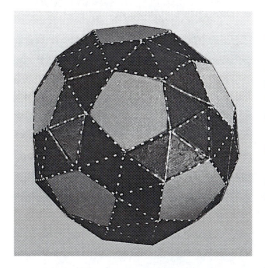

Child
Snub Icosidodecahedron
(Archi 3-3-3-3-5)
F = 14
V = 60
E = 36

Dual
Pentagonal Hexacontahedron

F = 60
V = 14
E = 36

Polygonal Analysis
The snub icosidodecahedron is derived directly from the the parent icosidodecahedron by a modified truncation in which there is a cutting, a twisting, and an inserting of equilateral triangles. There are no planes of reflection in this child which allows it to occur in right and left-handed forms.

Natural Connections: The Fullerenes

This page:
One of the branch of mathematics needed to fully understand the subject of Fullerenes is called Group Theory. A group is a set of elements together with an operation used for combining those elements.
With the buckyball, the group involves looking at symmetry elements and operations since this object is highly symmetric. The elements of a symmetry set are the basic rigid motions that can be performed on the figure such as rotation and/ or reflection. The rotational symmetry group of the buckyball has 60 elements.

Two other avenues of mathematical investigation involve the subjects of graph theory and topology. You might like to read up on these topics.

There is a connection to nature between the truncated icosahedron of the Archi Family and a family of carbon compounds called the "fullerenes". For the chemistry community, the discovery of the C_{60}, which takes the form of the truncated icosahedron, is the most exciting opening up of new avenues of exploration. This carbon molecule is related to the chemistry of the stars as well as the carbon compounds found within each living being. It is a newly recognized form of carbon joining the already familiar graphite and diamond. The former is the most common form of elemental carbon. It is composed of flat sheets of hexagons which stack in layers one on top of each other. These layers are spaced 0.335 nanometers (one billionth of a meter) apart and are able to slide easily over one another. Diamond has the familiar tetrahedral arrangement. Each atom is bonded to four others. This gives strength and hardness. Under the very right circumstances, however, graphite can be converted into diamond. The new third form of carbon, fullerite, is the first family of closed spherical structures. It brings a new form to chemical architecture.

In honor of Buckminster Fuller's work with geodesic spheres, the chemistry community has named the C_{60} "the Bucky Ball". Investigation into this new molecule is as recent as 1985. The third form of carbon became an issue when scientists began looking at molecules in interstellar space where temperatures are high and the atmosphere

carbon-rich. In researching, they found evidence that there was a carbon which had a 60 atom cluster and which seemed stable. But the question was: what shape could and would this carbon atom take? A long chain structure seemed inadequate; flat sheets of atoms stacked on each other seemed inappropraite; only a figure that could close up on itself might prove to be the answer. To one of the primary researchers, Harry Kroto, a memory of an architectural experience at Expo in Montreal, Canada, provided the key to the solution.It was the truncated icoshaedron. This object is extremely symmetric and spherical. It was the form Kroto had been searching for. The combination of pentagons and hexagons allows not only for a figure that could close up upon itself, but could provide 60 vertices where atoms could sit. The pentagons are not adjacent to each other but their presence allows the figure to close up. Carbon atoms need to have four bonds so one of the bonds had to be a double one.

Interestingly, this polyhedron is just one member of an infinitely large family of closed shells made up of only pentagons and hexagons. It was Euler who showed that twelve pentagons can be assembled with any number of hexagons, greater than one, to produce closed structures. This family provided an explanation for even numbered carbon clusters. Each time an additional hexagon is added to a successive member of the family, two new vertices occur where two more atoms can sit. One of the qualities that makes the fullerenes so special is the potential for forming them with atoms located on the inside. Some of the other fullerenes are $C_{44,}$ $C_{70,}$ C_{76}, C_{78}, C_{82}, C_{84}, C_{240}, C_{540}. Consider building models of any one of these carbon molecules remembering that they all contain just twelve pentagons and bunches of hexagons. Also, you might consider how long this process might take. (Hint: the C_{44} has 12 pentagons and 12 hexagons; the C_{70} has 12 pentagons and 25 hexagons; the C_{540} has 12 pentagons and 260 hexagons. Position as well as numbers accounts for the final form). How does nature seem to do it so easily?

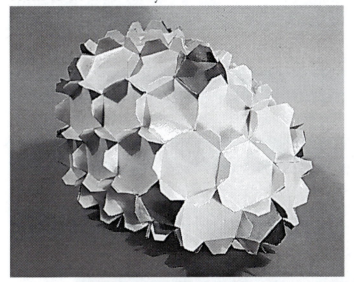

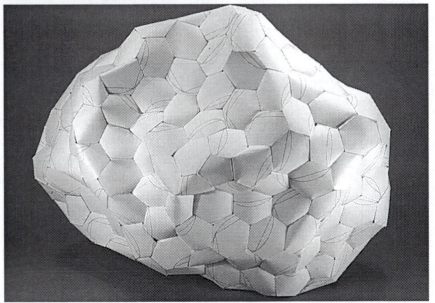

This page:
Student works exploring arrangements of pentagons and hexagons to produce closed shell three-dimensional objects. Try building any one of those given here. You might like to investigate the current literature on the subject.
Top right: Lillian Ng. Marker and graphic tape on paper.
Middle left: Heather West. Glue tabs placed on the outsdie. Colored cardstock paper.
Middle right: Jessica Gamache. Watercolr on paper.
Bottom: Keith Croft. Non-regular pentagons and hexagons. Photocopied random elements on paper.

Animal Architecture: Radiolaria

There are also spherical and polyhedral connections to microscopic animals called Radiolaria, marine protozoa, which number at least 4,000 species. These are all ocean-dwelling members of the amoeba family that are single-celled and have a skeletal structure. They are water inhabitants that float near the ocean surface. Although they belong to the amoeba family, their form is immensely different from them, radiolaria possessing great intricacy, variety and beauty. The body of each species has its own particular arrangement of spikes and pseudopods. Their fossil remains have been found, dating as far back as 600 million years ago. This is because the sandlike shells of these creatures resist chemical change. When the soft portion of the body dies, the hard element sinks to the ocean floor. Many of the species that exist today are identical in shape to their forbears that lived millions of years ago. Despite their longevity, elements of their form still remain a mystery to the scientists.

Typically, the body of these creatures consists of a spherical mass of protoplasm which lies within a meshwork of equally sized polyhedral cells. The openness of the skeleton, keeps them afloat in the water providing increased surface contact. The openings in the skeleton also allow for portions of the body to move in and out when looking for food. As you now know, no system of hexagons can enclosed a volume of space without the presence of another polygon such as the pentagon. Thus, the shells contain other polygons, some with fewer than six sides, and some with more than six.

The chemical composition of the nearly colorless skeleton is unusual in that it is composed of silica, a mineral related to quartz and glass of the inorganic world, but which rarely occurs in organic matter. At the outer surface of their forms, radiolarians secrete their skeletal material in the spaces between bubbles of a foam. The regularity of their skeletons is due to the physical force of surface tension in which bubbles tend to organize in symmetric ways. Radiolaria have been found to take on all of the five forms of the Royal Platonic Family as well as other polyhedra. Some of the forms you are already quite familiar with. If you make a wire frame tetrahedron and dip it into a soap solution, the soap film will cling to the edges of the frame. This same configuration can be found in the siliceous skeletons of Callimitra, a member of the Radiolaria group, which is a spherical tetrahedron. Try other wire frame structures.

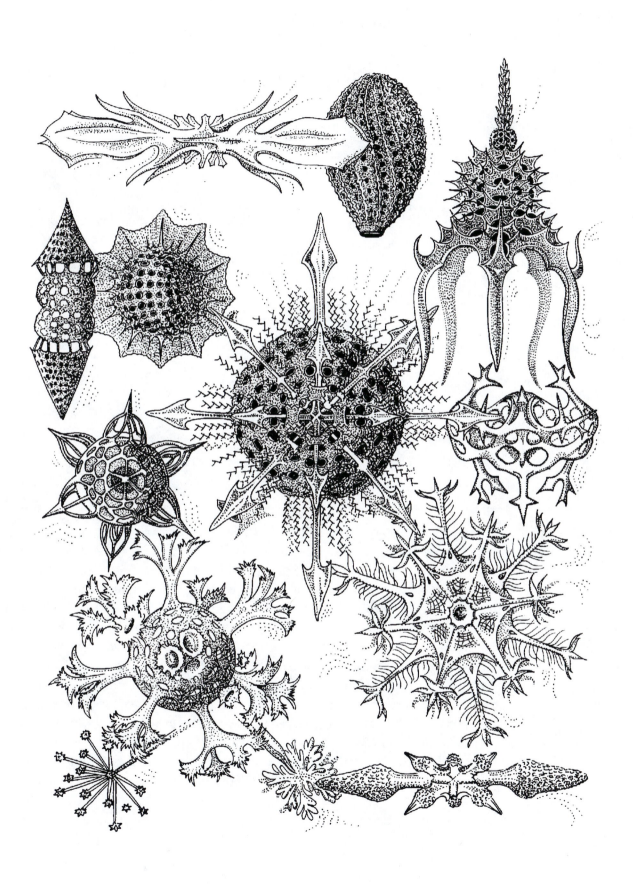

Dual Partners		Commonalities		Complementarities	
		Symmetries	Edges	Faces and Vertices	Vertex Nets
Platonic Pair	Cube and Octahedron	(6) 2-turn (4) 3-turn (3) 4-turn	12	6 ⟋⟍ 8 8 ⟍⟋ 6	4-4-4 3-3-3-3
Archimedean-Catalan Pair	Cuboctahedron and Rhombic Dodecahedron	(6) 2-turn (4) 3-turn (3) 4-turn	24	14 ⟋⟍ 12 12 ⟍⟋ 14	3-4-3-4 4-4-4 4-4-4-4
Platonic Pair	Dodecahedron and Icosahedron	(15) 2-turn (10) 3-turn (6) 5-turn	30	12 ⟋⟍ 20 20 ⟍⟋ 12	5-5-5 3-3-3-3-3
Archimedean-Catalan Pair	Icosidodecahedron and Rhombic Triacontahedron	(15) 2-turn (10) 3-turn (6) 5-turn	60	32 ⟋⟍ 30 30 ⟍⟋ 32	4-4-4 3-3-3-3

The Complementary Mesh

The Complementary Mesh

This page:
The chart above indicates commonalities and complementarities of the dual partners. Each face of a Catalan solid corresponds to a vertex of its Archimedean dual because of the fact that an Archi solid has all vertices equivalent and guarantees that its Catalan dual will have all its faces equivalent.

Throughout this chapter, we have woven an intricate mesh of complementarity and commonality. In so doing, we have shown that which is a complement, and is seen, is governed by that which is common and unseen. By this, we mean that the commonality of space determines the possible complementarity of form, and the commonality of symmetries determines the possible complementarity of structure.

We look at two particular figures to further illustrate this concept. They are the Catalan dual partners of two Archimedean Solids. The rhombic dodecahedron complements the cuboctahedron, and the rhombic triacon-

tahedron, the icosidodecahedron. If you look at the chart at the top of this page, you will see that the common threads throughout all of these figures are the rotational symmetries passed from parents to children, and then reflected in dual partners. Also the numbers of edges remain constant within the groups. The complementarity takes place through the exchanges of the numbers of faces and vertices. This is a result of having each face correspond to a vertex and each edge will correspond to an edge of the dual at right angles to the original. While an Archimedean solid has all its vertices the same, a Catalan solid has all its faces the same.

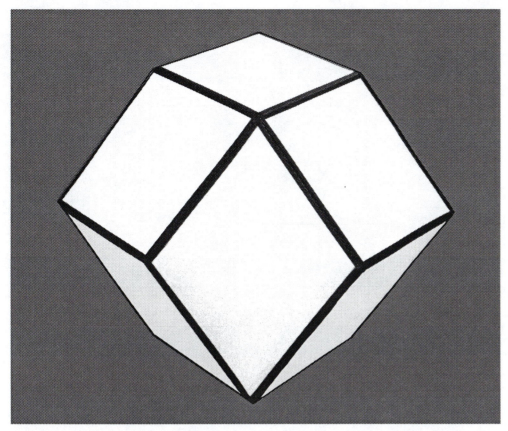

Left:
Donna Fowler. A model of the rhombic dodecahedron. Bristol paper and graphic tape.

Below:
Fig. 5.16 Template for the rhombic dodecahedron. You will need twelve of these.

The Rhombic Dodecahedron

This figure requires twelve rhombuses with two opposite angles of 70° 32' (A), and two opposite angles of 109° 28' (B).

Preparation
1. Duplicate the template in Fig. 5.16 twelve times.
2. Score and mountain fold all lines.
Assembly
This figure requires two different vertex nets.
1. Join four rhombuses together at A to form a *vertex cap* of 4-4-4-4.
2. Add one rhombus at a time at the B angles so that a 4-4-4 vertex is formed.
3. The remaining rhombuses can now be added one at a time until the form is compete. Make certain that all B's meet at a vertex of 4-4-4, and all A's meet at a vertex of 4-4-4-4.

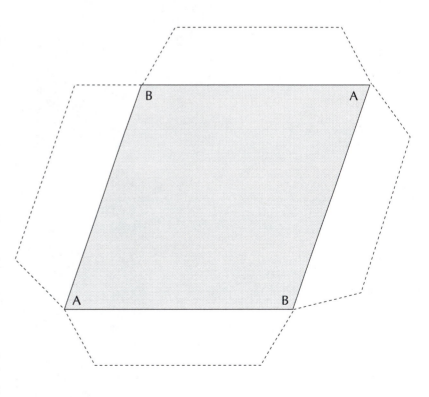

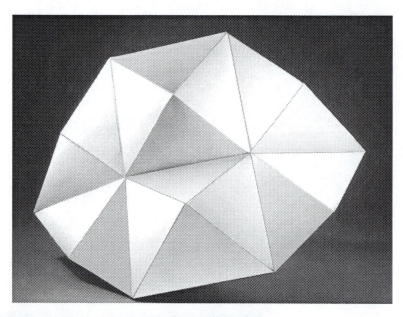

This page:
Student work. Cherie Cappelle. Three study variations on the template for the Catalan Solid called the tetrakis hexahedron. It is the dual of the truncated octahedron. Photocopied elements on paper.

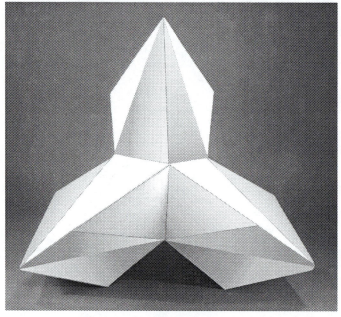

These two pages have models that relate to the Catalan solids. Notice that these forms have a relationship to both the Archimedean and Platonic solids. Each model is constructed from a particular template that has been duplicated a given number of times. Each template unit is composed of n-regular polygons which have been repeated around a vertex and joined along two edges to form a cap. If one subdivides the faces of the Platonics at midpoints of edges and/or of the entire polygon, new triangles and quadrilaterals appear that project slightly off the surface. The requisite number of caps are connected by using the arrangement around vertices that relate to the members of the Platonic Royal Family. If, however, you choose to use the templates in other vertex arrangements, you might obtain figures that look like those found on this page. Perhaps you would like to try a model for yourself. We suggest that you refer to the book, "Order in Space" by Keith Critchlow. There you will find the necessary nets for these objects.

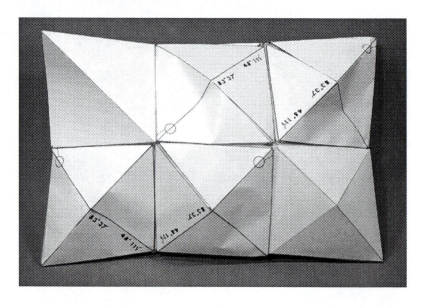

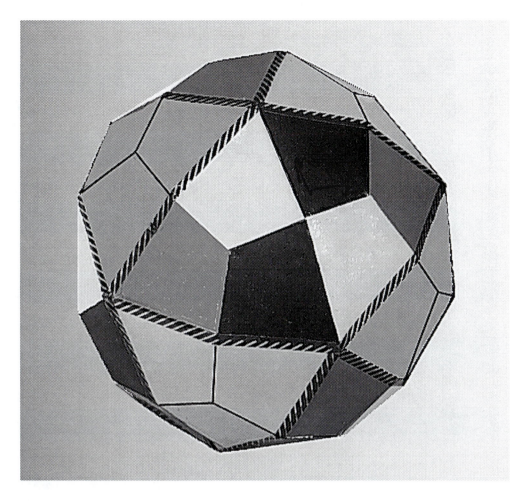

This page:
Student works. Top.
Mary Calnan. Trapezoidal
hexacontahedron. Dual of
the rhombicosidodecahe-
dron. Acrylic paint on paper
with graphic tape on the
edges.

Bottom:
Richard Wladkowski. Low-
er left is the tetrakis hexahedron, dual of the truncated
icosahedron. Acrylic paint
on watercolor paper.
Cappie Leake. Upper mid-
dle is the triakis tetrahedron,
dual of the truncated tetrahedron. Acrylic paint on
paper.

Andrea Dancer. Right is the
trakis octahedron, dual of the
truncated cube. Acrylic paint
on paper with collage elements.

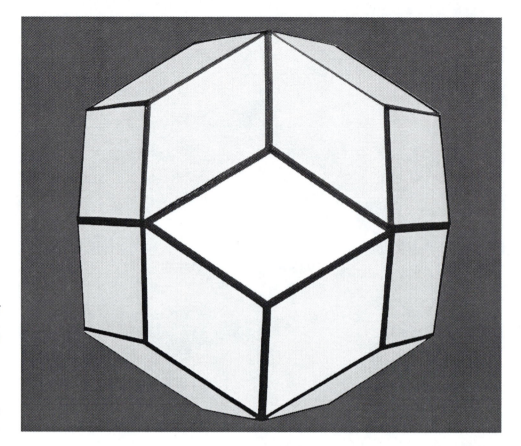

Right:
Donna Fowler. A model of the rhombic triacontahedron. Bristol paper and graphic tape.

Below:
Fig. 5.17 Template for the rhombic triacontahedron. You will need thirty of these.

The Rhombic Triacontahedron

This figure requires thirty rhombuses with angles of two opposite angles of 63°26' (A), and two opposite angles of 116°34' (B).

Preparation
1. Duplicate the template in Fig. 5.17 thirty times.
2. Score and mountain fold all lines.
Assembly
This figure requires two diffferent vertex nets.
1. Join five rhombuses together at A to for a *vertex cap* of 4-4-4-4-4.
2. Add one rhombus at a time at the B angles so that a 4-4-4 vertex is formed.
3. The remaining rhombuses can now be added one at a time until the form is complete. Make certain that all B's meet at a vertex of 4-4-4, and all A's meet at a vertex of 4-4-4-4-4.

Our polyhedra families like to partner with each other in very tight-knit communities of like-minded individuals. Once a bond is formed, it repeats in endless rows and stacks, back and forth, up and down. There are no gaps between members. They stand shoulder to shoulder and regard each other face to face.

The cube, the patriarch of the Royal Family, and the Rhombic Dodecahedron of the Catalan Clan, can simply go on and on mirroring themselves. Others need a one-to-one relationship. Our regular tetrahedron needs an octahedron for its significant other, but it can also find meaning with a truncated tetrahedron from the Archi Family. Some other Archi's join with the Platonics in trios, others in quartets in order to make beautiful music. The chart on the following page shows the space filling arrangements of the polyhedra that we have looked at throughout this book plus three prisms that we did not. They are the triangular, hexagonal and octagonal prisms.

Two of them are shown in the photograph below. You might like to do some research on the subject of space-filling. According to mathematicians, while there are only 17 groups that cover the plane in two-space, there are theoretically 230 groups that can fill three-dimensional space. These groups all depend upon rotational, reflectional, and translational symmetries. Filling three-space is analogous to tiling the plane in two-space. The essential requirement for space filling is that the sum of the interfacial angles around a common vertex must equal 360°. The same requirement holds true for tilings on the plane.

Mineral crystals are examples of natural forms that are built up from millions of space-filling layers of atoms It takes many, many, many of these layers before the crystal form becomes visible to the naked eye. The outward forms of crystals, however, are polyhedral and relate to the Catalans as well as other familiar faces.

In three-dimensional space, only a few basic shapes will combine to build stable structures or do useful work. These patterns prevail because they make the most efficient use of energy. They are purposeful.

Horace Freeland Judson

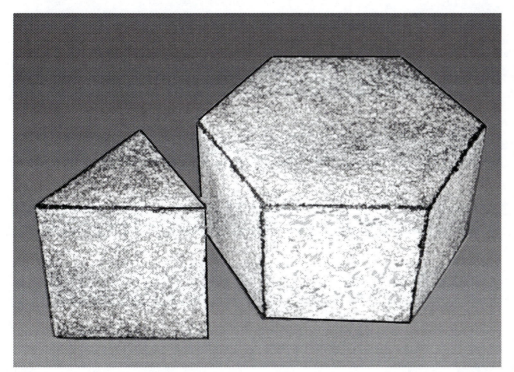

This page:
Rochelle Newman. Models of the triangular and hexagonal prisms.
The two objects can be considered a partnership pair if the lengths of the hexagons, triangles and squares are kept constant.
The triangular prism requires two triangles and three squares. The hexagonal prism requires two hexagons and six squares. by the process of stretching the squares could "grow" into Dynamic or Phi-Family rectangles. The space filling properties, however, would remain the same.
Six triangular prisms around a single vertex would give us the hexagonal prism.
Try constructing a right triangular prism or build a non-regular hexagonal prism. What would their space-filling properties be?

Uniform Space Filling With Polyhedra
(at each vertex, the number and kind of polyhedra stay constant)

One Type		
Triangular prism		
Hexagonal prism		
Cube		
Rhombic dodecahedron		
Two Types		
Tetrahedron	1	
Truncated tetrahedron	1	Unit 1:1
Tetrahedron	2	
Octahedron	2	Unit 2:1
Octahedron	1	
Cuboctahedron	1	Unit 1:1
Truncated cuboctahedron	1	
Octagonal prism	3	Unit 1:3
Three Types		
Cube	3	
Truncated cuboctahedron	1	
Truncated octahedron	1	Unit 3:1:1
Rhombicuboctahedron	1	
Cuboctahedron	1	
Cube	3	Unit 1:3:3
Rhombicuboctahedron	1	
Cube	1	
Tetrahedron	2	Unit 1:1:2
Truncated Cuboctahedron	1	
Truncated Cube	1	
Truncated Tetrahedron	2	Unit 1:1:2
Truncated octahedron	1	
Cuboctahedron	1	
Truncated tetrahedron	2	Unit 1:1:2
Four Types		
Rhombicuboctahedron	1	
Truncated cube	1	
Octagonal prism	3	
Cube	3	Unit 1:1:3:3

Do not let the information in this chapter mislead you into thinking that there are only a few polyhedra. Altering limits, changing definitions, and stretching faces all add to the possibilities.

Grab some paper, paint, and a pot of paste. Become a polyhedra playmate. Go for a stellation jaunt. Or take a rhombic ramble to discover what happens when all those square faces are tilted. Whichever partners you choose, partake of pleasure.

Particular polygons become polyhedra.
Pairs become partners.
Partners become parents.
Potentialities become probabilities.

At first glance, finite families.
At deeper seeing, endless fascination.
A fitness of forms.
　　No frills.
　　Simple.
　　Elegant.
　　Right.

The symmetry satisfies.

Caps become cups.
Squares tilt into rhombuses, right-handed and left.
Turnings, twistings, truncations.
One figure transforms into another.

Suddenly polyhedral puzzles lead to polyhedra passion.
　　　　　　　　　　Rochelle Newman

Above:
Donna Fowler. Models of a nonregular Golden Pair. These were introduced to us by artist/geometer, Vedder Wright.

Left:
A nonregular dodecahedron.

Right:
A nonregular icosahedron.

Problems

1. Make a chart that shows that Euler's Formula holds for the convex deltahedra.

2. Take two of the deltahedra, truncate all of the vertices in both forms, and construct the new polyhedra that are generated by the truncations. Make a template so that other people can build the forms.

3. Take one of the Archimedean Solids and open it at the vertices so that new polygons can be inserted. Build a model. Write up your procedure.

4. Look at the transformation of the Archi's on pages 261-265. Describe at least two other processes, such as chamfering and stretching, that can be used to explore the polyhedra.

5. Given your understanding of duality, determine the dual polyhedron of one other Archimedean Solid without resorting to research. Construct the model in order to see if your reasoning is correct.

6. Cap one of the Archimedean polyhedra using the necessary pyramidal cap.

7. Transform a Platonic or Archimedean Solid from a regular form into a nonregular one. Describe your process in writing. Could you write a general rule for this process?

8. Research the mathematics of the 59 stellations of the icosahedron. Write a short paper that describes the mathematical reasoning so that a layman might understand it.

9. Answer in writing: How does one go about constructing proofs for the existence of polyhedra? (This might take a lifetime of math.)

10. Using the polygonal templates on page 225, enclose a new volume of space.

11. Research the mathematical discoveries of Leonhard Euler. Write a summary of what you find.

12. Using the Golden Triangle with its angles of 72°, 72°, 36°, develop a new family of polyhedral forms.

13. Put pyramidal caps on the faces of the Platonic Solids. Have you seen any of these polyhedral transformations anywhere?

Projects

1. In materials of your choice, build a sculpture that joins the five Platonic solids in an aesthetically satisfying way. Consider varying the sizes, transforming the planar faces or using skeletal elements only.

2. Construct a helical column using octahedra. Develop and execute a pattern for the faces.

3. Imagine that you have been commissioned to design a public monument for the Washington, D. C. area. The focus of this work is to celebrate life and peace. Build a model using a member of the Archimedean Family and your creativity.

4. With Golden triangles, cap all or part of any two of the polyhedra that you have met in this chapter. Be sure to make them artful.

5. Use the concept of duality to create a model for an outdoor sculpture that celebrates both similarities and differences. Design an environment for your piece.

6. Use corrugated cardboard as your building material and one of the concepts from this chapter as

inspiration, to design and execute a special domicile for your pet dog, cat, or bird.

7. Using black illustration board and colored acetate, create a prototype for a stained glass ornament based on one of the forms in this chapter.

8. Create a prototype for a fantasy merry-go-round based on one of the polyhedral forms. Work with the idea of creating awareness of endangered species through this project.

9. Choose one of the figures in this chapter and transform it to represent a natural creature — its form and its pattern. Construct it from a sturdy material, and create a simple wheeled pull toy.

10. Do an illustration of a nursery rhyme or fairy tale that incorporates figures from this chapter. Add elements that take it out of the plane.

11. Do drawings and then build a model for an architectural complex that involves the stacking of uniform space-filling polyhedra.

Edible Architecture

12. Choose one of the forms from this chapter and cut out cardboard templates for a variation on a house for the old woman who lived in a shoe, Cinderella's coach and four, or a structure from a story of your choice. Execute it in gingerbread using the recipe below. Decorate it with frosting and candy.

Dough

8 cups all purpose flour
1 1/2 tsp. ground cinnamon
1 1/2 tsp. ground ginger
1/4 tsp. salt
1 3/4 cups light corn syrup
1 cup firmly packed brown sugar
1 1/2 sticks margarine

• Line three 12" x 15" cookie sheets with foil, making sure the edges are covered. Cut out pattern pieces from waxed paper.
• Stir 4 cups flour and the spices together in large bowl.
• In a 2 quart saucepan over low heat, melt margarine. Add corn syrup and sugar, and stir until sugar dissolves.
• With mixer at low speed, gradually beat syrup mixture into flour mixture. Increase speed to medium and add 2 cups flour. Add remaining flour and mix with a spoon or your hands. Add flour if dough is sticky. It should be firm.
• Divide dough into thirds and place one third on each cookie sheet. Roll into 11" x 14" rectangles. Refrigerate for at least one hour.
• Heat oven to 350°.
• Remove sheets from refrigerator and arrange the pattern pieces so that there is a half an inch between pieces. Use a sharp knife to cut out pieces.
• Remove patterns and all excess

dough. Reroll excess on cookie sheet later as needed.
• Bake for fifteen minutes or until forms are set and edges begin to brown.
• Cool completely before removing from foil.
• Repeat until all pattern pieces are used. If you need more dough, make the recipe again rather than doubling it.
• Brush a small amount of corn syrup over the surfaces of the cardboard pieces and secure them to the backs of the gingerbread pieces. Allow to dry thoroughly before assembling.

Icing

3 egg whites
1 lb. confectioners sugar
1/2 tsp. cream of tartar

• At low speed, in a small bowl, beat all ingredients together until blended. Beat at high speed until stiff. Add more sugar if necessary.
• Divide into smaller bowls and color as desired with food coloring. Adding powdered cocoa will help match the color with the gingerbread for the icing that is to be used as mortar to hold the pieces together. The stiffer the mortar, the faster it will dry. Place plastic wrap on all surfaces to keep the icing from drying out.
• Decorate pieces as much as possible before assembling. Support the structure while the mortar sets. Joining just a few pieces at a time will help to keep the structure from collapsing as you build. Gluing internal supports, such as cardboard tubes, to the cardboard pieces will also help solidify the structure. Make sure it dries thoroughly before you finish decorating. Enjoy!

Further Reading

Coxeter, H. S. M., P. DuVal, H.T. Flather, and J. F. Petrie. *The Fifty-Nine Icosahedra*. New York: Springer Verlag, 1982.

Cundy and Rollett. *Mathematical Models*. Oxford and New York: Oxford University Press, 1977.

Critchlow, Keith. Order in Space. New York: the Viking Press, 1970.

Holden, Alan. *shapes, space, and symmetry*. New York: Columbia University Press, 1971.

Hargittai, Istvan, editor. *Fivefold Symmetry*. Singapore: World Scientific, 1992.

Pearce, Peter and Susan. *Polyhedra primer*. New York: Van Nostrand Reinhold Company, 1978.

Pugh, Anthony. *Polyhedra a visual approach*. Palo Alto, California: Dale Seymour Publications, 1990.

Solit, Matthew A., Marvin Solit, and Charles Letovsky. *Exploring Math with Root Blocks*. Waltham, Massachusetts: Rhombics, Inc., 1990.

Wade, David. *Crystal & Dragon*. Rochester, Vermont: Destiny Books, 1993.

Wenninger, Magnus J. *Polyhedron Models*. Cambridge: Cambridge University Press, 1971.

6 Crystal Conclusion

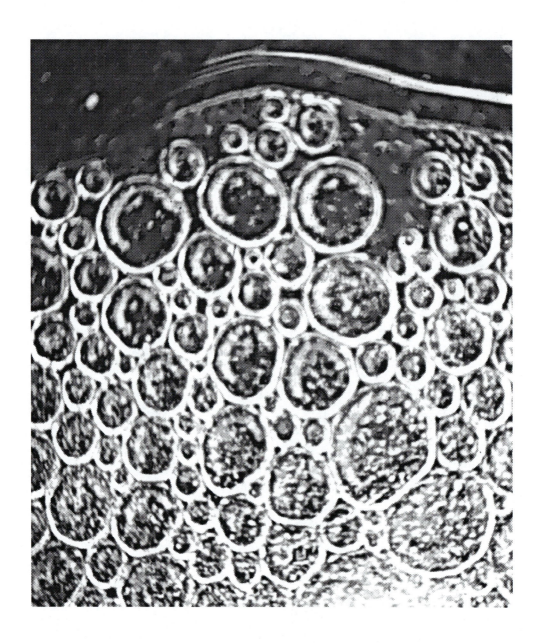

A crystal is ordered because of its very simplicity, but an organism is ordered for precisely the opposite reason-by virtue of its complexity. In both cases the concept of order is a global one; the orderliness refers to the system as a whole. Crystalline order concerns the way that the atomic arrangement repeats itself in a regular pattern throughout the material. Biological order is recognized because the diverse component parts of an organism cooperate to perform a coherent unitary function.

Paul Davies-Ecologist

We have come to the last section of this book. Each of the previous chapters only teases the appetite for having more. As we have, perhaps, only hinted at heretofore, we state emphatically. We believe that everything is connected to everything else in subtle and complex ways. Nothing exists in isolation. Everything is interdependent: space and form, a partnership; symmetry and structure, a partnership; microscopic and macroscopic, a partnership; organic and inorganic, a partnership; spheres and polyhedra, a partnership. Thus, we want to conclude with an example from nature that displays all this interconnectedness. The domain of crystals is our candidate.

Boulders, rocks, stones, pebbles, soil particles, and sand grains are the famililar components of the natural landscape that surrounds us all. They are part of the inorganic realm. We take them for granted and for the most part, ignore their existence. On the other hand, gold, diamonds, rubies, emeralds, and sapphires, all attract our attention as they conjure up images of beauty, luxury and opulence. They are savored worldwide by different cultures and throughout time. People have fought and died for the mining and purchase of them. Legends surround their acquisition. Persons who possess them sometimes believe that they have magic and power. They are given in courtship and in marriage. They are the rich relatives of mineral crystals which have been polished and refined. The poor relatives can be found on everyone's table. They are the sugar and salt of the earth.

The solid portion of this planet, Earth, is made up of rocks. These are composed of minerals, usually more than one kind to a rock, and these minerals are composed of natural crystalline materials. A minerals is a substance with a definite homogeneous chemical composition produced by an organic process. The greatest majority of minerals form as crystals. In fact, except for glass and organic matter, all solids are crystalline. Under the

> Ultimately all the regularities of form and structure that we see in nature, ranging from the hexagonal shape of a snowflake to the intricate symmetries of living forms in flowers and animals, are based upon the symmetries of these atomic patterns.
>
> Victor Weisskopf
> Physicist

Facing page:
These seven crystal systems are schematic building blocks that relate to the symmetries of the point groups discussed in chapter 1. All crystals can be related to one of these groups of blocks. Within each group, there are several different ideal polyhedral forms. For example, within the cubic system, you will find octahedral, dodecahedral, and tetrahedral forms. The blocks have rotational symmetry and rotations occur with 2-turn, 3-turn, and 4-turn axes. There are 32 point groups, called classes, that are derived from these building blocks. There are a total of 230 groups based on the internal arrangements within the blocks. Research the subject of crystallography if you want to know more.
The unit building block is the smallest volume that can be repeated indefinitely in three dimensions. It contains all the various ions, and their relationships, of the crystal structure.
These systems are defined by three or four axes of either equal or unequal length that intersect at the center of any "perfect" crystal form. The length of the axes and the angles between them define the shape of the crystal.

correct circumstance, even organic matter can form crystals.

There are at least 2,000 minerals that scientists have identified, yet 95% of the earth's solid crust contains only about twenty of them. While all crystals are homogeneous in their individual chemical compositions, most rocks are heterogeneous. A rock can be broken apart and the minerals separated out. These then can be identified by their purity, chemical composition, luster, and crystallinity. They are also distinguished by color, shape and hardness, but only crystals can be cleaved apart by breaking them along planes.

Minerals, as with all matter, are made up of collections of atoms organized in particular ways. The arrangement and electrical charges of the atoms give rise to the basic elements, as seen in the periodic chart, pg. 67, that are found in such substances as iron. It is the combination of these elements that gives the diversity that we see in everything around us.

Crystals have external form and internal structure. At levels where the unaided eye cannot see, atoms cluster together in layers and then in stacks, all dependent upon the atomic arrangements of their elements. A crystal is a cooperative community in which the overall stability of the group depends upon the cohesion of a fair number of molecules. These millions upon millions of atoms produce a form that can finally be seen by the naked eye. All of the faces of these forms are planar resulting from their atomic planes. A perfectly formed crystal, however, is a rarity since from the beginning the growth is not consistent. Natural crystals display pits, ridges, grooves, mottlings, and other manner of defects. These, however, allow for interesting things to happen to the forms. A crystal is extremely sensitive to minute changes in its growing environment; however, the final product, on detailed inspection, can always be related to the geometry of the basic atomic unit which is the smallest volume that maintains the chemical formula, atomic arrangement, and the geometric properties of direction and proportion of that particular crystal. Thus, crystals show a great many different forms. But all of these can be related to a system of seven basic three-dimensional forms based on common geometric features and symmetries. Like our transformed blocks in Chapter 3, these systems can all be derived from the basic cube. The chart on the next page shows how these forms are derived.

The Seven Crystal Systems

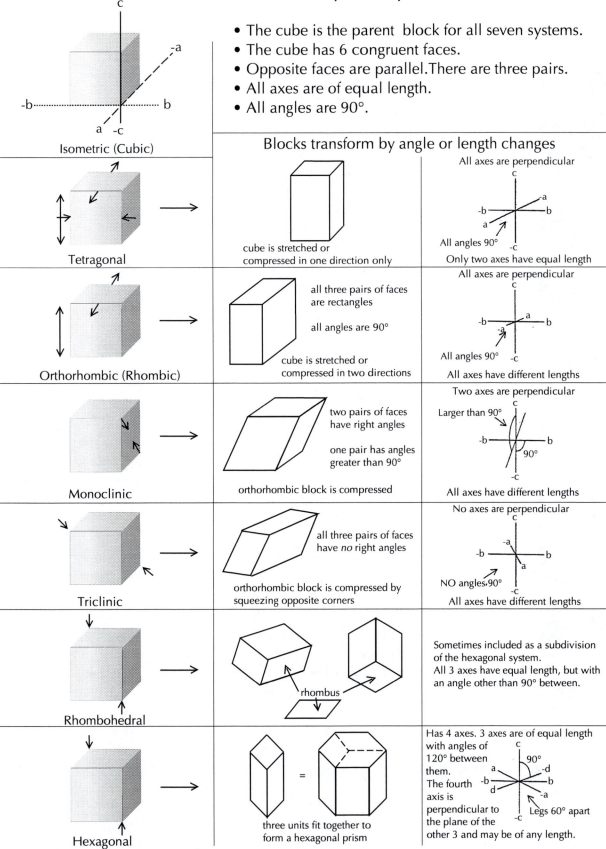

- The cube is the parent block for all seven systems.
- The cube has 6 congruent faces.
- Opposite faces are parallel. There are three pairs.
- All axes are of equal length.
- All angles are 90°.

Isometric (Cubic)

Blocks transform by angle or length changes

Tetragonal

cube is stretched or compressed in one direction only

All axes are perpendicular

All angles 90°

Only two axes have equal length

Orthorhombic (Rhombic)

all three pairs of faces are rectangles

all angles are 90°

cube is stretched or compressed in two directions

All axes are perpendicular

All angles 90°

All axes have different lengths

Monoclinic

two pairs of faces have right angles

one pair has angles greater than 90°

orthorhombic block is compressed

Two axes are perpendicular

Larger than 90°

90°

All axes have different lengths

Triclinic

all three pairs of faces have *no* right angles

orthorhombic block is compressed by squeezing opposite corners

No axes are perpendicular

NO angles 90°

All axes have different lengths

Rhombohedral

rhombus

Sometimes included as a subdivision of the hexagonal system.
All 3 axes have equal length, but with an angle other than 90° between.

Hexagonal

three units fit together to form a hexagonal prism

Has 4 axes. 3 axes are of equal length with angles of 120° between them.
The fourth axis is perpendicular to the plane of the other 3 and may be of any length.

90°

Legs 60° apart

Snowflake designs courtesy of Dover Publications.

For those of us who live in the Northeast United States, we get bombarded by crystal structures at least part of the year. Usually this happens somewhere between December and March. Minute miracles of magic moments, with symmetry and structure, moving through space, transforming from liquid to solid and back to liquid again. Water, snowflakes, and ice are all variations on a theme. Ice is crystallized water. If ice is heated to just above 0°C, it will start to melt and become water once again. The melting point of a solid, which is a temperature, is a point of balance between the two conditions of crystallizing and liquefying. Snowflakes are snow crystals. They begin with a tiny seed, such as a speck of dust, grabbing water molecules as they descend from on high. Individually they do not amount to much, but collectively they pack a wallop that can bring a halt to many things. But, for the most part, many of us are delighted by the presence of these ephemeral bodies.

Snow crystals form in the clouds. Vapor freezes into the first "seeds" of the crystal and gradually grow into the ubiquitous snowflake. At very low temperatures, the droplets of water become supercooled which means they are still liquid even though they are below freezing temperature. Under certain conditions, the supercooled droplets evaporate and the vapor freezes into minute ice crystals directly. In ice, the water molecules repeat in fixed arrangements. The freezing of a teaspoonful of water requires the precise orientation of about 10^{22} molecules. These water molecules are the basic building units. The moisture and the atmospheric temperature determine the shape of a particular flake. Because of the crystalline form, 90% of the snow is actually air. Flakes may take the form of flat hexagons, columns, cups or needlelike shapes. The more complex crystal shapes occur at higher temperatures when there is more humidity available. At this stage, crystals have more branching extensions. Small and simple crystals arise from slow growth, while relatively complex ones happen with rapid growth. No two snowflakes are ever exactly alike despite the underlying symmetry of their inherent structures. Because of the way the hydrogen bonds of the snowflake operate, crystals need less energy if they add new layers to the side faces and so the crystal becomes hexagonal. As humidity increases, the rate of growth does also. It occurs more rapidly at the vertices of the hexagon giving the familiar six-pointed star. Since each snowflake forms under subtly different atmospheric conditions, each flake becomes unique in its form.

As far back as 1611, Johannes Kepler, intrigued by the properties of snowflakes wrote an essay in which he believed that there was a link between the ways in which collections of spheres would arrange themselves in economic groupings and the snow crystal. But he did not have the kind of scientific equipment that would enable him to know that for sure. By 1929, scientists had worked out the way in which water molecules arrange themselves. By this time, it was known that snow crystals are dependent upon the symmetry of the atomic arrangement; the relative speeds at which each face of a crystal grows, and these differ; and the need to minimize the use of energy in maintaining the crystal surfaces.

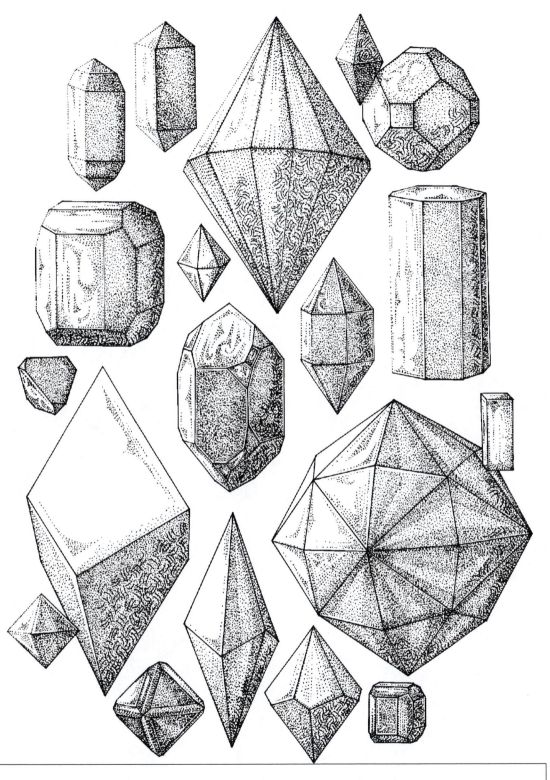

Sufficient has been said to show that crystal building, which is in principle so simple--a matter of stacking molecules or ions as a child stacks building blocks--turns out to be unexpectedly complex when we try to understand the precise way in which it happens and to find out what controls the speed of it. The transformation from chaos to order seems to be as difficult for molecules as for men.

Charles Bunn, Scientist, The Royal Institution, London

The crystal may be regarded as one of the basic form patterns, in which the component atoms or molecules are so spatially arranged that the unit can withstand the stresses of the environment, or be able to accommodate itself either to free space or to the pressures of confinement.

David Drabkin, Biochemist

Winter in New England--the road less travelled.

Snow-covered garden giving simplicity and silence to the moment.

".....snowflakes create beautiful, hexagonal patterns, none of which are precisely the same. These snowflakes and crystals, in turn, have inherited their structure from the way in which their molecules have been geometrically arranged. This arrangement is mainly determined by the electron shells of the molecule, which, in turn takes us back to the rotational symmetries of the quantum theory.......

Michio Kaku, Theorectical physicist

The Designer is found in the details.

This section concludes with questions:

Is there a Grand Design?

Is there a Grand Designer?
If the answer to either, or both, of these is "yes",
then another whole series of questions arises.

Is the Grand Design knowable by
humans?
Is the Grand Design comprehensible
through Reason?
      Or is it Faith?
      Or is it Faith in Reason?

Can Reason only tell us How? Not Why?
Or Who?
Or is it always Mystery?
Is the Grand Design simple but disguised
as complex?
Is it so simple that we cannot see it?
Is beauty the Way into the Grand
Design?
Is Beauty related to Truth, both leading
us to experience the Grand Design?

We can only say, that if there is a Grand Design, we are a part of it.

Rochelle Newman

Selected References

Atkins, P.W. *Creation Revisited.* Oxford and New York: W.H. Freeman & Co., 1992.

Baggott, Jim. *Perfect Symmetry.* Oxford, New York, Tokyo: Oxford University Press, 1994.

Ball, Rouse. *A Short Account of the History of Mathematics.* New York: Dover, 1960.

Banchoff, Thomas F. *Beyond The Third Dimension.* New York: Scientific American Library, 1990.

Bogert, L. Jean, Ph.D. *Fundamentals of Chemistry.* Philadelphia and London:W.B. Saunders Company, 1963
.

Boles/Newman. *The Surface Plane.: The Golden Relationship: Art, Math & Nature.* Bradford: Pythagorean Press, 1992.

Bruni, James. *Experiencing Geometry.* Belmont: Wadsworth, 1977.

Buffaloe, Neal D. and J. B. Throneberry. *Principles of Biology.* New Jersey: Prentice-Hall, 1967.

Capra, Fritjof. *The Tao of Physics.* New York: Bantam Books, 1965.

Capra, Fritjof. *The Turning Point.* New York: Bantam Books, 1983.

Carmen, Robert A and Hale M. Saunders. *Mathematics for the Trades A Guided Approach.* New York: John Wiley & Sons, 1986.

Companion, Audrey L. *Chemical Bonding*. New York: Bantam Books, 1983

Cotterill, Rodney. *The Cambridge Guide to the Material World*. Cambridge: Cambridge University Press, 1985.

Coulter, Merle C. *The Story of the Plant Kingdom*. Chicago: The University of Chicago Press, 1935.

Coxeter, H.S.M. *Introduction to Geometry*. New York: John Wiley and Son, 1961.

Critchlow, Keith. *Order in Space*. New York: The Viking Press, 1970.

Cundy and Rollett. *Mathematical Models*. New York: Oxford University Press, 1961.

DeDuve, Christian. *Blueprint for a Cell: The Nature and Origin of Life*. North Carolina: Neil Patterson Publishers, 1991.

Doczi, Gyorgy. *The Power of Limits*. Boulder: Shambala Press, 1981.

Feininger, Andreas. *The Anatomy of Nature*. New York: Dover, 1956.

Friday, Adrian and David S. Ingram, General Editors. *The Cambridge Encyclopedia of Life Sciences*. New York: Cambridge University Press, 1985.

Fuse, Tomoko. *Unit Origami*. Tokyo: Japan Publications Inc., 1990.

Gardner, Martin. *The New Ambidextrous Universe Third Revised Edition*. New York: W.H. Freeman and Company, 1990.

Ghyka, Matila. *The Geometry of Art and Life*. New York: Dover, 1977.

Cohn-Vossen. *Geometry and the Imagination.* New York: Chelsea Publishing Co, 1952.

Holden, Alan. *Shapes, Space and Symmetry.* New York: Columbia University Press, 1971.

Huntley, H.E. *The Divine Proportion.* New York: Dover, 1970.

Kaku, Michio. *Hyperspace.* New York and Oxford: Oxford University Press, 1994.

Kline, Morris. *Mathematics and the Physical World.* New York: Oxford University Press, 1953.

Kline, Morris. *Mathematics in Western Culture.* New York: Oxford University Press, 1953.

Lord, E.A. and C. B. Wilson. *The Mathematical Desription of Shape and Form.* New York: John Wiley & Sons, 1984.

McGilvery, Robert W., Ph,D. *Biochemical Concepts.* Philadelphia: W.B. Saunders Co. , 1975

Hilbert, D. and Pauling, Linus. *The Architecture of Molecules.* San Francisco: Freeman, 1964.

Mora, S. Rapsomanikis and W.R. Johnston. *Introductory Chemistry for the Environmental Sciences.* Cambridge and New York: Cambridge University Press, 1991.

Newman/Boles. *Universal Patterns: The Golden Relationship: Art, Math & Nature.* Bradford: Pythagorean Press, 1992.

Pearce, Peter and Susan Pearce. *Polyhedra Primer.* New York: Van Nostrand Reinhold, 1978.

Pugh, Anthony. *Polyhedra a visual approach.* Palo Alto: Dale Seymour Publications, 1990.

Seymour, Raymond B. and Charles E. Carraher. *Giant Molecules*. New York: John Wiley & Sons, Inc., 1990.

Sinkankas, John. *Minerology: A First Course*. New York: Van Nostrand Co., Inc., 1966.

Smith, Robert D. *Vocational Technical Mathematics*. New York: Delmar Publications, Inc., 1983.

Spielberg, Nathan and Byron I. Anderson. *Seven Ideas that Shook the Universe*. New York: John Wiley & Sons, Inc., 1987.

Stanley, Melissa and George Andrykovitch. *Living: An Introduction to Biology*. Boston:Addison-Wesley, 1984.

Thomas, Richard K. *Three-Dimensional Design, A Cellular Approach*. New York: Van Nostrand Reinhold, 1969.

Wenninger, Magnus J. *Polyhedron Models*. Cambridge: University Press, 1971.

Wenninger, Magnus J. *Spherical Models*. Cambridge: University Press, 1979.

Weyl, Hermann. *Symmetry*. Princeton: University Press, 1952.

Williams, Robert. *The Geometrical Foundation of Natural Structure: A Source Book for Design*. New York: Dover,1979.

Zee, A. *Fearful Symmetry*. New York: MacMillan-Publishing Co. 1986.

Zeier, Franz. Paper Constructions. New York: Charles Scribner's Sons, 1980.

Zelanski, Paul and Mary Pat Fisher. *Shaping Space*. New York: Holt, Rinehart and Winston, 1987.

Art Appendix: Materials and Techniques

Contents

This page:
Student work. Lillian Ng. Stacked Planes. White Formica surface covering on a pressed board.

Basic Materials for Working With Paper

Paper has been the material of choice throughout this book. It is versatile, easily found, easily manipulated, relatively inexpensive, and can be elegant as well as humble. We have encouraged you to use it first so that you can experiment freely and quickly. Its surface accepts a variety of coverings so that within the confines of the forms you build, you can also try out ways to create patterns and textures. The following is a very brief list of readily available supplies.

Acrylic Paints
This is a polymer paint which is soluble in water when liquid but which dries to a hard permanent finish. It can be manipulated in many ways so that it can mimic transparent watercolor, opaque gouache, buttery oil paint. It comes in jars or tubes depending upon the application required. It can also be used in conjunction with other materials such as pencil, crayon, oil based crayons, pastels, traditional watercolor, and gouache. There are many, many good books introducing acrylics. Check your local library and favorite bookstore.

Adhesives
Your choice of adhesive will depend upon the weight of the papers you are using as well as the required drying time. A glue stick will work well for a quick study provided that your paper is fairly lightweight. Apply to both surfaces of the work and hold together with binder clips until it sets. Acrylic medium, either matte or gloss finish, acts as an adhesive. It works well on light weight papers such as brown bags or magazine pages. White tacky glue is a thicker adhesive but in the same family as the acrylic polymer. It will hold on heavy weight papers such as bristol, cardstock, cardboard, illustration board, oak tag, etc. Apply to two facing surfaces, and hold together with binder clips or clamps. Rubber cement will work as a permanent bond if both surfaces are covered with it. Let dry thoroughly before joining together.

Construction Tools
Compass of good quality
Metal straightedge
Pencils of various degrees of hardness
Technical pens
Scissors
T-square and triangles
Utility Knife with extra blades
(computers and/or photcopiers can make some of the work go faster)

Papers
Acetate of various thicknesses
Bristol board, various weights
Cardboard
Cardstock
Construction, good quality
Copier type for rough studies
Illustration board
Mat board
Oak tag, manilla folders
Tracing paper for design work
Transfer paper
Watercolor of various weights

The Color Wheel

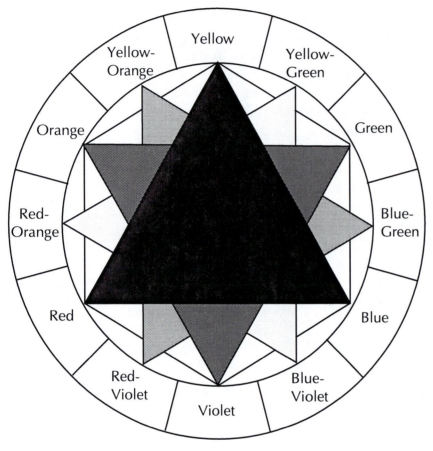

There are many systems used to describe color. This color wheel is based on a twelve tone structure. Each color has three characteristics: hue (its name), purity (the amount of saturation) and tone (the lightness or darkness of the color).

Yellow, Red, and Blue are the three primary colors. On computer programs, you will also find a system using Cyan, Magenta, and Yellow. In considering light, the primaries are Red, Green, and Blue. Theoretically, all the other colors can be mixed from only the three primaries.

It is best, however, when purchasing pigment colors to include white, black, and violets in order to gain the maximum flexibility when mixing colors. You must also take into consideration the amount of transparency and opacity of the colors you choose.

A secondary color structure is obtained by mixing together a pair of primary colors. The secondary colors are orange (red & yellow), green (blue & yellow), and violet (blue & red).

A mixture of a primary and a secondary color yields one of the tertiary colors which are the remaining ones on the wheel. For example, yellow & green gives yellow-green.

The colors in any artwork must have some relationship to each other, either by similarity or by contrast. The final effect is also influenced by the ratios of the colors.

Here are a few ways by which to obtain a color structure

1. Color (your choice) to a tone to a gray.
2. Color (your choice) to a tint to a white.
3. Color (your choice) to a shade to a black.
4. Tint to a tone to a shade.
5. Tint to a shade to a tone to a gray.
6. Shade to a tone to a white.
7. Color (your choice) to a tint to a white to a gray to a black.

The Tone Scale Related to Color

Tone, sometimes called value, refers to the degree of lightnessor darkness of a surface or an area. Black absorbs most light while white reflects it. Even though, in the natural world, there is an infinite range of tones between the extremes of pure light and pure darkness, the materials available to the artist at this point in time have a more narrow, finite, range. It has been suggested that the average human eye can distinguish among forty variations of tone, but for practical purposes, we shall use a scale of eleven steps. White and black will occupythe extreme positions on the scale while the nine other steps will move from light to dark grays. Every color, or hue, at its maximum purity (sometimes called saturation) has a corresponding value. In an artwork that uses color, the artist not only has to be sensitive to color choice but also to the tone of each color.

The choice of one manipulation will depend upon the inent of a particular work. Tones may be used in a highly representational work in order to create the illusion of actual three-dimensional forms. These will suggest the play of light and shadow across volumes. Or, in more abstract works, the tones may be used in a purely arbitrary way for emtional affect or form considerations.

Every material that can produce tone has its own value range. A black marker will differ from an HB pencil. It is a good idea, therefore, to set up a value scale using a particular material when deciding upon which material to use for a particular project.

Terms Related to Value:
Tint-when white is added to a color
Tone-when gray is added to a color
Shade-when black is added to a color.

Warm or Cool grays - When particular hues are added to grays. Orange will warm a gray while blue will cool the color.

Chiaroscuro - subtle modulation of tone from light to dark in order to create the illusion of three-dimensional volume on a two-dimensional surface plane.

Grisaille - an underpainting of tone that sets the light to dark relationships before color is applied.

Tenebrism - the use of extreme contrsting chiaroscuro to create highly dramatic effects.

1. High Contrast Range
One that uses the extremes of black and white only.

2. Neutral Range
One that uses black, white, and only a middle gray.

3. Light Tone Range
One that uses the grays at the light end of the value scale where middle gray functions as the darkest value.

4. Dark Tone Range
One that uses the grays at the dark end of the value scale where middle gray functions as the lightest value.

The Twelve Hues of the Color Wheel
and their Corresponding Tones

	Yellow	Yellow Orange	Orange	Red Orange	Red
White					
10%	Hansa Yellow Light Cadmium Yellow Light				
20%	Cadmium Yellow Medium				
30%		Azo	Cadmium Orange		
40%	Yellow Ochre				
50%					Cadmium Red Light
60%	Raw Sienna			Red Oxide	Cadmium Red Medium
70%					
80%					
90%	Raw Umber		Burnt Umber		
Black					

A richer black is produced by mixing Burnt Umber with Thalo Blue, Cadmium Red Deep and Thalo Green, and Acra Violet with Thalo Green. To make the black even darker, cover with a varnish or glaze.

Red Violet	Violet	Blue Violet	Blue	Blue Green	Green	Yellow Green
						Brilliant Yellow Green
Medium Magenta				Turquoise Green	Permanent Green Light	
Acra Violet						
		Cobalt Blue				
Deep Magenta	Prism Violet		Cerulean Blue		Permanent Green Deep	
			Thalo Blue	Thalo Green	Hooker's Green	

Every hue (the name of the color) at it's maximum purity (intensity, saturation) has a corresponding tone.

Glossary

acute angle
An angle that measures between 0° and 90°

acute triangle
A triangle having three acute angles.

algorithm
A mathematical rule.

altitude
In a triangle: the line segment from a vertex perpendicular to the opposite side. Every triangle has three altitudes which might not all be in the interior of the triangle.

In an acute triangle: all three altitudes lie in the interior of the triangle.

In an obtuse triangle: two of the altitudes lie in the exterior of the triangle.

In a parallelogram: the altitude is the distance between two parallel sides. Any line segment joining two sides and perpendicular to both is *an* altitude.

analogous color scheme
A color scheme that uses three to four hues that are next to each other on the color wheel. For example, you can use yellow, yellow-green, and green. Light and dark values of the hues may be included to extend the scheme.

angle
The figure formed by two rays having a common endpoint. The common endpoint is called the vertex of the angle and the rays are called the sides of the angle.

arc
The figure formed by two points and the portion of a circle between hose two points. The two points are called the endpoints of the arch. An arc is named by its endpoints.

area
The measure in square units of any bounded portion of a plane.

axis
A line used as a reference. In the Cartesian coordinate plane, all points are located with reference to two perpendicular axes: the x-axis and the y-axis.
An axis of symmetry: a line which divides the plane into two halves which are mirror images of each other (also called an axis of reflection or a mirror).

axis of reflection
See axis.

axis of rotation
In three-dimensional space, an axis serves as the center of rotation.

axis of symmetry
See axis.

base
The plane regions on either end of a cylinder.

bisect
To divide into two congruent figures.

bisector
The line or ray that divides a segment or angle into congruent figures.

bisector, perpendicular
A line that passes through the midpoint of a segment and is at right angles to that segment.

Cartesian coordinate plane
A rectangular system for locating points in a plane by using a pair of perpendicular axes: the horizontal line is the x-axis and the vertical line is the y-axis.

center
A point from which all points on a circle are equidistant.

center of rotation
In two-dimensional space, a point serves as the center of rotation.

central angle
The angle formed by two radii of a circle.

chord
A line segment whose endpoints lie on a circle.

circle
The set of all poins in a plane equidistant from a given point called the center. Although it is not part of the circle, a circle is named by its center. Circle O is a circle whose center is O.

circumference
The distance around a circle. The circumference of a circle is given by the formula C=d, where d is the diameter of the circle. It is also given by the formula C=2 where r is the radius of the circle.

compass
An instrument used for drawing circles and arcs.

complementary angles
Two angles whose sum is 90°.

complementary color scheme
A color scheme that uses two hues that are directly opposite each other on the color wheel. Red is the opposite of green, violet is the opposite of yellow, blue is the opposite of orange, etc.

concave polygon
A polygon that has at least one interior angle that measures more than 180°.

concentric
Having the same center. Two circles with the same center are considered concentric.

cone

A three-dimensional figure with a circular base and a surface generated by the lines passing through a point outside the plane of the cirlce and the points on the circle.

consecutive

In order, or in sequence. In a polygon, consecutive sides or consecutive vertices are those that appear in order as you travel around the polygon in either direction starting at any vertex.

convex deltahedra

A group of 8 polyhedra composed of only equilateral triangles.

convex polygon

A polygon whose interior angles measure less than 180°.

crenellated

Having notched projections.

cube

As a noun: A polyhedron having six square faces, sometimes referred to as an hexahedron.

As a verb: To raise to the third power. 3^3 = 3 cubed = 3 x 3 x 3 (27).

curve

A continuous set of points having only the one dimension of length. By this definition, a straight line is a curve.

cylinder

A three-dimensional figure generated by a circle whose center moves a long a line segment.

decagon

a polygon having ten sides. It may be either regular or non-regular.

deduction

See deductive reasoning

deductive reasoning

A method of reasoning that allows specifid conclusions to be drawn from general truths. This is the form of reasoning used in mathematical proof.

degree (°)

The unit of measure in angles. There are 360° in a circle. Thre are 180° in an Euclidean triangle.

denominator

In a fraction, this is the number that is written below the line. In the fraction two-thirds, 2/3, 3 is the denominator.

diagonal

A line segment that joins the non-consecutive vertices of a polygon. The number of diagonals that a polygon has is dependent upon the number of sides of the polygon.

diameter

A chord that passes through the

center of a circle is called the diameter. A circle has infinitely many diameters all having the same length. The measure of any one of them is called the diameter of the circle. A diameter cuts the circle into two semicircles.

distance

Between points: the length of the line segment joining the points.

From a point to a line: the length of the line segment from the point to the line and perpendicular to the line.

Between parallel lines: the length of any segment having one endpoint on each line and perpendicular to both.

Divine Proportion

The proportion derived from the division of a line segment into two segments such that the ratio of the whole segment to the longer part is the same as the ratio of the longer part to the shorter part.

dodecahedron

Any polyhedron having twelve faces which may or may not be regular. There is a pentagonal dodecahedron which has twelve congruent pentagonal faces. There is a rhombic dodecahedron that has twelve congruent rhombic faces.

Dynamic Parallelogram

Any parallelogram whose sides are

in the same ratio as one of the Dynamic Rectangles.

Dynamic Rectangles

A family of rectangles derived from the square through the use of diagonals. If the width is *1*, then the lengths of the rectangles are given by the square roots of the natural numbers. The Dynamic Rectangles are sometimes called the Root Rectangles and sometimes the Euclidean Series.

Dynablocks

A family of rectangular solids which are derived from the Dynamic Rectangles.

edge

In a polyhedron, the common side between two faces. In a cube there are twelve edges joining the eight vertices.

elements of symmetry

In three-dimensional space, the elements of symmetry are: the axes of rotation and the planes of reflection.

equiangular

Having angles of the same measure. In an equilateral triangle, all the sides and all the angles have the same measure.

equilateral

Having sides of the same measure. In a regular polygon, all the sides have the same measure. In an equilateral triangle, all the three sides have the same meas re.

even number
A whole number that is divisible by two. 2, 4, 6, 8....are numbers that are divisible by two. If *n* is any whole number, *2 n* will always designate an even number.

exponent
A number that indicates the number of times a quantity is to be used as a factor. In the expression b^3, 3 is the exponent. $b^3 = (b)(b)(b)$.

exterior
Of an angle or a closed curve: The set of all points in the plane that do not lie on the figure or in the interior of the figure.
exterior angle of a polygon: An angle formed by a side and the extension of an adjacent side in a polygon. There are two exterior angles at each vertex.

face
A polygonal shape, together with its interior, that forms part of the surface of a polyhedron. A square is the face of a cube. A triangle is the face of a tetrahedron.

factor
A number that divides another number without leaving a remainder. 3 is a factor of 9 since 3 divides 9 three times without

leaving a remainder.

Fibonacci Numbers
The summation sequence whose terms are: 1, 1, 2, 3, 5, 8, 13....

fractal
A curve that exhibits self-similarity at all levels of magnification.

generation
In fractal geometry, the figure determined by a particular number of iterations of the rule.

generator
In fractal geometry, the figure that results from one application of the rule.

glide reflection
The symmetry operation that combines moves of translation and reflection.

Goldbricks
A set of rectangular solids that are derived from the Phi-Family Rectangles.

Golden Cut
The point on a line segment that divides the segment into two segments whose lengths are in the Golden Ratio.

Golden Mean
the Golden Mean is the same as the Golden Cut.

Golden Ratio

The Golden Ratio is the same as the Golden Cut and the Golden Mean. The Golden ratio is the ratio of approximately *1.61803* to *1*, derived from the Divine Proportion. The Golden Ratio is sometimes known by the Greek letter ø (phi).

Golden Rectangle

Any rectangle whose sides are in the ratio of ø to *1* where ø is approximately equal to 1.61803.

Golden Triangle

Any isosceles triangle in which the ratio of a leg to the base is ø to 1, where to five decimal places ø = 1.61803. The triangle is also called the Triangle of the Pentalpha or the Sublime Triangle.

grid

A repeating pattern superimposed on the plane consisting of lines and/or circle.

polar grid: A grid consisting of concentric circles with radius vectors emanating from the center, or pole.

rectangular grid: A grid whose units are rectangles.

triangular grid: A grid whose units are triangles.

handedness

Referring to the orientation of right or left-handedness.

height

In a cylinder: The distance between the bases.

hexagon

A polygon having six sides which may be regular or non-regular.

helix

A spiral-like curve formed by wrapping a cylinder uniformly in a single layer. The thread of a metal screw is a helix.

hexahedron

A figure having six faces which may or may not be regular. A cube is a hexahedron. Plural is hexahedra.

hue

The name of a particular color. Red is a hue.

hypotenuse

In a right triangle, the side opposite the right angle is the hypotenuse.

hypothesis

A conjecture that requires testing for verification.

icosahedron

A polyhedron having 20 faces which may be regular or non-regular.

included angle

The angle formed by two specified

adjacent sides of a polygon.

included side
In a polygon, the common side between two specified angles.

induction
See inductive reasoning.

inductive reasoning
A method of reasoning that allows a generalization to be made from observing specific cases. Inductive reasoning can be likened to making educated guesses based on experience. Unlike deductive reasoning, it can lead to a false conclusion. This is the form of reasoning used in the Scientific Method.

initiator
In fractal geometry, the initiator is the original figure to which the rule is applied (the first generation curve).

inscribed angle
An angle whose vertex likes on a circle and each of whose sides intersects the circle.

inscribed circle
A circle lying in the interior of a polygon such that each side of the polygon is tangent to the circle.

inscribed polygon
A polygon whose vertices like on a circle.

integer
Any member of the following infinite set of numbers:....-3, -2, -1, 0, 1, 2, 3....

interior
Of an angle: The set of all points not on any angle having the property that if any two are joined by a line segment, the segment will not intersect the angle.
Of a closed curve: The set of all points in the plane that are enclosed by the curve.

interior angle
Of a polygon: An angle formed by adjacent sides of a polygon.

intersect
To have at least one point in common.

irrational number
Any number that cannot be expressed as the ratio of two integers. The Golden Ratio is an irrational number.

Isosceles Right Triangle
A triangle having a pair of congruent sides and one right angle (90°).

Isosceles trapezoid
A trapezoid in which the nonparallel sides are congruent.

isosceles triangle
A triangle having a pair of congruent sides.

isometric projection
This is a drawing system for representing three dimensions on the two-dimensional surface. This form of projection presents three faces visible to the viewer and the receding angles are congruent.

iteration
A repetitive procedure generally linked to a mathematical function wherein the prevous output becomes the input for the next term.

lattice
See space lattice.

lateral surface
The portion of the surface of a cylinder that lies between the bases.

leg(s)
   In an isosceles trapezoid: the nonparallel sides.
   In an isosceles triangle: the congruent sides.
   In a right triangle: the sides that form the right angle.

line
An undefined term in geometry. It has the properties of infinite length, continuity, and no width. It is a straight curve. A line is named by any two of its points or by a lower case letter.

line group
A line group is a linear pattern resulting from translating a unit in a single direction. The unit is developed by manipulating a two-dimensional motif with the symmetry operations of reflection or rotation or both. There are seven two-dimensional line groups.

line segment
The figure formed by two points on a line and all the points in between those two points. The two points are called the endpoints of the segment. A line segment is named by its endpoints.

midpoint
The point that divides a line segment into two congruent segments.

minute
One-sixtieth of a degree in angle measure. 60' = 1°. 35°12' reads 35 degrees and 12 minutes.

monochromatic color scheme
A color scheme that uses one hue and the light and dark values thereof.

mirror
See axis of reflection.

megalith
A large upright stone used in prehistoric architecture.

motif
A two-dimensional design that is asymmetric.

mountain fold
In the techniques of paper folding, the fold in which the peak points upward as a mountain is called a mountain fold. It is the reverse of a valley fold.

obtuse angle
An angle that is greater than 90° and less than 180°.

order of (vertex net)
The mathematical numerical notation that indicates what kind and how many polygons are found at a single vertex.

Parablock
A set of rectangular solids that are derived from parallelograms.

parallel
    Lines: two or more lines that lie in the same plane and have not points in common.
    Segments: noncollinear segments which lie on parallel lines.

parallel projection
This is a drawing system for representing three dimensions on the two-dimensional surface. A projection that sets a face parallel to the picture plane while the lines that recede are at angles to that picture plane.

parallelepiped
A three-dimensional solid that is composed of 6 faces with three pairs of parallel ones.

parallelogram
A quadrilateral in which opposite sides are parallel.

pattern
A repetition of units in an ordered sequence.

Penrose tiles
The tiling units discovered by the British mathematician Roger Penrose. These units can be used in pairs to form infinite nonperiodic tilings. Each is derived from the pentagram within a pentagon.

pentagon
A polygon having five sides which may or may not be regular.

perimeter
The distance around a figure.

perpendicular
    Lines: lines that meet to form a right angle.
    Segments: noncollinear segments that lie on perpendicular lines.

perpendicular bisector
See bisector, perpendicular.

phi
The number naming the ratio that appears in the Divine Proportion (approximately 1.61803). The Greek letter phi (ø) is used in this text, but the letter tau, O, is also used by mathematicians to name this ratio.

Phi-Family Rectangles
The group of rectangles related to the Golden Rectangle or generated by phi.

picture plane
Refers to the surface, usually rectangular, on which an artist constructs an image.

plane
An undefined term in geometry. A plane may be thought of as "a slice of space" having infinite length and infinite width but no thickness.

plane group
A pattern resulting from the repetition of a unit in two non-parallel directions in order to fill the plane. The unit is developed by manipulating a motif using one or more of the symmetry operations of rotation, reflection, translation. There are 17 plane groups.

plane of reflection
In three-dimensional space, the plane of reflection divides the object into mirror halves.

Platonic Solids
The five regular polyhedra that are associated with the Greek philosopher Plato. They are: the tetrahedron, the cube, the octahedron, the dodecahedron, and the icosahedron.

point
An undefined term in geometry. A point is often thought of as a location in space having no dimension.

point group
A pattern that results from the rotation of a unit about a pole.

pole
In a polar graph, it is the point corresponding to the origin.

polygon
A simple closed curve composed of line segments each intersecting exactly two others, one at each endpoint. A polygon is named by its vertices read consecutively in either a clockwise or counter-clockwise direction. The line segments are called the sides of the polygon. The points of intersection are called the vertices of the polygon.

polyhedron

A three-dimensional figure formed by polygons which intersect in such a way that vertices and sides are common. The polygonal figures are called the faces of the polyhedron. The common sides are called the edges of the polyhedron. The common vertices are called the vertices of the polyhedron.

primary colors

In pigments, the primary colors are yellow, red, and blue. These are the essential hues from which all other colors can be obtained.

proportion

A pair of ratios set equal to each other. a/b =c/d. In this proportion, *a* and *d* are called the extremes of the proportion while *b* and *c* are called the means. These words refer only to the position of the terms.

projection

See isometric and parallel projection.

protractor

A tool used for measuring the number of degrees in an angle. It is shaped like a semicircle.

Pythagorean Theorem

It is the theorem named after Pythagoras in which the sum of the squares on the sides of a right triangle equal the sum of the squares on the hypotenuse.

Pythagorean triple or triad

The integers that have the property that the sum of the squares of two of them equals the square of the third. 3, 4, 5 is a Pythagorean triple since 32 = 42 = 52, or 9 + 16 = 25.

quadrilateral

A four-sided polygon which may or may not be regular. A square is a quadrilateral. A rhombus is a quadrilateral.

radicand

The quantity under the radical sign.

radius

Of a circle: a line segment that joins the center of a circle to any point on the circle is *a* radius of the circle. The measure of any of these segments which are all congruent is *the* radius of the circle.

of a regular polygon: If a regular polygon is inscribed in a circle, *the* radius of the polygon is the radius of the circumscribed circle. A radius is a line segment from the "center" of the polygon to a vertex.

ratio

A comparison of numbers to each other. The ratio of 4 to 5 may be expressed as 4:5 or simply 4 to 5 or as a fraction 4/5.

ray
The figure formed by a point on a line and all the points on the same side of that point. The point is called the endpoint of the ray. The ray is named by its endpoint and any other point on the ray.

reflection
The symmetry operation that flips a motif changing both its position and its handedness.

rhombus
A parallelogram in which all sides are congruent.

rhombohedron
A solid composed of 6 rhombuses.

right angle
An angle that measures 90°.

right circular cone
A cone whose base is at right angles to its axis of rotation.

right circular cylinder
A circular cylinder whose bases are at right angles (90°) to its axis of rotation.

right triangle
A triangle having one right angle.

Rope Knotter's Triangle
The right triangle whose legs measure 3 and 4 respectively, and whose hypotenuse measures 5. Also known as the 3-4-5 Right Triangle. It was so named because it was discovered by the Ancient Egyptian rope knotters who prepared ropes for the purpose of measuring .

Root Rectangles
The rectangles derived from the square such that the width measures one (1), ands the length measures the square root of a natural number. These rectangles are the members of the family of Dynamic Rectangles.

rotation
The symmetry operation that involves the turning of a motif about a point or an axis.

rotocenter
A point about which a motif is rotated to create the two-dimensional point groups of symmetry.

scalene triangle
A triangle having no congruent sides.

secant
A line that intersects a circle in exactly two points.

second
One-sixtieth of a minute in angle measure. 60" = 1' or 3600" = 1°. 20° 40' 13" reads 20 degrees, 40 minutes, 13 seconds.

sector
A region in the interior of a circle bounded by two radii and the circle itself.

sequence
An ordered progression of terms. A sequence may have a finite number of terms, eg. 1, 2, 3, 4, 5, 6, 7; or an infinite number of terms, eg, 1, 1, 2, 3, 5, 8, 13, 21.....(This is known as the Fibonacci Sequence) .
If the notation $S_1, S_2, S_3, ...S_n$ is used to denote a sequence, the subscript names the position of the term, eg. S_{12} would be the 12th term.

side
Of an angle: see angle.
Of a line: either of the half-planes formed by a line in the plane.
Of a polygon: see polygon.

similar
Having the same shape. Two polygons are similar if corresponding angles are congruent and corresponding sides are in proportion.

simple closed curve
A plane curve that can be traced without lifting pencil from paper in such a way that the starting point and the ending point are the same. No point is traced more than once.

space frame
In three dimensions a repeating array of points or lines. Also known as space lattice.

space lattice
See space frame.

square
Noun: a rectangle in which all of the sides are congruent.
Verb: To multiply a quantity by itself. The number 2 used as an exponent indicates the operation of squaring, eg. $a^2 =$ (a)(a).

square root
a number that when multiplied by itself produces a given number. The operation of taking the positive square root of a number is indicated by a radical sign. The given numer, under the sign, is called the radicand, eg. $\sqrt{16}$ = 4 since 4 x 4 = 16.

Square Root Phi Rectangle
Any rectangle in which the ratio of the length to the width is phi to 1, or approximately 1.271.

straight angle
An angle measuring 180°.

symmetry operations

The symmetry operations are those of rotation, reflection, glide reflection, and translation.

tangent

A line lying in the same plane as a circle that intersects the circle in exactly one point.

template (for a polyhedron)

A two-dimensional prototype that has glue tabs added.

tessellation

a tiling.

tetrahedron

a polyhedronhaving four triangular faces which may or may not be regular.

tiling

   Noun: the resulting pattern when the plane is tiled.

   Verb: the process of covering the plane with closed units so that there are no gaps or overlaps.

transformation operations

The operations of chamfering, skewing, slicing, stretching, truncating, that alter a three-dimensional figure in a particular way.

translation

The symmetry operation which involves the sliding of a motif in two-dimensions, or a figure in three-dimensions without changing its orientation.

trapezohedron

A three-dimensional object that has trapezia for its faces.

trapezoid

A quadrilateral with exactly one pair of parallel sides. The parallel sides are called the bases of the trapezoid and the angles including either base are called the base angles. There are two pairs of base angles.

trapezium

A quadrilateral having no parallel sides. The plural is trapezia.

triangle

A polygon having three sides which may or may not be congruent.

triangulate

The operation of subdividing a figure into smaller triangular units.

truncate

To cut off either planar sections or three-dimensional sections in a systematic fashion.

unit

   In measurement: a length or volume that acts as a basic element of measure.

   In symmetry: a pattern

element determined by a motif or figure used with one or more symmetry operations.

unit measure
The length taken to represent the number *one (1)* in a given set of circumstances.

valley fold
This is a fold in the technique of paper folding that has the peak pointing downward as a valley. It is the reverse of a mountain fold.

vertex

> *Of an angle:* see angle.
> *Of a polygon:* see polygon.

vertex net
A numerical notation that gives the kind and number of polygons around a particular vertex, eg. 4 - 4 - 4 tells that three squares surround a vertex.

volume
The measure in cubic units of any three-dimensional object.

x-axis
The horizontal axis on the Cartesian coordinate plane.

y-axis
The vertical axis on the Cartesian coordinate plane.

z-axis
The oblique axis on the Cartesian coordinate plane.

Water always the alpha and omega of life.

Index

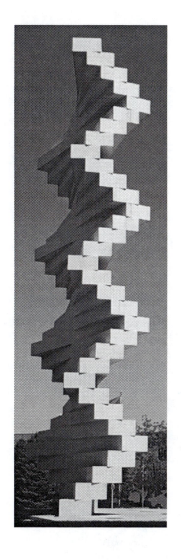

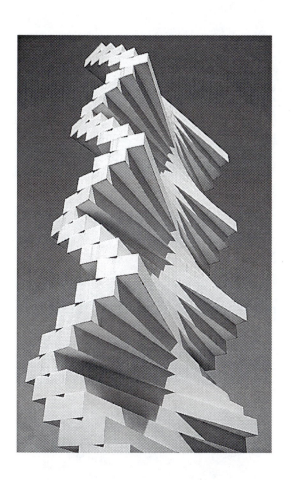

This page:
Herbert Bayer."Articulated Wall", 1985, 85' high, yellow prefabricated concrete sculpture at the Denver Design Center, Colorado.Three different views.Notice how a slight rotation in the position of each slab unit turns an essentially simple form into a complex structure.

Top Left:
Frontal View.

Right:
Side View

Lower Left:
Three-Quarter View

Notes

This page:
Student Work. Heather West.
Wire mesh form based on
the manipulation of the tet-
rahedron.

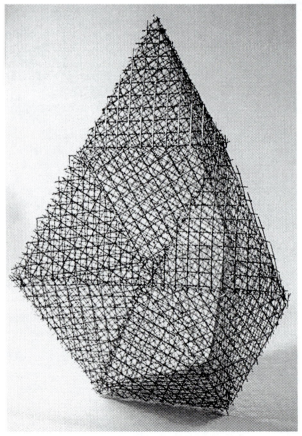

Notes

This page:
Student Work. Lillian Ng. Slit
work in paper.

To order copies of *Space, Structure and Form* (ISBN 0-697-33058-3), contact Times Mirror Higher Education Group, Inc. customer service at 1-800-338-5578

Volume discounts are available to Schools, Libraries, Bookstores, etc.

Other books are available from Pythagorean Press.

This page:
Gum drop and toothpick study
for a geodesic structure.

Pythagorean Press offers two other books that bring together art, math, and nature.

Book 1: *Universal Patterns* ISBN 0-9614504-4-4

This book looks at some of the constants in nature that can be described by geometry and given form through art. In the first chapter, readers are introduced to basic geometric constructions that give them a foundation on which to build a variety of forms in two-dimensions. The second chapter introduces the concept of the Golden Ratio which becomes the common thread that weaves the chapters on triangles, Dynamic Rectangles, Fibonacci Numbers, and Spirals together.

Book 2: *The Surface Plane* ISBN 0-9614504-2-8

This book continues the exploration of two dimensions with emphasis on pattern. In the first chapter, readers are introduced to the notion of the grid and its function. The second chapter describes in detail the aspects of point, line, and plane symmetry which become the underlying concept that weaves the chapters on circles, tilings, and fractals together. The last chapter, the Pliable Plane, is the lead into three dimensions.

This page:
Linda Maddox. Archimedean Solid (Archi 5-6-6). Face elements developed on the computer. Paper construction.

These books may be ordered by contacting:
Pythagorean Press
c/o Corporate Fulfillment Systems
1 Bert Drive
P.O. Box 339
West Bridgewater, MA. 02379-9970
1-800-344-4501 or 508-583-5239
Fax: 508-583-9904

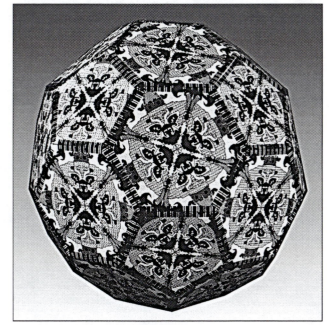